The Administrative Side of Coaching

Applying Business Concepts to Athletic Program
Administration and Coaching

— Second Edition —

The Administrative Side of Coaching

Applying Business Concepts to Athletic Program Administration and Coaching

— Second Edition —

Richard Leonard, PhD

Flagler College, Tallahassee Campus

FITNESS INFORMATION TECHNOLOGY

A Division of the International Center
for Performance Excellence

262 Coliseum, WVU-PE, PO Box 6116
Morgantown, WV 26506-6116

Library of Congress Card Catalog Number: 2008928086

ISBN 13: 978-1-885693-83-9

Production Editor: Matt Brann
Cover Design: Craig Hines
Typesetter: Craig Hines
Copyeditor: Matt Brann
Proofreader: Maria E. denBoer
Indexer: Maria E. denBoer
Printed by Sheridan Books
Cover images © Shelly Little (money/football collage) and © Brian Kelly (various ball collage at top and bottom), bigstockphoto.com.

10   9   8   7   6   5   4   3   2   1

Fitness Information Technology
A Division of the International Center for Performance Excellence
West Virginia University
262 Coliseum, WVU-PE
PO Box 6116
Morgantown, WV 26506-6116
800.477.4348 (toll free)
304.293.6888 (phone)
304.293.6658 (fax)
Email: fitcustomerservice@mail.wvu.edu
Website: www.fitinfotech.com

To my wife, Shuli Leonard, and my incredible family.
I could not have completed this without you.

Special thanks also to Fitness Information Technology
and Matthew Brann for their commitment
and hard work in helping me complete this project.

—Richard Leonard

Table of Contents

Preface

In developing the second edition of this text, I wanted to update the concepts of coaching administration to include the most recent business models and apply those theories to the profession of coaching. While the foundational information is still intact from the first edition, the new version of the text focuses on more practical application of coaching administration. Text changes encompass new chapter designs, contemporary support references, additional administrative philosophies, and a more comprehensive coverage of the individual topics of coaching administration.

While designing the original manuscript, I was confronted with two explicit questions. First and foremost, will this composition be received in the spirit that it was written? Secondly, will coaches and athletic administrators of today be interested in the sum and substance of it? Let's address the second question first: Will coaches and administrators be interested in the subject matter?

Anyone who has spent time in coaching and program administration (no matter what the sport or level of competition) realizes that while a competent knowledge of his or her sport is imperative for achievement and success, coaching goes far beyond diagramming Xs and Os, teaching innovative playing techniques, or designing unique variations of a practice drill. Whether one acknowledges it or not, all coaches perform the same obligatory duties as managers in the business world. Like business managers, coaches and athletic program administrators are individuals of responsibility who act as facilitators, decision makers, and resource allocators with both formal and informal authority. It is important to break down this last statement into its simplest terms so the connection between business management and athletic coaching/administration can be clearly seen.

As facilitators, business managers are responsible for the orderly operation of their respective division, facility, or company. Coaches and athletic program administrators are no different. They must ensure their program's consistent functioning in everything from practice to competition, player to player (or coach) relations, facility scheduling, fundraising, and countless other administrative elements. From the perspective of decision making, business managers are directly accountable for both primary and secondary decisions that not only influence the prevailing situation but the future direction of the organization. Coaches and athletic program administrators also make consequential decisions on a daily basis that determine a program's current and future success. Additionally, business managers and coach-administrators are also responsible for all types of resource allocations. Resources such as time, money, and manpower are important for both to distribute equitably and appropriately for the business or athletic program to function effectively. Finally, business managers and coach/program administrators are similar in regard to formal and informal authority. Whether one is a corporate manager or a coach or athletic administrator, there is certain, inherent, formal jurisdictional power in the organizational position and title. How one handles the explicit authority is determined by personal style and specific situation, but it is legitimized through job responsibilities and duties. Conversely, managers and coaches promote informal authority through their distinct personalities. Informal power is what motivates employees (or in the case of this text, athletes and staff) to achieve beyond required expectations. Successful managers and coaches/program administrators have the intangible talent to inspire and focus employees and athletes.

Another significant parallel that exists between the business world and the profession of coaching athletics relates to the intense search for a competitive edge. In every business environment, corporate managers understand the urgency associated with operational efficiency. They understand how a skillful deployment of administrative fundamentals can and will provide a practical advantage over the competition. The same philosophy applies to coaching.

Athletic programs, whatever the level or sport, are experiencing an exponentially increasing volume and concentration of competition. Coaches no longer have the luxury of managerial complacency. In simple terms, in order to thrive, athletic programs must be as administratively competent as possible. The application of business techniques discussed in this book could be the difference between survival and growth and deterioration and failure.

In response to my initial concern of whether this book will be received in the spirit that it was written, I would sincerely like to see it used as a generator of good ideas for improving a coach's/athletic administrator's work and personal life. Ideas produce movement. Good ideas create movement, which, in turn, creates progress. From that premise, the book could be utilized as a reference or as a cover-to-cover foundation for program and team administration. No matter how one utilizes this text, if it produces new good thinking, then it is a success.

CHAPTER 1

Program Planning for Coaches

CHAPTER OUTLINE

- To introduce the concept of planning as it relates to athletics.
- To delineate the pros and cons of athletic program planning.
- To identify the types and levels of planning.
- To provide a sectional structure to program planning.
- To elucidate the importance of the following components of a program plan:
  - Executive Summary
  - Mission Statements
  - Program Chronicled Description
  - Program Structure
  - Goal Setting
  - Rules and Operating Actions
  - Human Resource Systems
  - Marketing Formation
  - Financial Reporting
  - Supplementary Information

INTRODUCTION

While planning is conceivably the most significant ingredient in the management process, it is undoubtedly the one element that triggers the most frustration and anxiety. One often hears the expression "the future is uncertain." As human beings, we try to avoid uncertainty while attempting to prolong the established and known. However, the essential makeup of athletics forces coaches and program administrators to proactively recognize and take hold of the future. Planning is that practical managerial function that deals with strategies to minimize the impact of the unknown arising from the future. Planning also provides the athletic organization with a tangible shared vision that all stakeholders (people involved with the athletic program) can reference and follow. This collective focus reduces the unproductive use of time, materials, manpower, and finances.

Why Plan? Planning Pros and Cons

The ensuing list details the positive elements of athletic program planning as well as the drawbacks of athletic program planning.

Pros/Positive Elements

- Formalized planning provides a framework to look strategically into the future.
- Planning furnishes a structure for resource allocation and financial stability.
- Planning can enhance internal operational focus as well as enhance

the program's efficiency.

- A well-constructed program plan can develop strong inter-organizational cooperation between various departments/divisions.
- Appropriate program planning can be used as a strong controlling element . . . coaches and program administrators can compare how well a program is doing in contrast to how well it was projected to do.
- Planning can generate optimistic beliefs concerning organizational citizenship, teamwork, and loyalty.
- Formalized athletic program planning can present a sustainable competitive advantage over athletic programs that do not have a planning system in place.
- Planning can be a way to tangibly unite individual program members' personal goals with the overall athletic program goals.
- A solid athletic program plan conveys a sense of professionalism and legitimacy for internal athletic program staff and athletes as well as external supporters and administrators.

Cons/Drawbacks

- Planning accurately takes time and energy . . . with salaries typically being an athletic program's largest expense, time spent is money spent.
- The planning process has an enormous misconception . . . administrators take completed plans as inflexible documents. This, in turn, creates "tunnel vision" on goals and actions that may have become irrelevant or even counter-productive.
- Planning involves demanding, difficult choices. Some of these alternatives can influence the program's survival and everyone involved.
- Planning deals with the indeterminate future. This uncertainty can trigger program-wide apprehension and anxiety.

Types of Plans

The planning concept can go from wide-ranging and all-inclusive to distinct and specific. Plans can be generated by top level administrators as well as individual coaches. As a coach and athletic program administrator, one's task is to determine which plan is the most appropriate for the program and level of competition.

The two primary types of plans are single-use plans and stand-alone plans. "Single use plans are developed to achieve a set of goals unlikely to be repeated in the future. Standing plans are ongoing plans used to provide guidance for task performance repeated within the organization" (Daft & Marcic, 2006, p. 169). From an athletic program vantage, standing program plans need to be established for long-term operational goals. Single use plans are project specific with terminal time frames. It should be noted that the depth of a single use plan will be determined by the importance of the project to the athletic program. Additionally, all external and unique projects outside the program's standing plan need some type of single use plan (from a one-page synopsis to a detailed step-by-step blueprint) that all individuals in the program can utilize.

The strategic levels of planning for athletic programs parallel the three central levels in the corporate world. "The three strategic levels (for the corporate environment) are corporate, business, and functional . . . corporate level is the plan for managing multiple lines of businesses . . . business level strategy is the plan for managing one line of business . . . functional level is the plan for managing one area of business" (Lussier, 2006, p. 151). One example of how these three echelons of planning equate to athletics would be in college/university athletics. The corporate level plan would be the college/university institutional-wide educational plan. The business level plan would consist of each division in the college/university (medical, business, education, athletics, etc.). The functional level plan would be the individual athletic programs within the business level athletic department plan. To recognize which plan one will need, the coach/program administrator should identify the hierarchical plane in which the particular program operates.

Universal Factors of Planning

The planning function ranks among the most significant in thriving corporate settings. Athletic program administration can simplify planning into these "basic factors:

- Set goals
- Develop commitment to goals
- Develop effective action plans
- Track progress toward goal achievement
- Maintain flexibility in planning" (Williams, 2000, p. 127).

These five components are found in virtually every type of business planning process. The configuration and interpretation of each of these items as well as their utilization change from organization to organization.

ATHLETIC PROGRAM PLANNING

The most lucid and understandable way to structure the five factors of planning is through an instrument called a business operational plan or, for the purposes of this textbook, an athletic program plan. Table 1 is an illustration of how one could arrange an athletic program plan.

Before a clarification is given to these components of the athletic program plan, it is imperative that one recognize that program plans are group endeavors and they must have everyone's total pledge and commit-

Administrative Tip

When developing an athletic program plan, solicit ideas from all internal members of the program as well as key external associates. If possible, have a yearly "mission retreat" away from the program's standard working environment. This hideaway will furnish an uninterrupted mission and planning focus. As the program's coach/program administrator be equipped to guide the meeting sessions. Additionally, schedule and arrange downtime recreational activities to keep all participants engaged in the process.

Table 1. Athletic Program Plan Sectional Breakdown

Section 1: Executive Summary

Section 2: Mission Statement

Section 3: Program History

Section 4: Long-Term Program Goals (3-5 years)

Section 5: Short-Term Program Goals (1-2 year actions)

Section 6: S.W.O.T. Analysis

Section 7: Policies and Procedures

Section 8: Human Resource Plan

Section 9: Marketing and Promotional Plan

Section 10: Financial Projections/Fundraising Programs

Section 11: Appendix

ment. The document can not be a single person's perspective, but everyone's vision involved with the operation and administration of the program. Whether one is running a junior, high school, college, or professional program, the participatory involvement of coaches, parents, administrators, and athletes is vital for planning and goal fulfillment.

The following sections (based on Table 1) will help a coach or program administrator assemble an athletic program plan.

Administrative Tip

Because the executive summary is a synopsis of the entire athletic program plan, it is completed last after all other plan components are finalized.

Section 1: Executive Summary

The executive summary is an abridgment of the entire athletic program plan. This overview accentuates key sections of the program plan to provide readers with a summation (characteristically one or two pages) of the plan's core components. The executive summary can be composed of

- a condensed description of the program's sport, services provided, and products produced;
- an abstract view of the competitive market and proposed marketing tactics;
- main points of the operational plan;
- a rundown of the management team (program administrators and coaches); and
- an encapsulated picture of the financial condition the program operates under and any new projected budgetary/capital needs.

Section 2: Mission Statement

A mission statement is defined as "a broad declaration of an organization's purpose that identifies the organization's products and customers and distinguishes the organization from its competitors" (Jones & George, 2004, p. 177). In other words, a mission statement is an all encompassing affirmation that defines the overall purpose, philosophy, and vision of the organization and program. "The mission is the basic purpose and values of the organization, as well as its scope of operations. It is a statement of the organization's reason for existing" (Bateman & Snell, 2004, p. 116). All objectives, policies, procedures, and actions emanate from the mission statement.

There are countless books and related literature on business planning and the development of a mission statement. Each has its own style and design criteria for a mission statement. The format and wording used is a matter of individual partiality and style. However, in writing the program's mission statement, answer the following broad but indispensable questions:

- What is our program about?
- What is our principal purpose?
- What is our philosophy in running our program?
- What is our operational environment?
- What is the future of our operations?

A mission statement can be as succinct and brief as a few sentences or as lengthy as a multi-paged elaboration. A short, straight-forward mission statement could be advantageous if the program plan is to be utilized for external funding and support. A multi-page embellishment could be useful to motivate internal staff and players by providing a comprehensive operational rationale and a philosophical course of action.

Section 3: Program History

Developing a program history section of an athletic program plan might seem unproductive to some coaches and administrators. In actuality, this segment furnishes internal and external stakeholders, who are fundamentally defined as people who have any type of existing or future interest in the program (internal are players and staff and external are outside administrators and future sponsors), with a point of reference and a progressive framework that they can follow. There are many ways to arrange this section. It can be in narrative form, outline, or even in a timeline style. More importantly, it should be in ascending chronological order from beginning to the present. The justification for compiling events this way is because a program plan is futuristic in nature. The plan should reflect where the program was, where it is, and where it will be.

Sections 4 and 5: Long- and Short-Term Goals

The next sections of the program plan deal with substantial, tangible goals and objectives. Long-term goals are the program's aspirations while short-term goals are the sequence of specific actions to achieve those aspirations.

> A goal, also known as an objective, is a specific commitment to achieve a measurable result within a dated period of time. The goal should be followed by the action plan, which defines the course of action needed to achieve the stated goal. (Kinicki & Williams, 2003, p. 153)

In essence, these two sections are the substance and heart of the program plan. Obviously, long-term goals (three- to five-year projections) will be broader in outlook. Short-term goals will be decisive actions that will be utilized to reach long-term objectives.

The actual makeup of each unique goal is up to the coaches, administrators, stakeholders, and the sport's nature. However, there are some in-

Administrative Tip

Do not hesitate to study other athletic program or business mission statements to come up with ideas and inspiration. Benchmarking mission statement format and content is a very viable method to formulate the program's own individualized mission. Annual reports, which contain business mission statements, are readily available at major public and university libraries.

It is frequently asked,
"How many long-term
goals should our pro-
gram develop and
implement?" Because
of the generalized
nature and enormity
of long-term goals as
well as the limited
resources of most
sports programs, no
more than four or five
long-term goals should
be attempted. How
many short-term ac-
tions should be de-
vised for each long-
term goal? However
many it takes to ac-
complish that long-
term goal. Simply put,
it may take a few
short-term and imme-
diate actions to reach
a long-term goal or it
could take dozens. It
all depends on the
long-term goal.

tegral parameters and rules that should be placed on establishing goals. They are as follows:

1. All goals should ultimately emanate from the mission statement.
2. When formulating goals, long-term objectives should be defined first. Subsequently, short-term actions should be formulated regarding how to accomplish each long-term goal.
3. It is critical to base all goals in reality. It is necessary to ask the following questions:
   - Do we currently have the resources and funds to achieve our projected goals?
   - Do we have the future potential to acquire the essential resources and funds to accomplish goals?
   - Do we have the staff or the likelihood of acquiring the staff to attain goals?
   - Is the timeframe for the execution of the goals practical?
   - Will there be any internal or external confrontations or resistance to the goals?
4. Goals should be easily comprehensible by everyone in the organization. They should be straightforward, concise, and in common language.
5. Each goal should be distinctive and salient. In other words, are the goals repetitive or are they unique in origin?
6. Each goal should have the absolute endorsement and focus of everyone in the organization. In the athletic program setting, the players/athletes, coaches, and administrators should be involved in the goal-setting process. Without everyone's input, key internal stakeholders might not take an active interest in operations, which, in turn, may leave goals unattained.
7. Each goal/program objective should be as precise and measurable as possible. The advantage of quantifying goals is to supply coaches and athletic program administrators with concrete numbers to compare projected goals with actual results.
8. Goals should be challenging but realistic. Setting goals "beyond the reach" of current resources and capabilities could be profoundly discouraging to both athletes and staff. Conversely, setting goals that are too easily achieved will depreciate the critical value of goal setting and goal achievement. A coach/program administrator must balance these two factors to maximize the program's potential.
9. In order to be effective, goals need individual and/or group accountability. Simply put, a program goal without individual and/or group accountability will fail because assumptions will be made on who is to work on and accomplish the goal.
10. Goals need to be time precise. While the word "deadline" has a negative connotation in our society, in goal setting and achievement it is

tremendously appropriate. Once again, the time frame to achieve a particular goal must be challenging but realistic.

Section 6: S.W.O.T. Analysis

A S.W.O.T. analysis, which is the evaluation of an organization's internal strengths and weaknesses and external opportunities and threats, is an essential part of establishing the future direction of the athletic program. The analysis supplies a comprehensive, contemporary picture of the organization. "The elements of S.W.O.T. analysis are included in the general planning model, and in using strategic inventory to size up the environment. Given S.W.O.T.'s straight forward appeal, it has become a popular framework for strategic planning" (DuBrin, 2006, p. 148).

The true value in a S.W.O.T. analysis is when the coach/program administrator takes the internal elements of strength and weakness and combines them with the external elements of opportunity and threat. This is called a scenario analysis (which is detailed later in Chapter 12).

Section 7: Policies and Procedures

In their 2007 text *Crafting and Executing Strategy: A Quest for Competitive Advantage*, Thompson, Strickland, and Gamble highlight the acute importance of developing program policies and procedures by stating that new policies and operating procedures act to facilitate strategy execution in three ways:

1. Instituting new policies and procedures provides top-down guidance regarding how certain things now need to be done.
2. Policies and procedures help enforce needed consistency in how particular strategy critical activities are performed.
3. Well-conceived policies and procedures promote the creation of a work climate that facilitates good strategy execution. (Thompson, Strickland, & Gamble, 2007, p. 391–392)

While policies and procedures are ordinarily listed together in a program plan, they are two autonomous elements that facilitate an organization's achievement. In straightforward terms, policies are more in line with program rules that guide behavior (people oriented) while procedures are narrow-scope steps/methods that explain how to perform program functions (task oriented).

As coaches, the most consequential aspect for the development and the use of policies would be dealing with players and staff members. The different areas in policy formulation and implementation concerning athletes would encompass all types of behavioral expectations. Some of these behavioral expectations are found in Table 2.

The concentration and range of policy items within a program plan are determined by the team's philosophies, position, operational environ-

Administrative Tip

Policy and procedure manuals are only beneficial if they are acknowledged, established, and applied. The commitment displayed by the coach/program administrator to policy and procedure manuals will determine if they are to be effectual. Either through formal meetings or informal exchanges, constantly re-emphasize the program's commitment to its policies and procedures.

Table 2. Athlete and Staff Behavioral Expectations

Players

Academics
Practice Policies
Tardiness/Absenteeism
Alcohol/Drugs
On-Court/Field Disposition
Off-Court/Field Representation
Media Relations

Coaches/Staff

Player Relations
On- and Off-Court/Field Representation
Recruiting
Administrative Responsibilities

ment, history, and traditions. Some areas may be more accentuated than others. For example, an athletic program may be a university/college team where athletes have a documented history of alcohol abuse. In this case, the policies section of the program plan may want to elucidate specific policies on alcohol and drug abuse as well as detail a definitive warning/disciplinary system (verbal warnings, written warnings, suspension, expulsion) for violations. In such an environment, each program member should have an absolute understanding of the ramifications of alcohol and drug use. The program's alcohol and drug policies should be in lucid, plain language to avoid any misinterpretations.

Procedures are step-by-step actions taken to perform specific tasks. Coaches would like to see their programs have straightforward procedures in areas of travel, purchasing, budgeting, cash handling, registration, and other administrative functions. The biggest dividend in determining procedures for administrative functions is uniformity. Uniformity saves time, coordinates activities, and minimizes frustration and stress that arise from disorganization.

Section 8: Human Resource Plan

The human resource plan is a plan within the program's overall plan. The human resource planning process consists of four basic steps:

1. Determine the impact of the organization's objectives on specific organizational units.
2. Define skills, expertise, and total number of employees (demand for human resources) required to achieve the organizational and departmental objectives.
3. Determining the additional (net) human resource requirements in light of the organization's current human resource.
4. Develop an action plan to meet the anticipated human resource needs. (Byars & Rue, 2006, p. 89)

As stated, human resource plans need to delineate action plan systems that will be used to reach organizational goals. Action plan systems can consist of (but not limited to) the following:

* Equal Employment Opportunity compliance systems
* New employee recruitment and selection systems
* Internal promotional systems
* Information processing systems
* Organizational and departmental new employee orientation systems
* Training and design systems

- Performance appraisal systems
- Compensation systems (wage, benefit, etc.)
- Disciplinary systems
- Safety and health systems

Each human resource plan will selectively "pick and choose" human resource areas that will have the greatest impact on organizational goals.

Section 9: Marketing and Promotional Plan

While Chapters 7, 8, and 9 will be devoted to marketing concepts, it is meaningful to discuss them as a component of the program plan. The business discipline of marketing is broken down into four factors known as the 4Ps of marketing (or the marketing mix). The 4Ps are

- Product,
- Price,
- Place, and
- Promotion.

The first of the 4Ps, *product,* is the one component coaches spend the greatest effort in developing. All other marketing activities stem from it. The product is a quality athletic program and team. People (especially Americans) can occasionally be deceived into purchasing certain products that are of low caliber and value. The one product that this country seems to consume voraciously is entertainment. Athletics is entertainment. In the most elementary terms, if a team is not good, the public will stay away no matter what marketing strategies are employed. Does this mean that a program/team needs to be undefeated before people will pay notice or support it? No. It simply means that the program/team needs to be competitive and stimulating in various other ways to attract consumers and supporters.

The second of the 4Ps, *price,* derives from the same logic. The more in demand the product, the more flexibility in the price the consumer will pay for the product. Simply put, the more competitive the team, the more predisposed the consumer will be to pay a higher price to watch and support it.

The third of the 4Ps, *place,* is commonly determined by other external factors in athletics such as in what league, conference, or geographic region one's program is located. Place (or product distribution) proceeds from the logical reality that the more conspicuous and in-demand a program is, the more places it can be sold.

The final member of the 4Ps, *promotion,* is the one facet that coaches and administrators can, if properly directed, have the most effect on and is the one area of the marketing mix that needs to be expressly spelled out in program plans. If one has a competent, quality product at an acceptable price and locale, then it is up to the administrator's own resourcefulness, creativity, and effort to promote it. Is funding consequential in promotion? It is significant but not imperative. Any advertising executive will communicate that the ultimate aspiration of any promotional campaign is to secure and enlarge positive word-of-mouth about the product. Can a program achieve this without major funding? Yes. Would it be easier to implement promotion with relevant funding? Undoubtedly. Yet, coaches can not let funding be the stumbling block of promotion.

It should be restated that marketing will be presented in more detail later in the text. However, from a program plan perspective, one needs to distinguish what resources are going to be available for marketing and then formulate a strategy to augment every dollar allotted. For athletic programs with minimal dollars, concepts such as utilizing athletes (and families), developing distinct logos, composing and distributing fliers, and verbally publicizing the program and/or special events is pivotal. Additionally, one can persuade student groups, participate and attend charitable functions, make publicity speeches, utilize alumni groups and former players, build a rapport with local media, and develop a news release system. These are all cost-effective techniques for program promotion. Once again, coaches and program personnel must be enterprising and imaginative.

After the foundations of the marketing mix have been developed, the marketing component of a program plan needs to be assembled. A coach or program administrator has two choices. The marketing section of an athletic program can

1. Embody and incorporate the entire comprehensive marketing plan of a program. These detailed documents break down the marketing mix:
   - Target marketing and demographics
   - Evaluation of competition
   - Customer profiles
   - Detailed elaboration of the marketing mix
2. Summarize the marketing plan. This strategy keeps marketing and its planning as an independent, particular document while providing a broad overview in the program plan.

Section 10: Financial Projections/Fundraising Programs

Financial projecting is budgeting. There are two direct ways of budgeting:

Method 1: Assess and evaluate all of the program's expected expenditures, total the amount, and that result is the targeted income (break-even) amount.

Method 2: Estimate the realizable income (or total money available) then attempt to adapt expenditures within that amount.

The budgeting concept is that simple. The quandary comes from how to arrive at one's conclusions and how precise one can be at predicting the future. For a lucky few, they just know how to "guesstimate" and their ap-

Administrative Tip

Never blindly leap into a marketing and promotions campaign. Too much is riding on the success or failure of marketing. It is the fastest way to squander a program's limited and most precious resource of money. Learn as much as possible about marketing theories. Enlist people with backgrounds in marketing to lend a hand to the program. Gain knowledge from the marketing achievements and disappointments of others. The time will be well spent.

proximations are, in general, accurate. For the majority, they need to budget through concrete calculations.

While the budgeting concepts are covered later in the text, there are some customary rules for deriving calculations and budget.

1. Base beginning projections in recorded facts. Usually the amount spent or received in previous years is a good basis.
2. Always forecast high on projected expenditures and low on projected income/revenue.
3. Get solid dollar amounts whenever possible. This might mean additional phone calls and leg work, but the effort will provide substantially more dependable projections. Furthermore, whenever conceivably possible, get all quotes in writing.
4. Always anticipate miscellaneous expenses. The amount of miscellaneous/float dollars should be projected at 5–10% of the total amounts.
5. Contemplate all budget line items before computing dollar amounts. Attempt to incorporate every realistic expense and income source.
6. Triple check all calculations.
7. Keep organized files for back-up and confirmation of budget amounts.

Administrative Tip

Knowing and recognizing one's distinctive limitations when it comes to program administration help to achieve a thriving program. If one is not detail oriented, delegate the financial task to someone with the appropriate background who is. The importance of financial accuracy should never be underestimated.

The program plan should not only include the budget and projections, but also a short narrative explanation on each item and how those estimates were derived. While financial projections are future oriented, financial statements are historic records of what actually was received and expensed. The importance of including this type of information is in the validation of the current budget projections. Additionally, the quantitative comparison of what happened during the last fiscal period and what is predicted to happen this fiscal period provides the coach/program administrator an opportunity to explain variances.

The extent to which a coach budgets depends greatly on the type and size of the program as well as the level of expertise a coach has in budgeting and financial statement accounting. The explanation of all of the different possible financial statements and quantitative forecasting techniques moves beyond the parameters of this manuscript. However, a fundamental working knowledge of budgeting (discussed later in Chapter 6) is critical for all coaches and program administrators.

Section 11: Appendix

The appendix section of a program plan can be just as important in providing salient information to stakeholders as the other sections. Information such as fundraising programs, travel itineraries, conditioning/training programs and schedules, booster programs and events, and volunteer activities are just a few of the elements that could be included in this sec-

Administrative Tip

The appendix segment of a program plan is not a "junk drawer" section. Keep only salient information in it and maintain its organization.

tion of the program plan. Once again, the extent of information provided in the appendix depends on numerous variables that are sport and program specific.

Other Elements of an Athletic Program Plan

Title Page

The title page/cover to the athletic program plan is a considerable informative ingredient as well as a relevant presentation component. Features can include

- Athletic program name (school, university, club name),
- Operational address, phone, e-mails,
- Date of plan,
- Program logo,
- Primary program administrators and coaches, and
- Copy numbers (which is essential for tracking program plans).

Table of Contents

Because of the extensive dimensions of athletic program plans, a table of contents is an indispensable component. A table of contents provides readers with an easy way to access specific information without going through the entire document.

Key Players/Organizational Chart

The program plan segment titled Key Players/Organizational Chart has two independent but closely interconnected elements. The subsection of key players is a conventional job description behind each staff position in the organization (program director, head coach, newsletter publisher, public relations director, etc.). The second subsection is a standard organizational chart. The diagram should display the hierarchical structure of the organization/program, who is accountable to whom, and who is answerable for each division below (chain of command). When combined together, these elements furnish everyone with clearly defined roles, positions, and program structure.

SUMMARY

There are distinct benefits and applications associated with developing a program plan. The predominant are

1. To furnish stakeholders with a concrete, tangible focus for the future;
2. To project professionalism to external groups and individuals;
3. To provide a valuable and useful tool for acquiring financial backing for the program;
4. To give staff members a sense of continuity;
5. To recruit new staff members or to recruit new athletes; and

6. To provide the organization with a reality foundation. In other words, it simply distinguishes what can or can not be accomplished.

The program plan is not a stagnate document. It should be considered an alterable and flexible athletic organization component that needs constant progressive updates and amendments. While most revisions will be minor modifications, they are indispensable in maintaining the ongoing benefits. The ability to adapt and amend the program plan to the changing environment in athletics could mean the difference between a program's success or collapse.

KEY TERMS

planning	goals (long- and short-term)
program plan	policies
mission statement	procedures
program history	human resource systems
executive summary	marketing mix
S.W.O.T. analysis	budgeting
organizational chart	

Review and Discussion Questions

1. What does the indispensable function of organizational planning provide an athletic program?

2. Define single use plans. Define standing plans.

3. What are the three levels of planning?

4. What are the five basic factors of planning?

5. List (in sequential order) the primary sections of an athletic program plan.

6. What is a mission statement?

7. What are some integral parameters and rules on establishing goals?

8. What are the four steps in the human resource planning process?

9. What are the four ingredients of a marketing mix?

10. What are two direct ways to budget for athletic programs?

11. What are some of the informational components that can be included in the appendix section of an athletic program plan?

APPENDIX 1A

Athletic Program Plan Outline

The following is a detailed sectional outline of an athletic program plan that can be adopted by any athletic program. Note: There is no single standard format for a program plan. General sections are consistent but not order or format.

Athletic Plan Outline

    I. Title Page
      –Program name
      –Logo
      –Program business plan
      –Completion/distribution date
      (unpretentious creativity is a plus)

    II. Table of Contents

    III. Company/Program Conceptual Description
      –1-Page Synopsis of
        –Nature of the program
        –Primary philosophy
        –Historical development
        –Location, competitive level, etc.

    IV. Executive Summary
      –Overview of
        –Products and services
        –Marketing strategies
        –Operational systems
        –Management team
        –Financial status and need

    V. Mission Statement (vision, philosophy, major goal)
      –An all-encompassing statement of philosophy, future vision, and major operational goal.

    VI. Long-Term Goals (3–5 years)
      –4 to 5 total long-term goals of the athletic program.
      –Broad but quantitative if possible.

    VII. Short-Term Goals (1–2 years)
      –Take each long-term goal and have specific actions (this year or next) to reach long-term objective.

　　　　　–Precise and measurable
　　　　　–No set number—as many as needed to fulfill each long-term objective

VIII.　S.W.O.T. Analysis
　　　　　–Strengths, weaknesses, opportunities, and threats
　　　　　–Scenario analysis

　IX.　Human Resource Plan
　　　　　–All aspects of human resource to include
　　　　　　　　Hiring procedures
　　　　　　　　Staffing requirements
　　　　　　　　Disciplinary/separation
　　　　　　　　Compensation/benefits
　　　　　–Policy and procedure manual

　　X.　Marketing Plan
　　　　　–Marketing mix (product, price, place, promotion)

　XI.　Financial Projections and Financial Statements

XII.　Appendix
　　　　　–Supplementary information and materials
　　　　　–Support data

CHAPTER

Personal and Athletic Program Organization

CHAPTER OUTLINE

CHAPTER

2

OBJECTIVES

- To describe the foundations of personal and program organization.
- To analyze personal organization through time management methodologies.
- To describe auxiliary tools for time management such as goal setting, daily schedules, list of things to do, supplies management, travel time organization, and delegation.
- To examine office organization through filing and office flow.
- To illustrate the importance of personal organization and computerization.
- To develop program organization by means of a step-by-step process.
- To investigate the organization of internal stakeholders through hierarchical systems/organizational charts, departmentalization, and job descriptions.
- To delineate between a centralized management structure and decentralized management structure.
- To discuss the importance of accountability as an element of structure.
- To evaluate external stakeholders and to organize, manage, and control them.

INTRODUCTION

Chapter 1 in this book reviewed the first of the five managerial tasks—planning. This chapter accentuates the managerial function of organization. The section probes personal organizational techniques as well as athletic program organization and design structure. In the truest meaning of the organizational function in the management process, the concept of organization is formally associated with the blueprint configuration of the business (in our case, athletic program). However, for our purposes, the meaning of the term *organization* encompasses personal as well as athletic program organization. The relevant rationale is that one's personality and individual performance can have a direct correlation on the prosperity of a program. Simply put, if the coach or program administrator is an organized and structured individual, the program will be organized and structured. Unfortunately, in this scenario, the inverse is also true.

PERSONAL ORGANIZATION

Personal organization is an exceptionally subjective topic. Tactics that can be useful for enhancing one person's performance might not work well for another. To discover if one is personally organized, ask some elementary, point-blank questions:

1. Is work getting done in a timely manner?
2. Is there spare time during the day to sit back and examine overall

When inquiring into one's personal organization, do not take the findings as positive or negative. Critical introspection should be as non-emotional as possible. One's aspiration should be to mature into the most professional, competent coach/program administrator that he/she can be. Ask for other program personnel's opinions of one's organizational skills and use that information to improve organizational techniques.

program direction and goals or is one constantly inundated with daily assignments that seem endless?

3. Can pertinent materials and data be retrieved instantaneously?
4. Is one always rushing to get to critical engagements and meetings?
5. Is it possible to manipulate and control the length and content of meetings? Of phone calls?
6. When leaving the program at night, does one feel prepared for the next day?

If not satisfied with the answers to the above questions, a coach or program administrator can explore the potential of improving personal organization in two important areas—time management and office organization.

Time Management

The most precious commodity we all have is time. In some cases, the sheer magnitude of work will dictate the availability of coaching and professional time. In most other instances, a coach can have a direct influence on time control and planning. This is where the much elaborated concept of time management comes into play.

The business concept of time management can be analyzed by saying:

> The problem is not a time problem. We all have the same amount. It's a choice problem. The choices you make determine if you're running your life, or is your life running you . . . sure there may be consequences to saying no, establishing boundaries or reordering priorities. But there are also consequences if you don't . . . you can do 50 things today and get little, if any, results for having done them. Or you can do one or two things that bring a big return, be it emotional, financial, physical or psychological. People who are winning at work know the difference and operate accordingly. (Russell, 2006, p. 28)

Making choices can literally take a matter of seconds to complete. For larger roles and responsibilities, one will need to outline a course of action on making logical time choices to complete assignments/tasks/responsibilities. These choices are strictly seen from a situational and contemplative personal standpoint. In other words, only an individual can determine how his or her choices and how his or her time is being applied and if the application is adequate. If it is perceived that one's choices are lacking, the development of an improvement strategy would be advantageous.

The repercussions of time management and the effective utilization of time has been a source of managerial focus and research for decades. As the program administrator, consolidate and emphasize time planning in all operational functions.

In the 2007 article titled *Finding Connection and Creativity in Craziness*, Hallowell proposes some distinct tips and tactics to create balance in one's hectic personal and coaching lives. The following are an extrapolation of his time management tips.

Tip 1: Do what matters most to you. Accept that time is limited and finite. . . . Learn how you spend yours and determine which time is allocated toward what matters most to you and which is not. You must choose. A person not doing what matters most to him or her is the most common cause of an excessively busy life.

Tip 2: Cut out those activities that are not important, while focusing on those that are. I call this "cultivating the lilies and getting rid of the leeches." Cultivate what is positive and matters most to you. Give yourself permission to get rid of what hinders you, whether they're projects, people, or ideas.

Tip 3: Create a positive emotional environment wherever you are.

Tip 4: Think of time as something you invest . . . and invest it for maximum return. Try not to let time be stolen from you or let yourself fritter it away.

Tip 5: Don't waste time "screen-sucking." Engage with your computer, PDA, videogames, television, and other screens when necessary, but make sure to turn them off when you can . . . screen-sucking is a modern addiction and a difficult problem to solve.

Tip 6: Identify and control sources of what I call "gemmelsmerch." This is the sticky force that distracts you from what you want to be or should be doing.

Tip 7: Don't multitask. Your brain is not wired to multitask effectively except in very specific cases that require virtually no thinking. Give what you are doing your full attention. You will do it better and you will do it faster.

Tip 8: Delegate what you don't like to do or aren't good at if you possibly can. Your goal shouldn't be to be independent, but rather effectively interdependent.

Tip 9: Slow down. . . . Take time to stop and think deeply. Ask yourself, "What's my hurry?"

Tip 10: Play. Imaginatively engage with what you are doing. This will naturally lead you to use the best part of your mind and help you stay focused. (Hallowell, 2007, p. 11–14)

There are auxiliary tools that can be utilized to systematize time and activities.

1. Personal Goal Setting: Personal goal setting is a powerful technique to actively control the use of one's time. Personal goals can range from major life goals to daily tasks and responsibilities. While spelling out major life goals might not seem a good use of time, it provides an individual with daily focus and responsibilities that will save time and effort in the long run.

Administrative Tip

Ask diligent, industrious people outside the program how they manage their time. Pose specific questions that relate to the program's operations and how they would handle the time constraints. Inquire what one of their typical days is like. From these explorations, form time management improvement techniques.

2. A List of Things to Do: Once goals have been broken down into daily tasks/assignments to reach those goals, a coach/program administrator needs to frame a comprehensive list of things to do. This list can be ordered by function, priority, or duration of assignments and tasks. The simplest, most valuable method is the three-point priority system. On a daily basis, write a master list of things to do. Even if the list is practically identical to the day prior, rewriting it on a daily basis reaffirms responsibilities and appointments. While writing the list, leave the left margin open. After the list is completed, go through each line item and numerically order them on importance and gravity. An item or task that has critical consequences should be numbered with a *1*. A *2* responsibility is a midrange element that has significance but is not an imperative priority. Obviously, a *3* duty is a low concern that does not necessitate immediate attention. The other purpose for rewriting the list on a continual basis is to re-rank objectives and duties. For example, a *3* priority task could suddenly become a *1* priority overnight or vice versa. Another modification could be to date each item or responsibility on its projected or required completion date. As soon as a task is completed, mark it off. It is often a good idea to maintain a file of preceding lists to substantiate task completion and dates.

3. Daily Schedules/Daily Planner: Breaking this concept down, arrange the day alongside the list of things to do. It does not have to be an intricate, minute-by-minute timetable; rather a generalized time schedule. When planning out the day, one should always attempt to leave an open-door period during which the program's staff and athletes have an opportunity to discuss their concerns and problems.

   A new technological practice for time management and daily scheduling is incorporated into most organizations' e-mail systems. "Use Outlook to schedule your work and down time. Outlook (or your office's equivalent) has a method to remind you of tasks and/or meetings; it can be audible, visual, or both" (Time management, 2007, p. 3). The major advantage of using integrated e-mail scheduling calendars is the ability to remotely access your schedules from any location, at any time.

4. Screen Calls: Plan in the daily agenda time to return calls. If possible, screen calls for their importance. An urgent message warrants immediate attention, while a low priority message should be returned afterward.

5. Re-Channel Unscheduled Visitors to Open Time Slots: This is more precarious than screening calls simply because of the face-to-face predicament. Initially, weigh the cost and benefit of an unscheduled "drop in." If it is perceived that an unscheduled visitor could have

a substantial benefit, the conversation mandates direct, uninterrupted attention. It should be noted that if one evaluates the benefits of a conversation and feels that it is necessary, give that individual your undivided attention. If not, the conversation will be costly in respect to time as well as detrimental to the future relationship with that individual.

6. Alternate Work Site: Try to maintain a discrete, alternate work area if possible. As devious as this seems, attempt to find an inconspicuous and obscure corner to get away from "no win" time periods. A "no win" time period is one where priorities are outstanding and interruptions are many. Have an office or staff confidant involved at all times in case of any contingent emergencies.

7. Managing Program Supplies: While having adequate supplies might seem a trivial matter where time management is concerned, running out of vital program items (such as printer cartridges, copy paper, file folders, etc.) at the wrong time can turn out to be a monumental time waster. In the most basic terms, know the program's supply room and what supplies it will take to operate the program efficiently. A common sense rule in supply room management is to overstock rather than run out.

8. Travel Time Organization: Much of a coach's or program administrator's time is spent traveling. This travel time, while regarded a "necessary evil" of the profession, is a wonderful way to get various program tasks accomplished. The salient key to exploiting this technique is to know (or estimate) the time one will have available during travel and what program items can be completed during that time. For example, an East Coast to West Coast flight can take anywhere between four or five hours (not counting airport time). With the continual convenience and usefulness of laptop computers, program correspondence, practice and game planning, revisiting program goals, and recruiting obligations are just a small number of the items that can be a part of the productive use of travel time.

9. Devise Checklists for Program Personnel: A coach and program administrator should devise program checklists for program members (both staff and athletes) to discharge routine tasks. The construction of these checklists, with the actual staff member's or athlete's input, will cost front-side time but prevent tremendous follow-up effort. Besides the time-saving benefit, these comprehensive checklists can strengthen a program's quality control and value.

10. Delegation: Delegation is defined as "the process of assigning managerial authority and responsibility to managers and employees lower in the hierarchy. To be more efficient, most managers are expected to delegate as much of their work as possible" (Kinicki & Williams, 2003, p. 256). The notable time management key to this

definition is to delegate as much as possible. Does this statement endorse the delegation of all responsibilities? No. However, it does sanction allowing subordinates to do their jobs, with managerial authority, and to save the coach/program administrator's time for more significant program needs. The worst time management statement associated with delegation is "if you want something done right, do it yourself." This mindset toward delegation and time management not only decreases the program's work output, it breaks down any potential division of labor essential to program operations.

11. Positive Work Habits: Developing positive work habits has an immediate correlation to time management and personal organization. The ensuing list has some of the workable tactics a coach/program administrator can use to maximize his/her time and organization.

- Arrive on time or a few minutes before a meeting or appointment.
- Do first things first and respond quickly to requests for information.
- Take careful notes and keep track of deadlines.
- Meet all deadlines.
- Write down all appointments.
- Review procedures in small groups.
- Project the most likely consequence of a decision.
- Assess and adjust when necessary.
- Be a follow-through person.
- Write notes to yourself.
- Return phone calls.
- Write action steps for projects.
- Follow up on details.
- Do the unpleasant but necessary things that you tend to avoid.
- Remind team members, tactfully, to finish projects.
- Don't make promises you can't keep. (Ferrett, 2003, p. 217)

Office Organization

Once again, how one arranges one's office or work area is purely a subjective preference. Does a clean office necessarily mean an organized, proficient office? Not necessarily. Everyone has known people whose work areas could be pronounced disaster zones, but when asked, they could find an obscure object or document processed six months earlier. On the other hand, there are people whose offices and desks are so tidy that they could land a plane on them, but they never seem to be able to locate anything that they are looking for. *Whatever works* is the primary consideration.

The following are principal factors and components of office organization:

1. Filing systems
2. Pitch method

3. Office flow
4. Computers

Filing Systems

Because of the escalating popularity of personal computers, filing now has evolved into a question of which floppy disk, hard drive, or CDs contains which file of information. However, even with the most reliable computer systems, it is crucial that a "hard copy" filing system (tangible backup copy, typically a print out or other paper document of pertinent data) be maintained. These materials must be cataloged in such a way that they can be located instantaneously with little or no effort by all staff members associated with the program. The cardinal rule of filing is "the simpler the better." Expenditures associated with filing systems can be minimal. If ordered correctly, a five-drawer cabinet with basic hanging file folders can be more than sufficient to meet one's filing needs.

To install a filing system, one needs to identify paramount program categories first and work toward smaller details within each classification. Hopefully, the program will not have more than five or six dominant classifications. For example, for most athletic programs, some of the major categories could be *player files, travel files, home event files, recruiting files,* and *staff and general administration files.*

Player files can be sub-sectioned into groups (age, position, school status) or could be filed aggregately. Whether sub-sectioned or not, these files should be in alphabetical order and as comprehensive as possible. Attempt to standardize basic information for each file and player. For example, a coach or program administrator might consider it essential that each athlete's file incorporate class schedules, medical information, emergency contacts, conditioning plans, etc. After the standardized data has been uniformly filed, supplement each file with other subsequent individualized information.

Travel files must be maintained with diligence. These files should be categorized by dates in ascending order. Pertinent information such as confirmation documentation, contracts, directions, itineraries, and emergency phone numbers could be included.

Home event files are not as essential to most athletic programs as player and travel files but are still meaningful to sustain. Home files, like travel files, should be in ascending order of event dates. They could incorporate schedules, event protocols, competition contracts, and miscellaneous data on incoming teams.

The materials contained in recruit files are often ordered by the governing body of the organization in which the program competes (State High School Association, NCAA, National Leagues, NJCAA, professional organizations, NAIA, etc.). These files could be arranged by recruit class and contain information on each prospect's individual strengths and significance.

Administrative Tip

Precision and orderliness in a filing system can never be overstated. A disorderly and haphazard filing system can actually be worse than having no filing system at all. Reiterate to every staff member who has access to the program's filing system that not only is security a primary ingredient of filing but so is neatness.

Staff and general administration files can comprise an extensive variety of data. Program components such as budgeting and financial information, promotional activities, mailing lists and booster/alumni contacts, and updated departmental memos can be included in this filing category. It is also recommended that these files be sorted alphabetically.

Once the system has been refined, it is imperative that all files are intermittently cleaned out. Files have a tendency to get cluttered with obsolete materials. Appropriate maintenance means going through each one and "thinning out" non-pertinent information. Additionally, at the end of the fiscal or competitive year, pull out yearly files and archive and store them for future reference. Even though it is up to one's personal preference, it is advisable to retain archived files for at least three years.

To conclude this section, the 2001 article titled *Filing . . . like the beat . . . goes on . . . and on* has a list of pointers on managing paper and filing. The following is a summarization of its concepts:

- Have a simple but complete filing system . . . one that makes sense to you.
- Always alphabetize. No matter what the structure of your filing system is, alphabetize within in it. It will save you time.
- Always color code for easy, quick identification. . . . Apply color coding even for a few files. As the number of files grows, the color system will make it easier to determine where a new file will go.
- Duplicating a document for filing in two different places creates more work, more bulk and is seldom useful. Resist.
- Place most recent documents in the front of the file folder . . . the oldest documents will be in the back when it is time to purge files.
- Sometimes deciding where to file a document is tricky. Always ask yourself, "Where would I look for this if I need it?" Never ask, "Where should I put this?"
- File each document as you finish with it or file at the end of the day. Don't let filing pile up.
- Staple together documents on the same subject with the most current information on top. Don't use paperclips . . . they can come off or catch on other papers in a file.
- Mark a discard date if you know when a document will become obsolete. Later you will know that you can throw it away without having to take time to read it. (Filing . . . like the beat . . . goes on . . . and on, 2001, p. 24)

Additionally, to keep track of the categories of items filed and to be filed, post a single sheet of paper alongside the file cabinet with the categories and their breakdown. The filing breakdown could be in a simplified outline form. In addition to being a reference, the sorting document could act as a method of designating file names appropriately. To maintain the filing system and adequately purge files, schedule times to routinely review the filing system. The times could be standardized from week-to-week or could be by a once-a-month open time schedule. It is advisable not to let files go unattended for longer than one month.

Pitch Method

As with businesses, athletic programs at all levels of competition become engulfed in mounds of paper. Memos, fliers, newsletters, and brochures are just a small number of items accumulating on our desks on a routine basis. There is an uncomplicated solution to this problem: it is called the pitch method. The pitch method is based on a three-step evaluation process. For example, when a departmental memo is generated and distributed to the program, a coach or program administrator can do one of three things: act on it, file it, or pitch it. If we originate our paper flow thinking process with the third component (pitch it) first and work backwards, our offices would be less overrun with paper. If a memo or other item is meaningless (which half of them typically are), toss it and the problem is solved. If there is a piece of critical data in the document, there are two alternatives. It can be filed for future reference and subsequently thrown away when it becomes irrelevant, outdated, or obsolete, or it can be acted on by consolidating it into a list of things to do. It is that easy. The most significant consideration with this paper flow technique is that the program does not amass piles of documents and papers. Simply address each document as soon as it arrives. This approach also has the beneficial side effect of timely responsiveness to all memos rather than accumulation and omission by fault.

Office Flow

The concept of office flow and workspace design is an exacting science that examines acoustics, lighting, safety, and temperature. To investigate the details of these highly specialized areas is beyond the scope of this text. However, office flow and design can be looked at strictly from an administrative perspective. In other words, how can coaches/program administrators make their offices and work areas conducive for the best use of their time and effort?

Because most coaches and program administrators have departments that would be considered small by most business standards, the work place evaluation process can be done in minutes. When defining the operational goals, simply ask the following questions:

- What is the program's office(s) used for and what does it produce?
- Is record storage a priority?
- Is the office a meeting area?

The easiest way to tackle this problem is to make a list of all of the things created and accomplished in the office and prioritize that list. From there, examine the office's current operational status. Ask another basic question: Is the current office flow satisfying the program's office priorities? If not, document what user-requirements the office lacks and determine what would fulfill those requirements. The first step is probably the most overlooked in the process. Most administrators do not define what they want to produce from their work areas, so they really do not have them arranged very logically or effectively.

From there, there are only two other cardinal rules associated with office flow. The first provision is that *all of the actual work areas should be as far away from people traffic as possible.* The second is that *the work areas should be ordered and designed so that one can access everything in the office* (desks, files, fax) *while seated and on the phone.* If the coach or program administrator observes these two fundamental rules, the rest of the layout is up to one's personal disposition and usable space.

Computers

The final area of office organization is computers. There is only one requirement in regard to the use of computers in a coach's personal and professional life—get one and learn to use it. Costs are rapidly declining, the program workload can be cut in half, the operating systems and software are becoming increasingly user friendly, and the quantity of online data that can be utilized by the athletic program is increasing exponentially. The benefits far outweigh the costs.

In choosing the program's computer software, major considerations should be uniformity, consistency, and usability. It is strongly recommended that a popular, universally recognized, integrated software package be utilized. An integrated software program is one containing a word processor, spreadsheet, database, and presentation software. This all-inclusive package is not only cost effective, but also encompasses most, if not all, of the athletic program software needs. Currently, the most accepted and generally known integrated software package is Microsoft Office. This integrated package has numerous training courses associated with its use as well as abundant support literature. It has upgrading capabilities and should have a long software life.

No matter how powerful/updated the program's computer and office technology, basic organizational procedures must be followed. One of the major areas of computer use and effectiveness deals with the orderliness and retrieval of computer files and documents. A strong office organization practice for managing computer files parallels the techniques used for "hard copy" filing. The program's computer files should be arranged in a "tree like" frame with core file headings, sub-file headings within these core headings, and specific files/documents within these sub-headings (see Figure 1). For documents and files outside the major file categories, a desktop miscellaneous file should be utilized and maintained. As with the program's hard copy file system, make sure the appropriate personnel know how the file and document tree is set up. If information in the program's computer filing system is confidential, establish "for you eyes only" security protocol.

Finally, for the program's safety and computer file integrity, it is strongly advised to furnish program personnel with portable flash drives. Flash drives, which connect through the USB ports, provide formidable protection from the fallibility of computers. Flash drives can be transported easily (most can be connected to key chains) and have sizable memory capacities. Because they are portable, confidential information should be for in-house flash drives only.

COMPUTER DESKTOP

MAJOR FILE HEADINGS

Player Files	Travel Files	Home Events	Recruiting Files	Staff Files	General Admin. Files	Miscellaneous Files

SUB-FILE HEADINGS

Freshman Sophomore Junior Senior	2008 2009	2008 2009	2008 2009 2010	Coaches Support Staff	Memos Meetings Schedules Forms Reports Budgets Alumni	Open Items

DOCUMENT LEVEL

Conditioning Plans Medical Class Schedules Etc.	Directions Confirmations Itineraries Contacts Etc.	Each Event Breakdown Etc.	Correspondence Rating Charts Contact Info. Visit Info. Legislative Complications Etc.	Résumés Job Descriptions Other H.R. Info. (as required)	All General Administration Documents

Figure 1. **Practical Computer File Tree for Athletic Programs**

ATHLETIC PROGRAM ORGANIZATION

The coach is the manager of the athletic program. To be successful, one should consider the program, no matter how large or small, a business. To think of it as anything else would be to restrict its capacity for expansion and ultimate success. From the management functional standpoint, planning is the initial and foremost priority in establishing the business. To recapitulate, planning is the future oriented function of determining strategic goals for the program's operation. From this plan, the manager must mold and configure the enterprise to achieve the stated goals. This is the underlying thought behind organizational development and design.

Step-By-Step Organizational Structuring Process

There is a logical step-by-step process to structure one's athletic program. While uncomplicated in concept, the construction and application can be, at times, tedious and demanding. With that being said, it is crucial that the process be followed and a program structure established (or re-established if re-organizing an already existing program). Without a sound, plausible organizational structure, an athletic program will, most likely, never realize its potential and have success.

The step-by-step process is as follows:

Step 1. Lay out and re-visit all of the athletic program's goals created in the program plan. The principal rationale for this is to concentrate the structure on the objectives that are directly related toward the program's achievement.

Step 2. From the goals (both long-term and short-term actions), assemble a detailed inventory of all the major jobs and action-oriented tasks/assignments to accomplish each specific goal.

Step 3. This is the extracting and grouping of tasks stage. Individually or in a collective session with athletic program personnel, craft job positions (job designing) from items grouped. First and foremost in constructing these job positions should be effectiveness and the ability of the position to achieve organizational goals.

Step 4. The forth step in the progression is taking each position and building hierarchical departments. Additionally, this stage should have profound emphasis on resource allocation, span of control for each department and job position, and accountability.

Step 5. This stage encompasses the formulization of the structure. A well-defined hierarchal chart as well as complete position/job descriptions should be completed. The coach/program administrator will need to meet with all program personnel to illuminate positional responsibilities and to define the reporting chain of command. It is imperative that every individual in the athletic program understand completely his/her status and duties along with the resources available and supervisory authority in the organization.

Step 6. The final step in the process is monitoring and adjusting, when necessary, the organizational structure for goal realization. In most cases, if the first five steps in the process are adhered to, this stage will have some positional "tweaking" of obligations and assignments. However, a substantial environmental change (or changes) will need scrutinizing as to the current and future effects on the program and the projected goals. If in these cases the external circumstance has a profound influence on the program, the re-structuring process (steps one through five) will need to be addressed.

Job Descriptions

As stated in step three of the six-step program organizational process, individual job descriptions/positions need to be constructed prior to departmentalizing positions. In other words, each internal position, from strictly a program viewpoint, needs a detailed and precise job description (see Appendix 3A). In this job description, list

1. The official title of the position and summarize its placement in the organization;
2. The functions of the position in order of the most significant to the least;
3. If feasible, an approximate range of time, in percentage form, of each function (50% of the position is recruiting, 25% is team training, etc.);
4. The empowerment of the position. In other words, the sanctioned authority delegated by the program coach/manager for the position;
5. The accountability of the position; and
6. The reward system for the position.

Departmentalization

Step four in the six-step process for structuring an organization to accomplish goals is to group constructed positions into departments. How a coach/program administrator assembles these departments is by individual preference as well as a desire to put together the best possible work units. There are four key ways businesses establish departments. These four departmentalization systems can easily be adapted to athletic programs.

Today the most common bases for organizing a business into effective departments are by function, by product, by location, and by type of customer.

- Departmentalization by function—grouping jobs that relate to the same organizational activity
- Departmentalization by product—grouping activities related to a particular product or service
- Departmentalization by location—grouping activities according to the defined geographic area in which they are performed
- Departmentalization by customer—grouping activities according to the needs of various customer populations (Pride, Hughes, & Kapoor, 2002, pp. 214–215)

Smaller athletic programs might find that one departmentalization method (customarily by function) would be more than sufficient to structure their programs. Larger programs with numerous customers, locations, and services may employ more departmentalization groupings under an all-encompassing athletic program structure.

Organizational Charts

> Organizational charts help employees understand how their work fits within the overall operation of the firm . . . it is a visual representation of a firm's structure that illustrates job position and functions . . . an organizational chart depicts the division of a firm into departments that meet organizational needs. (Boone & Kurtz, 2006, p. 284)

The types of organizational charts in today's businesses are numerous. For a majority of athletic programs, an uncomplicated classical method with direct lines of command will be more than adequate. This traditional format (or vertical hierarchical chart) has distinct advantages even as it has some limitations. Its advantages include being a top-down blueprint that has clear lines of authority and communication, minimization of formal jurisdiction power struggles between different staff members, and the provision of status to primary areas necessary for program survival and prosperity. Its disadvantages include minimal coordination and interaction between nonaligned positions, lack of horizontal training (which promotes well-rounded employees), potential for informal power friction between positions of the same level, and reduction of the ability of the staff to progress and advance in the program because all occupational promotions are on the vertical axis.

Organizational structure clarification should be a top priority for coaches and administrators. Staff members will perform better if they know the expectations of the job, their employment duties, the importance of the assignments in the hierarchical design, and their position's compensation and rewards.

Job descriptions along with hierarchical charts should be readily accessible and always utilized in staff evaluations. Take time to create them. In the long run, it will save countless hours of miscommunication, supervision, and frustration. The aggregate total of all of the job descriptions should encompass every known element of the operation. Regard them as adaptable documents that can be molded to fit the program's needs if the situational environment changes.

Centralized versus Decentralized Management/Structure

Another organizational structure concern relates to the concept of centralized or decentralized management. The philosophies are easy to understand. Centralized management is when a coach or program administrator (at the top of the hierarchal chain of command) retains the greater part of the program's authority, decision making, and power. Centralized management is a top-down theory in which prominent decisions are controlled by top level administrators while routine, day-to-day actions are completed by lower level personnel. Decentralized is diametrically opposite.

Administrative Tip

Whatever the organizational configuration one's program uses, underscore simplicity and clarity for all involved. Have no hidden agendas. Make sure all internal stakeholders know precisely where they are positioned in the organization. If a coach/ program administrator takes for granted and assumes that the internal staff and athletes know their power and structural position, he/she is exposing the program to destructive interpersonal conflicts within its operations.

Formal authority, decision making, and power is "push down" or "spread out" to the positions in the lower level of the organization's structure.

Centralized versus decentralized management and structure is a philosophical outlook as well as an operational situation. If the coach/program administrator believes he/she has a capably trained, loyal, and mature staff, he/she might choose to, during the construction of job positions and duties, assign tasks to program positions that have an elevated deal of autonomy and program authority. Conversely, a new and inexperienced staff could need a centralized management structure until they acquire program experience and maturity. A special note—a miscalculation in constructing jobs and structure could have disastrous consequences. For example, if a coach/program administrator chooses a centralized management structure with a mature and experienced staff, there is a strong chance that some (if not all) program members will be dissatisfied and unmotivated. This, in turn, will contribute to goal breakdown. However, if a coach/program administrator chooses a decentralized power structure and bestows critical job responsibilities and influence to inexperienced staff members, there is also a strong chance that jobs will be inadequately completed and this will contribute to goal breakdown.

Organizational Structure and Accountability

A concluding remark on internal athletic program structuring . . . no matter what the concentration and complexity, design and construction, or centralized or decentralized style, an organization's structure will not facilitate the achievement of program goals without accountability. In the 2007 text *Introduction to Business*, Madura succinctly summarizes the magnitude of accountability in organizational structure by stating:

> While organizational structure indicates job descriptions and the responsibilities of employees and managers, the firm also needs to ensure that its employees and managers are accountable. One of the important duties of the firm's managers is to evaluate employees and make them accountable for fulfilling their responsibilities. The job descriptions provide direction for the positions, but the managers above the positions must determine whether the employees performed according to their job descriptions. (Madura, 2007, p. 282)

External Influencers

Internal influencers are people over whom the coach and program administrator have sovereignty and control, including formal authority and legitimate power. External influencers are people who have a stake in the athletic program and have formal or informal authority over the program. One's first impression after reading the previous statement is, "How can a coach

Administrative Tip

When dealing with an individual's authority and influence, never forget that power is linked undeniably with people's egos. Be sensitive to the program stakeholder's personalities and egotistical composition. By no means should one ever disregard the potency of self-esteem and sense of worth. To overlook it would open a "Pandora's box" of personality conflicts.

Administrative Tip

An imperative key in dealing with external influencers is perceptive empathy. An insensitive act (even unintentionally) could do enormous damage to the support structure of the program. Try to know the program's influencers and anticipate their possible reactions to certain situations.

or program administrator have organizational control and structure over people who have power or jurisdiction over the program and its operation?" There are two solutions:

1. Pleasant avoidance.
2. Aggressive incorporation.

Pleasant avoidance is almost self-explanatory: Endeavor to make the program as self-sufficient as at all possible and evade/avoid (pleasantly) external influencers. This is also known as diffusing external influencer's power. In predicaments of conflict and confrontation with the external influencer, promptly and calmly resolve the problem or requirement and proceed with the program's regular operations. In some circumstances, this might be the only technique for organizing and dealing with incompatible and demanding external influencers. Fulfill all requirements requested and stay away from that individual. The chief advantage of this technique is less trepidation, aggravation, and stress for everyone involved in the operation (internal influencers). The disadvantage is the loss of a potential program patron and supporter.

The second program tactic involves aggressively incorporating the external influencer into the organization's structure. In other words, the coach or program administrator's management obligation is to develop and organize a continuous public relations plan that summons people of influence and power into the program. The danger is evident; once inside the organizational structure, without tactical supervision and control, these individuals could use their power to bring about internal disorder and destruction.

To organize the external influencer, a coach or program administrator's goal should be to prioritize and structure the individuals and what they require and want out of the program. Make an inventory of external stakeholders and develop particular listings of each of their expectations, requirements, and agendas. At that point, have a systematic game plan for providing each one with generalized data in a timely manner. The benefits from this are plentiful. The external influencer will perceive that he or she has a vested interest in the program and will then use resources and capabilities to improve and help the athletic program.

SUMMARY

Both personal and professional program organization are essential operational components for successful athletic programs. Through organization, one can reasonably employ all personal and program resources to the program's mission and its achievement of operational goals. The program will be able to effectively utilize personal and program power as well as control and develop external patrons and followers. A properly ordered professional environment can do several positive things:

1. Convey professionalism that, in turn, inspires confidence.
2. Minimize stakeholder and influencer apprehension about the operation and their specific role.
3. Provide a competitive edge in the arena by furnishing the coaches, staff, and players more time to concentrate efforts on improving skills and capabilities in their particular field rather than catching up on a disorganized workload.

KEY TERMS

time management	office flow
list of things to do	computer software
daily schedules/daily planner	job descriptions
screening calls	departmentalization
alternate work site	organizational charts
hard copy filing system	centralized management/structure
supply management	decentralized management/structure
delegation	accountability
pitch method	external influences

Review and Discussion Questions

1. What direct questions should be asked to discover if one is personally organized?

2. What time benefits come from personal goal setting?

3. Describe the three-point priority system used to create a list of things to do.

4. How can e-mail systems help with time management?

5. Why would a coach or program administrator want to utilize an alternate work site?

6. How does supply management help with time management?

7. Define the term *delegation*.

8. What are the four components of office organization?

9. Why is it important to maintain a hard copy filing system and how would one create and develop it?

10. What is the *pitch method* of office organization?

11. What questions should a coach or program administrator ask when defining the administrative goals of office flow?

12. What should one consider when choosing an athletic program's computer software?

13. What are flash drives and how can they be important?

14. What are the six steps to structuring an athletic program?

15. What are the six components of a job description?

16. What are the four ways to departmentalize an organization?

17. What are organizational charts?

18. What is the difference between centralized and decentralized management?

19. What are the two solutions associated with external influencers?

CHAPTER

3

Human Resource Management for Coaches and Athletic Administrators

CHAPTER OUTLINE

CHAPTER

3

OBJECTIVES

- To define human resource practices used by contemporary businesses and apply those techniques to athletic programs
- To outline some of the basic employment/human resource laws/acts that can affect athletic programs
- To present an understanding of staffing systems as they relate to tracking demand shifts, manpower planning, and recruiting concepts
- To explain the five-stage selection process as it relates to athletics
- To review organizational orientation and departmental orientation programs
- To explore concepts of human resource training and development
- To clarify human resource evaluations (MBOs and 360 Degree Evaluations)
- To assess the fundamentals of athletic program rewards, compensation and benefits
- To illuminate step-by-step methods of employee discipline and grievance policies and procedures

Administrative Tip

Never disregard the crucial reality that the people in one's organization are the lifeblood of productivity. A coach/program administrator could never achieve any of the program's goals if it was not for their dedication and hard work. Consciously focus on the concept of lifeblood of productivity when dealing with the program's most valuable resource ...its people.

INTRODUCTION

Human resource management "is the process of providing an adequate mix of employees for achieving organizational goals. It includes forecasting employee skill needs, comparing them to present skill base, and determining the appropriate human resource actions" (Bedeian, 1993, p. 340). In other words, human resource administration is a hands-on, people-oriented function. It directly correlates to the productivity of the program. Productivity can be thought of as the acquisition and effective utilization of resources to maximize organizational worth. Undoubtedly, the most indispensable resources in any program or business are its human resources.

This chapter highlights the managerial component of human resource planning and management. Because these principals are generically applicable to all businesses, situations, and industries, they can be freely adapted and applied to athletic programs. Inside a particular athletic program, the two sources of human resources come from program staff (coaches, secretaries, managers, volunteers, etc.) and athletes. The following tactics can be utilized throughout program operations to support these two internal stakeholder groups.

LEGAL ASPECTS OF HUMAN RESOURCE MANAGEMENT

Before one can examine the business models and applications involved in human resource management, it is first essential for coaches and program administrators to recognize, comprehend, and appreciate the basic legal aspects and responsibilities that go along with this managerial function.

While the field of human resource management law is considerably beyond the capacity of this text, it is important that a coach and program administrator be cognizant of the legal foundations and ramifications of proper human resource management. As with all specialized fields, it is advisable to discuss any and all legal concerns with trained experts. For coaches and program administrators operating within educational institutions, the human resource department is characteristically a knowledgeable informational and advising asset. For individual, autonomous athletic programs,

---

Table 1. Summary of Equal Employment Opportunity Laws and Executive Orders

Law/Acts/Year	Purpose or Intent/Coverage
Equal Pay Act (1963)	**Purpose**: Prohibits sex-based discrimination in rates of pay for men and women working in the same or similar jobs. **Coverage:** Private employers engaged in commerce or in the production of goods for commerce and with two or more employees; labor organizations.
Title VII, Civil Rights Act **(1964/1972)**	**Purpose:** Prohibits discrimination based on race, sex, color, religion, or national origin. **Coverage:** Private employers with 15 or more employees for 20 or more weeks per year, institutions, state and local governments, employment agencies, labor unions, and joint labor-management committees
Age Discrimination in Employment Act (1967)	**Purpose:** Prohibits discrimination against individuals who are at least 40 years of age but less than 70. An amendment eliminates mandatory retirement at age 70 for employees of companies with 20 or more employees. **Coverage:** Private employers with 20 or more employees for 20 or more weeks per year, labor organizations, employment agencies, state and local governments and federal agencies, with some exceptions.
Pregnancy Discrimination Act (1978)	**Purpose:** Requires employers to treat pregnancy just like any other medical condition with regard to fringe benefits and leave policies. **Coverage:** Same as Title VII, Civil Rights Act.
Immigration Reform and Control Act (1986)	**Purpose:** Prohibits hiring of illegal aliens. **Coverage:** Any individual or company.
Americans with Disabilities Act (1990)	**Purpose:** Increase access to services and jobs for disabled workers. **Coverage:** Private employers with 15 or more employees.
Older Workers Benefit Protection Act (1990)	**Purpose:** Protects employees over 40 years of age in regard to fringe benefits and gives employees time to consider an early retirement offer. **Coverage:** Same as Age Discrimination Employment Act.
Civil Rights Act (1991)	**Purpose:** Permits women, persons with disabilities, and persons who are religious minorities to have a jury trial and sue for punitive damages if they can prove intentional hiring and work place discrimination. Also requires companies to provide evidence that the business practice that led to the discrimination was not discriminatory but was job related for the position in question and consistent with business necessity. **Coverage:** Private employers with 15 or more employees.
Family and Medical Leave Act (1993)	**Purpose:** Enables qualified employees to take prolonged unpaid leave for family and health related reasons without fear of losing their jobs. **Coverage:** Private employers with 15 or more employees.

(information extrapolated from Byars & Rue, 2006, p. 30)

contacting/retaining a lawyer(s) with a solid emphasis in employment law can provide indispensable legal counsel.

Table 1 is a synopsis of some of the key human resource-related laws and acts that can affect athletic programs.

It is imperative that a coach/program administrator know that there are specific state and local employment laws and regulations in addition to the federal laws/acts listed in Table 1. Once again, consult with human resource managers and/or legal counsel to review these particular laws and regulations.

HUMAN SYSTEMS IN ATHLETIC ORGANIZATIONS

In today's business world, organizational philosophies and obligations toward the human element have gone beyond the simple duties of hiring, firing, and filling gaps. Modern human resource management systems embrace concepts such as employee enhancement and satisfaction, increased productivity though empowerment, and providing positive social environments for long-term commitment. This new perspective on developing and maximizing human potential should be a part of each athletic program's agenda and operation. Coaches need to perceive that each program (no matter what the extent or competitive level) is a business and that staff members and players are employee stakeholders. If coaches, as the program administrators, commit to this basic premise, they will need to construct a system that comprises six vital human resource operations:

- Staffing—recruiting, selection, and placement.
- Orientation—new hire organizational and departmental orientation.
- Training and Development—training activities, counseling, and career planning.
- Performance Evaluations—joint analysis of performance expectations and accomplishments.
- Rewards, Compensation, and Benefits—wages, performance incentives, and miscellaneous benefits.
- Disciplinary Procedures—disciplinary processes and grievance procedures.

Staffing Systems

From the standpoint of athletic administration, a coach's skillful use of staffing systems is related to acquiring the precise number and the highest qualified staff and athletes. This segment analyzes the human resource concepts of demand shift analysis, manpower planning, and recruitment and selection.

Demand Shift Analysis
When initiating a discussion on staffing, one must first examine the internal organizational demand for human resources and the external factors

that affect that demand. External factor questions that can affect human resource demand encompass the following:

- How will a fundamental shift in our local, regional, or national economic condition affect our program? Since athletic programs rely on disposable income for funding (either through paid attendance or donations), will an economic change in our operating community result in a financial change in our internal operating system? In turn, will this shift our financial situation affecting our staff?
- How do EEOC, Affirmative Action, Disabilities Act, and other governmental regulations affect us? Is our program considered socially responsible in its staffing and athletic recruitment? What does our governing athletic association state about staffing and athletic recruitment?
- Will we be able to increase our program's staffing and operations through effective use of technology?
- What are our competitors doing in terms of staffing and athletic recruitment? Are they growing or downsizing? Are they focusing their human resource efforts on a certain individual with particular strengths and areas of expertise?

These are just a few of the questions that could be asked when examining the external factors that can affect a program's staffing demands. It should be noted that whenever one is examining any external environmental element that could affect an athletic program (not only from a human resource perspective, but from the perspectives of all areas of operation), look at each factor as an opportunity or a threat. If it is an opportunity, strategize how to exploit it. If the environmental element is a threat, minimize it.

Internal elements that might shift a program's demand for human resources are organizational forces and workforce. These internal factors need continuous oversight and management. Organizational elements such as a program's strategic plan, budget and forecasted projections, new ventures, and job designs are all explicit elements that have a direct relationship on human resource needs.

Budgeting and *forecasting* (which will be covered in Chapter 6) are the most obvious and immediate determinants for staffing and players. Budgeting and forecasting delineate and place into focus what an organization can spend fiscally and what it projects to spend and earn in the future. They determine the program's size, operational limits, equipment and facilities, and human resource limitations.

Another organizational planned strategy is *new ventures*. If planned properly, not only will these ventures have goals and structure, but they will also have human resource demands within specific timeframes. New ventures are directly related to the program plan and should be included within that document.

The last of the internal organizational elements that affect human resource demand is *job design*. Job design refers to the initial development of positions in a new venture or the restructuring of positions in an ongoing operation. Either way, new job designs and descriptions typically mean a fundamental change in internal human resource demand.

The second internal element that might shift human resource demand is the program's *current workforce*. Coaches and program administrators should see the program's staff and players as a workforce. This workforce must be thought of as a flexible, flowing component of an operation that could change daily. Some changes can be anticipated in advance and planned for, such as, for example, a scheduled retirement or an anticipated leave of absence. However, other changes might not be so easy to predict. Sudden and critical demand can arise from resignation, employment termination, or severe illness and injury. To compensate for abrupt shifts in a program's human resource demands, a program will need to have in place a well defined staffing system.

Once a need for human resources has been determined through staff and player demand analysis, a coach or program administrator must apply a systematic staffing strategy. Staffing strategies for athletic programs (for either players or staff members) can be isolated into three types: manpower planning, recruiting, and selection.

Manpower Planning

Manpower planning (which is similar to human resource demand planning but more specific and narrowly defined) is

> the process of anticipating and making provisions for the movement of people into, within, and out of an organization. Its purpose is to deploy these resources as effectively as possible, where and when they are needed, in order to accomplish the organization's goals. (Bohlander, Snell, & Sherman, 2001, p. 122)

From a staff outlook, the manager needs to carefully analyze both long-term goals, which are future-oriented by nature, as well as short-term objectives, which call for more immediate actions. One must prioritize which of these goals (short and action-oriented or long and future-oriented) are critical and in need of quality staff members or players. Two scenarios may emerge from this process. The first is that the existing manpower position is deemed sufficient for the program's future goals and direction. In this case, the administrator or coach might need to do some adjusting of job responsibilities and workloads, but the staff and athletes will remain essentially the same. The second scenario is that the program's manpower needs are deemed insufficient and will require additional staffing to attain the future program projections.

The one inherent constant in all athletic programs is that there will always be player turnover. Turnover can come from age limitations, grad-

Table 2. Manpower/Human Resource Planning for Athletic Programs

Step 1

From the athletic program plan, lay out and revisit all of the projected goals and actions for the entire program.

Step 2

Lay out and revisit all of the departments and job positions in the athletic organizational structure. Each job should have a comprehensive listing of all current and future duties and responsibilities.

Step 3

From each individual job listing of duties and responsibilities, analyze what human resource skills, education, and experience each duty and responsibility requires (both now and in the future). This is commonly known as the job analysis process.

Step 4

Complete a current skills inventory for each person in those job positions. The skills inventory will examine the individual's ability to fulfill the job duties and responsibilities based on Step 3's analysis of the skills, education, and experience required performing the program's job duties and responsibilities.

Step 5

The concluding step is to construct an action plan. This action plan is used to align the goals and objectives of the athletic program with the current human resource asset of the program.

uation, quitting, injury, or other situations. Manpower planning for athletic programs can be accomplished simply through a diagram known as a depth chart. A depth chart is a versatile diagram that lists the positions in the program and the people in each position. How the coach delineates and designs the graph is entirely subjective. One possible design is as follows:

1. Across the topmost section of the chart, list the positions in the program or on the team.
2. Arrange the program players under each category in order of significance and value. If there are players who are multi-skilled, classify and index them under their primary area.
3. After placing players in descending order, color code them for age, grade, or other critical criteria. For example, in a college setting, all seniors could be highlighted in one color, juniors in another, and so forth.

This diagram will furnish the coach a visual picture of future recruiting requirements as well as where each player is currently situated in the program. Always consider this document a flexible chart. Players can progress up and (unfortunately) down as their abilities increase or decrease.

Recruiting and Selection

After manpower planning assessments have been outlined and there is a definite internal human resource need, the next logical procedure in staffing is recruiting. "Recruiting is the process of developing a pool of qualified applicants who are interested in working for the organization and from which the organization might reasonably select the best individual or individuals to hire for employment" (DeNisi & Griffin, 2001, p. 170).

Sources of Recruiting

There are two principal resources for attaining a pool of competent applicants—internal sources (known as promotion within) and external sources. Internal sources can include

- current employees/staff members already in the athletic program;

- prospective employees recommended by current athletic program members/staff; and
- former re-hirable staff members and athletes.

External sources can include

- media advertising in wide-ranging or targeted mediums (newspapers, trade publications, radio, TV, governing athletic bodies, etc.);
- college/university graduates with a focused degree in sport management/coaching education and a concentrated sports level knowledge;
- networking sources in the particular sport in which the athletic program competes; and
- other external sources such as walk-ins, transfers, agencies, etc.

Which source a coach/program administrator selects hinges upon the recruiting situation as well as the benefits and drawbacks of each method. The following list is an itemization of the benefits and drawbacks of internal and external recruiting.

Internal Recruiting Benefits

- Internal recruiting (promotion within) is a persuasive motivational tool for current program members and staff. For example, a second assistant coach is going to execute his/her current position to the best of his/her ability if he/she knows the first assistant position is attainable.
- There is a considerably reduced amount of risk with internal sources. Simply put, a coach/program administrator is already familiar with, through a working relationship, the aptitude and potential of a present staff member. That staff member is an established quantity.
- The learning curve, which is characterized as the time an employee/staff member takes to become proficient at their position, is significantly less for a current staff member. While the individual being promoted will need to cultivate additional skills and learning in their new position, he/she is already accustomed/familiar with the program's operating systems as well as internal operational policies and procedures.
- Promotion within leads to a cascading outcome throughout the entire athletic program. For example, if a first assistant coaching position is filled by a current program second assistant, that second assistant's position could be filled by a volunteer coach or graduate assistant. In turn, their position could be filled by a graduating athlete/retiring athlete.

Internal Recruiting Drawbacks

- The first negative aspect associated with internal recruiting relates to what most human resource theorists call "inbreeding." A staff member who is promoted within an athletic program could either be "set in their ways" or so "programmed" (from long-term habit) that he/she does not envision or recognize there are innovative and more resourceful methods of completing tasks.

- If there is more than one eligible candidate for an open position, promotion within can lead to an exceptionally competitive work environment. Some would argue that this internal competitiveness drives individuals to function better while others would say that it fractures the cohesiveness of the "team" atmosphere.
- If an athletic program has an open position with several qualified candidates, the individual staff members not acquiring the open position could have irreparable morale and employment-related issues in the future.
- Other internal source recruiting obstacles encompass
  - Employees who are promoted only because they've worked with the organization a long time
  - Pressure from someone inside the organization to see a favored, but unqualified individual promoted
  - In the case of a supervisory position, a promotion that is based upon skill alone, without consideration of leadership abilities
  - "Popular" people who are promoted because they get along well with people even though they are not necessarily qualified (Hacker, 1996, p. 9)

External Recruiting Benefits

- External recruiting (or bringing someone in from the outside) has an overriding benefit of infusing the athletic program with innovative ideas, work processes and procedures, novel talents and skills, and fresh energy.
- External recruiting, with a suitable pool of candidates, can legitimize and bring attention to an athletic program.
- An external recruit is not embroiled and entangled in the internal political/bureaucratic structure of an athletic program. He/she can bring about more substantive change with being involved less.

External Recruiting Drawbacks

- The first obstacle (and possibly the most internally damaging) from external recruiting is the existing employees' perception of how they were "stepped over" or given "false hope" of being promoted. This scenario can be exceptionally detrimental with long-term staff members who have been steadily productive and dedicated to the athletic program.
- The expenditures associated with external recruiting are a great deal higher than an internal promotion. Additionally, while internal promotion can take literally days or even minutes, external recruiting can take weeks and conceivably months.

- There is substantially more risk in external recruiting than internal. While recruiting and selection have logical step-by-step processes to follow, there are no assurances that the selection of an external recruit will be successful.
- External recruiting not only has a positional learning curve but an organizational learning curve. This organizational learning curve adds time and a shortfall of productivity until the newly hired staff member understands the organization's operating systems.

Selection Process

Now that the sources have been clarified, the next stage is the selection process. The selection process (which can be terminated at any time) customarily proceeds as follows:

Phase One: Phase one consists of an informal preliminary evaluation. In other words, it is the assessment of the talent of a potential staff member or athlete. It can be as informal as the program manager and other staff members verbally assessing a candidate's qualifications or as formal as charting detailed selection criteria and quantifying the results.

Phase Two: Phase two consists of applications/questionnaires and a review of résumés. These two types of instruments are accepted and recognized techniques for gathering pertinent information regarding a specific individual. The design of application and questionnaire instruments is limited by legal boundaries. For staff members, employment applications must conform to all Equal Employment Opportunity Commission and Privacy Information Act provisos and stipulations.

Player questionnaires are characteristically legislated by the governing body under which the program operates (NCAA, NAIA, high school, etc.). When discussing types of applications,

> some organizations have developed weighted application blanks, in which responses to questions on the application form are compared to with measures of job performance . . . thus, certain items found to be more important than others in regards to performance. The important or "predictive" items are then weighted and used to help select future employees. (Anthony, Perrewe, & Kacmar, 1993, p. 283)

Phase Three: Phase three consists of face-to-face conferences. Coaches and program administrators initiate this meeting through a conventional interview process. The intensity and format of the interview is determined by the significance and gravity of the position in the organization's operating scheme. Athlete face-to-face meetings can be home visits, campus visits, program meetings, individual counseling, etc. Once again, the controlling athletic association will deter-

Administrative Tip

Some application and questionnaire categories are more noteworthy in the selection of an employee/ athlete than others. Depending on the volume of applications and questionnaires received, a coach/program administrator must prioritize which categories to survey and measure for an applicant's program suitability. In other words, in critical classifications, establish ranges that must be met for a candidate to be considered. This technique can eliminate hours of tedious review.

mine the composition and duration of the encounters. Additionally, throughout this phase, contacting players in the form of written correspondence as well as additional evaluations is advisable.

There is characteristically one way for a coach and/or athletic program administrator to become a skillful and adept interviewer . . . by doing legitimate interviews. It is a routine that takes time and practice to utilize and become skilled as an interviewer. However, there are some fundamental steps that can be taken to assist a coach/program administrator with becoming a more accomplished interviewer.

Step 1: A coach/program administrator must conscientiously prepare for each and every interview. Interview preparation is a mental state as well as a logistical structure. The mental preparation for an interview correlates to "clearing ones mind" of other distractions so absolute attention can be given to the candidate being interviewed. Logistical interviewing components can encompass times and locations, a thorough examination of each individual candidates credentials and history, and pre-established questions.

Step 2: The second step in the interviewing progression is the actual interview. Actual interviewing is the

> core of the hiring process. No matter how long the interview lasts, there is still only a short period of time in which to assess the worth and value of another person and to make the decision as to whether or not you want to work side-by-side with that person for many years to come. (Curzon, 1995, p. 46)

The actual interview can have a multitude of formats and participants. A coach/program administrator can conduct the interview over a meal, with his/her supervisor, in his/her office, or a separate conference area. Additionally, a coach/program administrator can ask pre-established questions that have predetermined answers or he/she can use open-ended questions that elicit more probing reactions/responses. Special significant notation—it is imperative that a coach/program administrator circumvent at all costs questions that are illegal or discriminatory. Prior to interviewing, it is strongly advised to analyze areas and questions that can or can not be asked during an interview. Sources for this type of information are human resource departments, human resources text, and legal counsel.

Step 3: Post-interview assessment is the last step in the interviewing process. After the conclusion of the interview (or interviews),

Administrative Tip

Before conducting a face-to-face dialogue with a prospective staff member or athlete, prepare a list of appropriate questions that will prioritize vital information needed to evaluate the candidate. Outline the presentation but encourage open dialog. Keep in mind that the more one is practiced at interviewing, the better he/she will become at it. Another critical aspect of interviewing is to avoid letting the conversation go too far out on tangential topics. These interviewing digressions will lead the conversations to irrelevant subjects instead of program operations and the interviewee's fit within those operations.

a coach/program administrator needs to unemotionally scrutinize all the facts and data gathered during the all-inclusive interview process. Items such as re-reading notes taken during interviews, annotations and comments given by other interview participants, responses to questions asked, and overall behavior of individuals are just some of the elements a coach/program administrator must evaluate.

Phase Four: Phase four consists of reference checks. This step in the selection process is habitually disregarded, but is crucial in affirming the character of the staff member or player. The coach or program administrator should have a slate of definite questions ready for all reference communications.

Phase Five: Phase five consists of negotiations and hiring or acquisition. After all the germane information has been assembled and references checked, the decision is made to offer the position.

There are two consequential rules that must always be applied whether securing additional staff members or recruiting players. The first standard is to always convey the truth in all recruiting practices no matter how much the program might desire or need a particular individual. The second principal is to never "negative recruit" against another organization for a staff member or player. Negative recruiting is basically identifying other competitors for a potential staff member or athletic recruit and verbalizing derogatory remarks about their program, coaching methodology, and overall organization. Violating these basic rules will always come back to "haunt" the program one is trying to maintain and build.

Athletic Program Orientation Systems

After going through the arduous recruiting and selection process, the coach and/or program administrator has hired who he/she believes is the ideal, best suited candidate. The new staff member's first organizational impressions are the most noteworthy component in determining the length and productivity of the individual's tenure. The first initial weeks "set the tone" for the individual on what work ethics, policies and procedures, and overall organizational culture exists in the athletic program. To achieve the right atmosphere, a professional, appropriately structured orientation program is indispensable. Conversely, a haphazard and incomplete orientation program can have a destructive and often long-term influence on the new hire.

There are two types of orientation programs; organizational orientation and departmental/job orientation.

Organizational Orientation
Organizational orientation (in larger athletic programs) is typically conducted by a human resource specialist. The new hire is presented with

> **Administrative Tip**
>
> Before a negotiation of any kind, evaluate which elements are negotiable and which factors are not. Have the attitude that negotiations, by their very nature, are accommodating interactions. However, one needs to declare up front which items in the meeting are open for discussion and which items are "deal breakers." Not only will a coach/program administrator avoid critical personnel errors by using this technique, he/she will set the tempo of the interview and have total control of the negotiation.

a complete picture of the entire organization during this orientation session(s). In the text, *Keeping Your Valuable Employees*, Dibble's chapter titled "Retention Starts with Orientation" imparts bullet points on what organizational orientation programs should provide new employees. The following is an extrapolation of her orientation points.

Overview

Personal Welcome from Chief Executive Officer
Mission Statement
Annual Report
Employee Handbook
Tour of the Facilities

Forms

Personal Information
Personalized Forms for Benefits Enrollment
I-9, W-4, Direct Deposit, and Other Forms

Getting Started

Map of Organization's Locations
Directions to Them
Samples of Products
Employee Publications
Schedule of Group Orientation Session
Organizational Chart
Pictures of Key Leaders
Computer and Other Passwords
Telephone Book, Including Locations and E-mail Addresses
Attendance Expectations
Planner with Pages on the Organization

About The Job

Job Description
Career Opportunity Services
Mentoring Program
Individual Development Services
Feedback Tools Used to Assist in Development
Compensation Philosophy and Details
Performance Management Process
Training Catalog

Orienting The Workplace

Flextime Policies
Neighborhood Features
Fitness Facilities

On-site Services
Opportunities for Involvement with Volunteer and Community Programs
Recreational Facilities
Restaurants in the Neighborhood

Fun

Video to Take Home and Show the Family
Work and Family Programs
T-shirt with Logo
Sport Leagues/Team Sign-up Sheet
Invitation to Annual Picnic

Evaluation of Orientation

Evaluation Process
Evaluation Forms
(Dibble, 1999, pp. 71–72)

From the opposing organizational orientation perspective, Branham in the text *Keeping the People Who Keep You in Business*, elaborates on five common mistakes employers make when welcoming new hires.

- Having assembly-line orientations—during which new hires attend long lecture sessions and fill out forms.
- Not having the new employee's desk, phone, computer, and other office supplies in place prior to first day.
- Ignoring the new hire or leaving the person to read manuals without one-to-one contact.
- Making new hire orientation a strictly HR run affair with little involvement of the new hire's manager and department.
- Failing to have the new hire's manager set specific performance objectives. (Branham, 2001, p. 143)

Departmental Orientation

Departmental/Job orientation is the production-centered initiation in which the new hire acquires job-specialized knowledge and departmental systems understanding. The important question relating to this type of orientation is "Whom should conduct it?" Should it be administered by a current staff member in a hands-on, on-the-job configuration or should the coach/program administrator be the sole contact to review departmental activities and responsibilities? The answer is both. There should be a balance between the involvement of fellow staff members and coaches and/or program administrators. The specific position the new hire is filling will impact job orientation interaction. Some position will be heavy in employee-to-employee orientation while others will stress supervisory influence in the orientation.

Regardless of who performs the departmental/job orientation sessions, a detailed outline (or job-related check-off list) of all of the posi-

---

Administrative Tip

No matter what type of training is being performed (skill, knowledge, attitudinal), never undervalue the influence of "fun." The more a coach/program administrator can balance his/her training goals with a pleasurable environment, the more productive the training sessions will be.

Administrative Tip

Whether one is block training (repetition training) or random training (real-life training), make sure new learning is programmed as early as practical in the training session. New learning takes a focused concentration, which is easier for the learner at the outset of a training session when he/she is fresh.

tion's tasks and obligations as well as the operating systems employed by the department should be utilized. The advantage in utilizing a pre-determined departmental/job outline is the avoidance of omitting/overlooking vital operational items necessary for the new hire's productivity and effectiveness.

Training and Development Systems

The one competency on which all coaches concentrate is the training of techniques and skills. It is the teaching aspect of the profession that most coaches enjoy. Training and development augment the program's most valuable resource—people. There is a wealth of instructional methodologies that a coach can utilize.

Skill Training

Skill training is the refining of specific dexterities and corporal abilities. In the coaching of athletics, this equates to instructing the physical portion of sports. Skill instruction can take on various forms. Two primary methods are *block training* and *random training*.

Block training is teaching skills through the unremitting repetition of a particular movement or activity. Simply put, the movement is completed over and over again until it is proficiently and adeptly displayed. It should be noted that there are no set number of repetitions to achieve competency. Human beings learn at disparate rates. As a coach, recognize this fact and, through pragmatic observation and distinct evaluation, analyze each person's progress accordingly.

Random instruction is the teaching of a particular skill or action through game-like situations and competitive activities. In random training, the exercises, drills, and teaching techniques are scenario driven, which means that the game or competitive condition is defined specifically for the individual(s), then the activity is conducted in a contest-like, live-action state. Random training has some distinctive advantages in its application. Following are some of the benefits:

1. It is as close to real-world competition as training can be.
2. It has participative learning in unsystematic conditions.
3. It combines the whole of the skill or activity rather than block training, which trains parts to make the whole.
4. It has the capacity to be dynamic and can keep the athletes' cognitive focus longer.

Knowledge Training

Knowledge training guides and teaches an individual to think. Knowledge training in athletics is as individual as each sport. The range of knowledge instruction can go from the basic Xs and Os to complex strategizing and conditional analysis. The concept of intelligence training and development encompasses business and psychological theories such as individual cognitive analysis, preconditions of learning (acceptance and motivation), creative cognitions, and rationality among others.

Attitudinal Training

Attitudinal training is concerned with the character, disposition, and mindset of an individual. This is by far the most difficult type of training for the obvious reason that attitudes are immeasurable and are by individual perspective. However, there are ways in which leaders can instruct their staff and players on attitudinal expectations.

1. Candidly discuss what attitudes are anticipated and expected.
2. Document the behaviors and attitudes projected so each individual has a tangible reference.
3. Lead by example.

The third component could be the most potent of the three. If a coach or program administrator displays an impoverished, pessimistic, and unenthusiastic attitude, then his/her players and staff will more than likely adopt the same stance. Conversely, if a coach or program administrator exhibits an encouraging, optimistic attitude, the staff and athletes can observe, reference, and follow that behavior.

No matter what type of training (skill, knowledge, attitudinal), the instruction of a program's personnel (staff and players) can strongly enhance consistent and competent results by applying a straight-forward, systematic approach. In the text *Training for Non-Trainers*, there are three basic tasks that all training programs must follow.

> Your first task as a manager is to precisely define your employees training needs . . . the second task is to figure out the best way to present the training information to each employee so that only such training as is required is presented and so that it is learned in an appropriate amount of time . . . your third task as a manager is to get the right training to the right people so that the resources it uses up are an investment in productivity. (Nilson, 1990, p. 3)

The various training methods to choose from encompass (but are not limited to) the following:

On-the-Job/Real World Application Training
Supervisory Consultations (one-to-one)
Peer Subordinate Training
Group Collective Training
Virtual/Distance Training (Self-Directed Training)
Classroom/Lecture Series Training
Understudy/Apprenticeship Training
Case Study Training
Job Simulation Training

Administrative Tip

Take into account when discussing and training attitudinally that idiosyncratic personalities are involved. Any time personalities are scrutinized and discussed, as a leader, mentally emphasize understanding and empathy for the individual involved in the training. Special note: Each person handles attitudinal instruction and debate differently. Spend time appreciating the human being and their reactions before embarking on attitudinal training.

Once again, the training technique a coach or program administrator selects depends on the aspirations of the training, the resources accessible for the training (time, money, training knowledge, etc.), and the productivity expectations of each technique.

Training Program Evaluation

For continuous improvement, training programs need to be objectively and subjectively scrutinized as to their value. While skills and knowledge training lend themselves toward quantitative evaluation (numerical measurements that contrast before and after training outcomes), attitudinal training is much more challenging to objectively measure. Typically, attitudinal training is evaluated by empirical observation of the individual's attitude/behavior before and after the training.

No matter which goal one has for the program's training, the evaluation can be based on four simple steps:

Step 1: Reaction. How well did the conferees like the program?

Step 2: Learning. What principles, facts, and techniques were learned? What attitudes were changed?

Step 3: Behavior. What changes in job behavior resulted from the program?

Step 4: Results. What were the tangible results of the program in terms of reduced cost, improved quality, improved quantity, etc. (Craig, 1996, p. 295)

It is pivotal to understand that most managers (coaches/program administrators) unquestionably go straight to Step 4: Results to appraise the efficacy of a training series. While "bottom line results" are a decisive factor in the appraisal of any training program's effectiveness, the elements in Steps 1–3 (Reaction, Learning, Behavior) are also valid measurement criteria for training programs. Simply stated, if reaction to a training program is positive, if learning from a training program increases, and if behaviors and job/work ethics are changed from a training program, there is a strong presumption that the by-product of results should increase.

Performance Evaluation Systems

The primary intention behind the evaluation of a program's staff and its players' productivity is to supply feedback to internal stakeholders, standardize goals, and to improve productivity outcomes. There are abundant methodologies that can be employed when completing performance evaluations. One of the most contemporary practices for evaluating employees is based on the concept of management by objective appraisals (MBOs).

Management by Objectives (MBOs)

MBO assessments are a more cooperative, motivational, and constructive method of staff and player evaluations than the traditional one-way critical judgment analysis.

Administrative Tip

Whatever evaluation technique utilized, when assessing and commenting on a staff member or athlete's shortcomings and inadequacies, always start off the criticism with a sincere positive comment about a constructive action that the subordinate has contributed to the program. From there, discuss the area that needs improvement. The reason to start with a positive comment is to keep the staff member or athlete in the "right frame of mind." A positive mindset is receptive while a negative mindset is blocked.

The MBO process is as follows:

1) Job review and agreement. The employee and the supervisor review the job description and the key activities comprising the employee's job. The idea is to agree on the exact make-up of the employee's job.

2) Development of performance standards. Specific standards of performance must be mutually developed. This phase specifies a satisfactory level of performance that is specific and measurable.

3) Guided objective setting. Objectives are established by the employee in conjunction with, and guided by, the supervisor.

4) On-going performance discussion. The employee and the supervisor use the objectives as a basis for continuing discussion about the employee's performance. While a formal review session may be scheduled, the employee and the manager do not necessarily wait until the appointed time for performance discussion. Objectives are mutually modified and progress is discussed during the period. (Mathis & Jackson, 1982, p. 303)

This process is a perpetual and repeating system. From the four-step process, a key term must be emphasized: mutual. This collaborative type of evaluation process is in the best interest of the staff member, the athlete, and the program. From the vantage point of the athlete or staff, the system is good because it supports individuals with clear objectives that have been established with their own input. Furthermore, coaches will find that this method bolsters staff and player confidence and levels of motivation, it creates strong lines of communication, and it cultivates teamwork.

Two other key points should be emphasized in employing MBO evaluations. Remember that evaluations are a collaborative effort. At first, the coach might have to "draw out" the player or staff member in the partnership aspects of clarifying objectives. It should also be clear that the player or staff member is accountable for his or her performance. The second key point is that there should be intermittent checkpoints. These checkpoints can be in the form of formal meetings or informal updates.

360 Degree Evaluations

An evaluation method that has gained momentum in the business world that can be adopted by athletic programs is called a 360 degree performance evaluation. The concept differs from traditional one-way performance assessments in that an individual is given work-related performance evaluations from all possible people the individual works with and for (peers, supervisors, subordinates, customers, etc.). Additionally, a true 360 degree evaluation also examines the individual's own perspective of how he/she performed. There are three key assumptions on which 360 degree feedback is based:

Administrative Tip

Often the most difficult aspect of an MBO evaluation is "drawing out" the staff members or athletes to contribute to the process. To have them collaborate in their own productivity and future, uncover what motivates them. Start the MBO process there in order to get them vested into all aspects of their position. Then explain to them the critical importance of items that might not be individual motivators.

(1) Multiple viewpoints from multiple sources will produce a more accurate picture of one's strengths and weaknesses than would a single reviewer's evaluation;

(2) The act of comparing one's own self-perception with others' perception will lead to enhanced self-awareness and greater self-awareness is a good thing;

(3) People who are effective at what they do will have self-perceptions that match other's perception of them fairly closely. (Carson, 2006, p. 395)

All performance assessments systems have distinct drawbacks. The drawbacks of the 360 degree system are as follows:

- Personalities can be overemphasized. In other words, the individual's actual job performance could become secondary if the evaluators emphasize one's likeability rather job skill and productivity.
- If the peer environment in an athletic program is competitive, 360 degree evaluations will likely provide an inaccurate picture of an individual's work quality and productivity.
- 360 degree evaluation forms need to be constructed separately for each evaluation group. The evaluation criteria that a supervisor(s) might feel is important might not necessarily be what a subordinate(s) is concerned with.
- An individual's self-assessment might not be based on reality.
- 360 degree evaluations take time to compile and "number crunch" the accumulated data from all of the sources.

Rewards, Compensation, and Benefits

The final human resource system in the program relates to the compensation and benefit packages proposed to potential and current staff members and players.

Intrinsic and Extrinsic Rewards

When discussing the human resource elements involved in rewards, compensation, and benefits, a coach and/or program administrator must understand the concepts of intrinsic and extrinsic rewards and benefits. Intrinsic rewards (or intrinsically motivated behavior)

> is performed for its own sake; the source of motivation is actually performing the behavior, and motivation comes from doing the work itself. Many managers are intrinsically motivated; they derive a sense of accomplishment and achievement from helping the organization to achieve its goals and gain a competitive advantage . . . extrinsically motivated behavior is behavior that is performed to acquire material or social rewards or to avoid punishment; the source of motivation is the consequences of the behavior, not the behavior itself. (Jones & George, 2006, p. 457–458)

Intrinsically motivated rewards and behavior differs from individual to individual. Each program member (or athlete) will have different feelings of accomplishment/achievement when completing a task. A major function of the interview process is to find individuals who have a strong level of intrinsic motivation to complete the position they are hired for.

Extrinsic rewards, which are tangible rewards/compensation such as salary, benefits, and job related "perks," are dictated by the financial status of the athletic program, the job position, and the qualifications of the individual. Contrary to the three previous human systems (staffing, training, evaluations), compensation in coaching and playing arenas will also be determined by the rules regarding professionalism. Staff members, however, can qualify for the same compensation rewards as any other business employee. Their compensations, awards, and benefits can include salaries or wages, commissions, performance bonuses, vacation and sick leave, pension and retirement, profit sharing, and workmen's compensation. In other words, the level and detail of the program's employee compensation package is dictated by the operational environment and specific situation.

If an individual has the opportunity to coach athletes in a professional setting, the above employee criterion for compensation would apply. However, a majority of coaches are bound by the rules of amateurism and the sport's governing organization under which compensation for athletes is strictly controlled. Colleges have a compensation system supported by scholarships. The governing organizations (NCAA, NAIA, NJCAA, etc.) have determined a very detailed set of rules regarding scholarships. Junior Olympic levels as well as high school programs are also strictly bound by the rules of amateurism for athletes.

Performance Bonus Systems

If an athletic program has the financial and bureaucratic flexibility, a strong consideration should be given to the development and implementation of a performance based bonus system. Bonus systems can be centered on individual performance, group achievement, or a combination of both. Constructing a lucid, structured, and fair/equitable bonus (pay-for-performance) system initially takes time to develop and implement. A valid consideration must be given to the fact that some job performances are difficult to quantify/measure. Furthermore, a coach/program administrator must dissect job performance goals and decide which elements warrant pay-for-performance measures. For example, a coach and/or program administrator in a college/university athletic setting might feel that a major job goal of an assistant recruiting coach is to recruit student-athletes with strong academic credentials. A quantitative bonus system could be devised around that specific job criteria by measure in-coming student-athletes' grade point averages, test scores, advance placement class grades, etc.

When developing a bonus/pay-for-performance system, a number of desirable preconditions have been identified and generally accepted:

1. Trust in management. If employees are skeptical of management, it is difficult to make a pay-for-performance program work.
2. Absence of performance constraints. Since pay-for-performance programs are usually based on an employee's ability and effort, the jobs must be structured so that an employee's performance is not hampered by factors beyond his or her control.
3. Trained supervisors and managers. The supervisor and managers must be trained in setting and measuring performance standards.
4. Good measuring systems. Performance should be based on criteria that are job specific and focused on results achieved.
5. Ability to pay. The merit portion of the salary increase budget must be large enough to get the attention of the employees.
6. Clear distinction among cost-of-living, seniority, and merit. In the absence of strong evidence to the contrary, employees will naturally assume a pay increase is a cost-of-living or seniority increase.
7. Well-communicated total pay policy. Employees must have a clear understanding of how merit pay fits into the total pay picture.
8. Flexible rewards schedule. It is easier to establish a credible pay-for-performance plan if all employees do not receive pay adjustments on the same date. (Byars & Rue, 2006, p. 245)

An equitable pay-for-performance bonus system can not only boost performance and tangible results, but employee morale can be substantially increased. Often times the extrinsic bonus reward becomes secondary to the intrinsic feeling of recognition for "a job well done."

Human Resource Disciplinary Systems

Disciplinary Process
The following is an escalating, stage-by-stage disciplinary system for athletic programs.

Stage 1: Oral/Verbal Warnings

Level 1: Oral/Verbal Warning (No Documentation)
This form of warning is for lesser/minor program offenses. No follow-up or written documentation is associated with this type of warning.

Level 2: Oral/Verbal Warning (Documentation)
This disciplinary discussion warrants some manner of supporting written documentation for referencing. It should be kept as a permanent record in the staff/athlete program file.

Stage 2: Written Warnings

Level 1: Written Warning (Internal Documentation)
This phase and intensity of disciplinary action has a formal, signed form retained in the staff/athlete's program file. It should be dis-

cussed at an official meeting with other program members in attendance. All who participate (including the violator) should sign off on the document.

Level 2: Written Warning (Internal and External Documentation)
The subsequent level of written warning is the same as Level 1 except that the written portion is maintained not only inside the staff member/player's program file, but also in the overall organization's and department's operation records. Because of the gravity of this violation, it is advisable to have a departmental administrator present to observe the meeting.

Stage 3: Suspensions/Dismissals

Level 1: Suspensions
This critical disciplinary situation involves the staff member/athlete receiving a participative suspension from all program activities. The length of the suspension could be predetermined or could be set through an advisory meeting with the organization's administration. All suspensions must be entirely documented with the full knowledge and support of all organizational administrators. The staff member/athlete can bring in outside counsel if so desired.

Level 2: Dismissal
This terminal stage involves the staff member/athlete's permanent discharge/release from all program activities and functions. Because of the definitive severity of this type of response to an infringement/violation, all parties should be well represented. Once again, comprehensive documentation is mandatory. It is also prudent to videotape the dismissal conference.

A few salient points about the workings of the disciplinary system:

1. Continued offenses move up the stage-by-stage process.
2. Major offenses skip the lower levels of disciplinary actions.
3. Define, in writing, typical (and if possible specific) offenses in each category and level.
4. Provide all staff/athletes with a copy of the disciplinary system and discuss it with them periodically.

Grievance Policies and Procedures

All disciplinary systems should have pre-established grievance procedures to allow individuals a chance to rebut/challenge the discipline incurred. Thus, a grievance process, which should be spelled out in the athletic program's policies and procedures manual, should be straight forward, clear, and all-inclusive.

If an athletic program does not have a spelled-out grievance process, one could be constructed as follows:

Step 1: The staff member/athlete being disciplined must 1) notify all relevant parties (human resource department, supervisor, divisional manager, administrator, etc.) in writing that he/she is contesting a disciplinary action and 2) must re-count his/her side of the disciplinary issue.

Step 2: The human resource department or athletic department administration will coordinate a timely grievance meeting with internal athletic program personnel (as well as persons outside the athletic program) to review the validity of the individual's claim. Additionally, the human resource department will issue a written confirmation to the disciplined individual stating that a grievance committee meeting will convene.

Step 3: If the committee feels that the individual's situation warrants further attention, an official meeting/hearing will be called. If the committee judges the discipline to be in accordance with athletic program policies and procedures, a written notification will be issued to the staff member/athlete detailing their findings/decision.

Step 4: The official meeting convenes with all relevant parties and witnesses. It is strongly recommended that the meeting be recorded by an independent third party.

Step 5: After the official meeting, the committee will make its final decision concerning the disciplinary action. The individual will be informed in writing (and in a timely manner) of the final decision.

Critical Notes:

1) Depending upon the severity of the disciplinary issue, legal counsel (for both the individual and the athletic program) may be advisable.

2) To reiterate, the organization should include independent outside individuals on the disciplinary committee for objectivity and impartiality.

3) The direct supervisor (who issued the discipline) should provide the committee with all internal documents supporting his/her decision to discipline the individual. The supervisor should have no contact with the committee while the process is proceeding.

4) As with all human resource systems, the grievance process prior to its inclusion in the athletic program's policy and procedure manual must be reviewed by human resource specialists and legal counsel. This review will ensure that every step in the process is within permissible legal requirements.

SUMMARY

For a business (in this case athletic program) to be prosperous, one pervasive truth must pervade the organization's philosophy and thinking: the program is only as good as the people in it. The selection, training, evaluation, and compensation of a program's staff and athletes have an absolute and unequivocal impact on all aspects of the program. The competent utilization of human resource applications can fortify this imperative resource. The deficiency of human resource management can spell complete failure.

KEY TERMS

human resource management

staffing systems

demand shift analysis

manpower planning

recruiting

skill training

block training

random instruction

knowledge training

attitudinal training

orientation

evaluations

MBO evaluations

compensation

benefits

disciplinary system

employee-generated separation

Review and Discussion Questions

1. What is human resource administration and why is it important?

2. What are the six human resource operations?

3. What are the five steps in manpower planning?

4. What is a program depth chart and how would it be constructed?

5. Name some internal and external sources for personnel recruits.

6. List the five phases in the selection process (in sequential order).

7. What are the three fundamental steps that can be taken to become a more accomplished interviewer?

8. What are two consequential rules that must be applied in securing staff and athletes?

9. What should organizational orientation programs provide new employees?

10. What are the benefits of random training?

11. What are the four steps to evaluating a training program?

12. What are the steps in an MBO evaluation?

13. What are the drawbacks to a 360 degree evaluation system?

14. What are the desirable preconditions that have been identified and generally accepted when developing a pay-for-performance system?

15. Name the stages in a disciplinary system for athletic programs.

Appendix 3A

Construction of a Job Description

The following layout is the core structure of a job description. This design can be easily modified to fit all types of athletic programs. The detail in each job description will be influenced by the complexity of the organization and the intricacy of the position.

Job Title

The first division of the job description is the formal and specialized name for the position in the organization. Other information in this section can include

- job number;
- operational division;
- creation date of job description;
- position in hierarchal scheme—accountability and reporting responsibilities; and
- salary range and compensation package associated with the position.

Occupational Overview

This is the narrative synopsis of the position and its practical importance in the program. While broad in scope, it should give the reader a sense of the details associated with the position.

Job Specifications

The job specifications portion of a job description is the demarcation of the primary activities involved in the position. It is advisable to do the following:

- Put all tasks, responsibilities, and functions in priority order.
- Bullet tasks, responsibilities, and functions for clarity.
- If possible, place estimated percentages of time for each task, responsibility, and function as they relate to the overall position.

Knowledge and Ability Requirements for the Position

This segment stipulates the mental and physical aspect mandated to execute the position. Educational minimums, size and weight requirements, and diverse prior job experience are all components of this part.

Appendix 3B

Employee-Generated Separations

(Co-authored by Richard Leonard, John Meis, and Robert Garner)

Introduction

The days when a coach/program administrator could expect employees to spend their entire career with the same athletic organization are over. Statistics show that today's college graduates will average between eight and 10 jobs and as many as three careers throughout their lifetimes (Byars & Rue, 2006). Management (in this case, program administrators and coaches) must adapt to capitalize on this new, dynamic workforce. One area that holds promise for both improving employee retention and enhancing a positive corporate culture is employee-generated separation.

Traditional approaches to employee-generated separation have taken on a reactionary management posture. Typically, once the employee gives notice of separation, the coach/program administrator focuses solely on filling the vacant position and training the replacement. Little attention, if any, is devoted to easing or supporting the departure of the current employee. More commonly, the employee's decision to leave the athletic program is met with feelings of resentment or even open hostility. This can be traced to an established organizational culture that values (and depends on) employee loyalty (Fuqua & Newman, 2004). An interesting paradox exists that many athletic organizations expect loyalty *from* their employees but fail to demonstrate loyalty *to* their employees. An unsupportive or even hostile reaction from a coach/program administrator toward an employee who has announced his/her intention to leave the athletic program (a response more appropriately found in a jilted lover than a program administrator) provides a glaring example of the program's lack of devotion toward its employees. This type of management response can cause a cascading effect of dissent within the athletic organization, potentially resulting in a variety of negative consequences for the program, including decreased productivity or further employee departures. The purpose of this human resource appendix section is to discuss catalysts of employee-generated separations, detail the needs of both the employee and the coach/program administrator during the separation process, and to suggest best practices in managing employee-generated separations. In order to better understand the potential impacts, both positive and negative, of employee-generated separation, we must first explore the different systems that interact both during and after employment.

System Interaction During and After Employment

Several distinct systems interact during an individual's period of employment—the economy, surrounding community, the industry, the organization, and the individual (Fuqua & Newman, 2002). At all times, the athletic organization is immersed within these systems. The employee exists as a separate, intact system that functions both within the other systems as well as independent from them (see Figure 1). Thus, while the athletic organization may fill a relatively stable role within these interactive systems, employees continually circulate throughout the systems, both surrounded by and apart from their involvement in the athletic program. As such, employees may influence the program through systems both internal and external to the organization.

During employment, the employee is largely absorbed in the athletic program and exerts his/her most powerful influence over its daily functions from within. However, the employee's community and industry interactions outside the program may also have measurable effects. Within the

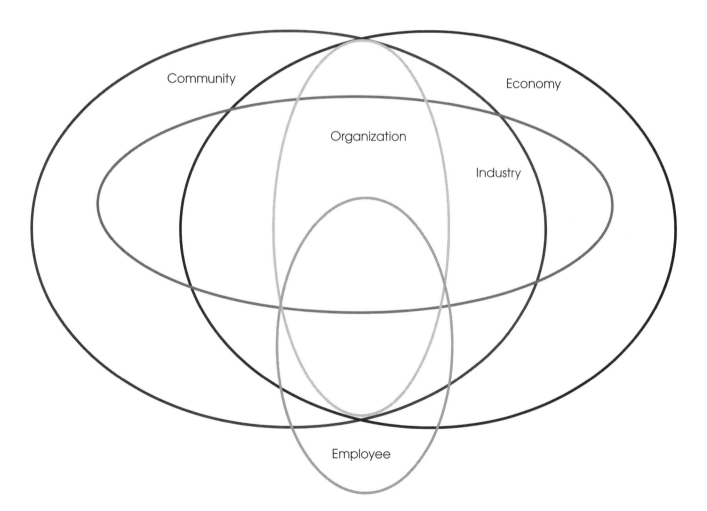

Figure 1. Systems Interacting during Employment

community or industry, employees are seen as representatives of the athletic organization. Therefore, the way in which employees are perceived can have a powerful impact on the public opinion of the program. When considering an individual and the athletic organization they represent, a variation of Woody Allen's classic line, "I wouldn't want to be part of any group that would have me as a member" is often called to mind: "Do I want to be involved with an organization that would have *that* person as a member?" Perception of employees within these external systems may lead to several possible consequences for the organization discussed later in this appendix.

After employment, the same systems are present and operational (see Figure 2). The only significant difference is the degree to which the employee directly impacts the inner functioning of the athletic organization. It is naïve to assume that simply because an employee has ceased to work for an athletic program, he/she no longer has any influence. Employees develop dedicated friendships within the organization, business contacts, and industry-wide reputations. These interactions do not cease simply because their employment has ended. The ex-employee's relationships within the organization, his/her productivity (or lack thereof) during the last days

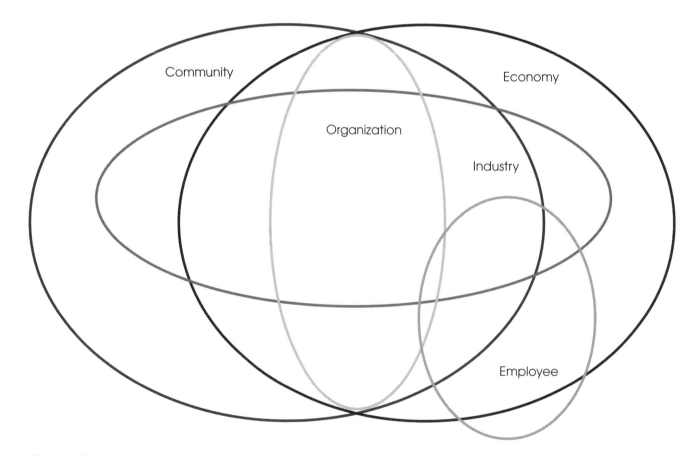

Figure 2. Systems Interacting after Employment

of their employment, and the emotional atmosphere surrounding his/her departure all continue to influence the inner functioning of the program long after the employee has left. The more amicable the separation process, the greater the likelihood that those system interactions will be positive.

Several questions naturally arise from the previous discussion. What needs do the employee and coach/program administrator have to each other during the employee-generated separation process? What are the various costs and benefits of the traditional system compared to a more employee-centered system? What are the "best practices" in employee-generated separation that will be most likely to produce positive results for both parties? What kinds of tangible and intangible benefits will the organization receive by having a sound, equitable separation process? The following sections address these questions.

Employee/Athletic Program Obligations

The recent cultural change to employment "free agency" mandates that coaches/program administrators reevaluate what obligations they have to their employees and what could be done to facilitate employee retention. Furthermore, coaches/program administrators must strive to understand what the employee currently perceives as his/her obligation to the athletic program. To better understand these obligations, we must examine employees' expectations of their athletic programs and the reasons why they would seek separation.

Controllable and Uncontrollable Organizational Elements

Within every athletic organization, there are clear operational tools and instruments that can be employed to enhance productivity, employee satisfaction, and worker retention. Some controllable factors that can affect employee retention and separation include

- flexible work schedules;
- job coaching, counseling, and career planning;
- job training (on the job, apprenticeships, classroom, cross training, etc.) to enhance employee performance;
- open door policies;
- cooperative evaluation systems;
- fair compensation, benefits, and incentive systems;
- job empowerment with reasonable accountability factors;
- job enlargement and substantive responsibilities;
- wellness programs and employee assistance plan; and
- perceived potential for advancement.

In today's workplace environment there are many unavoidable situations that spawn an employee-generated separation despite management's best efforts at retention. Although employee-generated separations have historically been perceived by management as employee disloyalty, it is important for coaches/program administrators to recognize these situations as an unavoidable product of today's complex marketplace and to respond with appropriate consideration for their employees' welfare. Several such instances are as follows:

- Certain vocations (especially athletics) inherently dictate long hours and high levels of stress that may cause employees to change careers to adjust their quality of life.
- Dual income families now make up a large percentage of the work force. A change in the employment of one family member may also necessitate a change in their spouse's employment.
- The globalization of business has created many opportunities for athletic programs to expand, forcing employees to be shifted to other branches within the program.
- Because of the contemporary (and often unparalleled) success of entrepreneurial ventures over the past 25 years, many industrious, creative, and well-trained employees are inspired to abandon coaching and athletic program administration to pursue their own personal and professional self-interest.

Employer and Employee Needs during the Separation Process

For effective management of the separation process, both parties must have a clear understanding of their obligations to each other. The following segment enumerates the needs of both the athletic program and employee during the employee-generated separation process.

Athletic Program Needs

- To be notified in writing of the employee's intent to leave the program
- Time to hire and adequately train a replacement
- Availability of departing employee to train a replacement
- Satisfaction or completion of contractual obligations and work-in-progress
- Exit interview process

Employee Needs

- Maintenance of safe, effective working environment
- Provision of appropriate references, credentialing, etc.
- Development of a system for transferring/maintaining healthcare benefits, retirement accounts, sick/vacation time, etc.

Taking into consideration the needs of both the employee and the athletic program, the subsequent segment describes best practices in managing employee-generated separations.

Best Practices in Employee-Generated Separation

An organizational climate of reasonable and equitable treatment of all employees (even the ones departing) develops open, non-confrontational interpersonal relationships. Brandt, in his article *Staying Together*, is quoted as saying

> a new social contract is needed between employer and employee that recognizes the fragile, possibly temporary nature of interactions and that enables both to live and work together as if the relationship was permanent. This social contract should be centered on three overriding principles: competence, engagement, and loyalty. (Brandt, 2004, p. 27)

An environment with a resilient social contract and sound interpersonal relationships augments operational productivity, market share, profitability, and strategy achievement. Consequently, this type of atmosphere can distinctly separate the athletic program from other competitors.

The uncertainty associated with a change in career can provoke a great deal of apprehension. As such, athletic organizations need to establish consistent, mutually beneficial systems and procedures for the separation process that should be communicated to the employees throughout their tenure of service. Nevertheless, the success of these systems will be no better than the attitude of the coach/program administrator executing the process. Coaches/program administrators must be informed, through ongoing training, of the importance of an amicable separation process. This training should be specific and include helping the coach/program administrator understand the long-term benefits of a smooth separation. It is critical that the individual realize that his/her emotions will greatly impact the perception of the sincerity of the process. A well-crafted system that is constantly reinforced throughout the athletic organization should eventually help ease separation anxiety.

Any system of control must have measurements in place to ensure its effectiveness. Upon receiving information from an employee regarding his/her intent to resign his/her position, a counseling session should be performed by the direct coach/administrator and recorded in writing. The coach/administrator should request written formal notification of the intent to leave the organization that includes the employee's time frame for leaving and availability to assist in training his/her replacement if athletic administration so desires. A separation checklist should be generated by the coach/program administrator and given to the employee to make sure that any operational issues are completed prior to the employee's last day of work. Any work-in-progress projects should be completed when possible. If there is not time to complete the project, a smooth transition to other designated employees should be facilitated. The coach/program administrator and the employee should agree that all contractual obligations of the employee and the organization are completed before the employee's final day of employment.

Once the coach/program administrator is satisfied that all operational issues have been addressed, an exit interview should be requested. The interview should be conducted face-to-face with the employee and a representative of the human resource department. The session should be informative in nature and communicate to the employee his/her status with any 401K plans, retirement benefits, health insurance, and eligibility for rehire. Issues of importance to the athletic program can be measured with standardized quantitative survey instruments (such as attitude scales, Likert scales, graphic rating scales, etc.). It is important that this section of the exit interview cover not only the reasons for the separation but also the employee's perception of the separation process itself. There should also be a qualitative aspect to the interview that allows the employee to address any issue not covered by the quantitative analysis. At a minimum, the following areas should be covered in the exit interview:

- Evaluation of employee's past position, separation process
- Job analysis
- General suggestions for improvement of organization as a whole
- Reason for leaving
- Eligibility for re-hire
- Tailored portion pertaining to position, time of service, etc.

It is important that this portion of the exit interview be handled by the human resource department. In many cases the reason for separation may include issues that the employee has had with his/her direct supervisor or the line management team. The probability of receiving a candid response to questions on the exit interview will be greatly enhanced if the interview is handled by a neutral third party.

The exit interviews should then be reviewed by the human resource department to determine if any trends exist that might require corrective action or more intense training. In this ever-increasing competitive environment, it is imperative that athletic organizations realize the benefits that can be achieved with an amicable separation process, and conversely, that nothing positive can be gained from a hostile separation.

Benefits of the New Attitude

The benefits of an athletic organization's supportive behavior toward employee-generated separations are three-fold. The first constructive area concerns a program's internal functions and the tangible and intangible consequences a supportive separation process has on its operations. The second issue deals with the external public relations and organizational perception a cooperative, pleasant, and productive employee separation practice can produce. Finally, the third distinct advantage that comes from a positive separation process involves the particular employee and his/her future influence on the organization.

Organizational Operations (Internal)

There are distinctive tangible and subtle intangible advantages a program can realize in its in-house operations by changing to an accommodating, helpful employee separation process. While the tangible benefits can have an immediate "bottom line" impact, the intangible aspects can have a more powerful and enduring influence on an athletic program's future. It should be emphasized that to secure these tangible and intangible benefits from a supportive employee-based culture (and separation process) athletic program administration must be conscious of the inherent danger in the difference between professing a corporate culture and living a corporate culture. "Getting managers to live the company culture can be difficult when they are allowed to play by different rules . . . employees immediately pick up on the differences between what managers say and what managers really do" (Babcock, 2004, p. 45). Athletic organizational support for its employees, both current and departing, must be unconditional and at every level of operation, especially management.

Tangible Operational Benefits
Several internal tangible benefits encompass the following:

- If an employee encounters a sincere helpful attitude toward his/her employment separation, there is a greater probability that his/her productivity will be uninterrupted and even enhanced between the time he/she give their termination notice and his/her last day of employment. "In business, as in personal relationships, commitment is a two-way street. If employers want loyal employees, they need to be loyal as employers. Demonstrating fairness, trust, and concern for employees is a good place to start" (Bragg, 2002, p. 20). If the athletic program has demonstrated commitment to the employee, he/she will likely reciprocate during the separation process. This consideration should result in the customary period between the employee's separation notice and final employment date going from a period of fractional/limited exertion to one that meaningfully contributes to the athletic program's operations.

- Another noteworthy organizational benefit obtained from an employee who is experiencing a positive separation experience is the cooperative exploitation of the employee's competencies and capabilities to train his/her replacement. "These individuals understand the organization and the tasks to be performed and are thus extremely qualified to present instructional material aimed at those skills and requirements" (DeNisi & Griffin, 2001, p. 278). If an enterprise can utilize the refined knowledge, job intricacies, and functional specialties of the person who held the position prior to the replacement, the new employee's learning curve could be substantially reduced. This, in turn, will get the replacement to an acceptable output capacity faster while shortening the athletic organization's transitional loss of productivity. Additionally, if the position is exceedingly intricate, the departing employee could be retained as an official (compensated) or unofficial (non-compensated) consultant until the replacement is suitably trained.

• A fair and congenial separation process can lessen any potential internal sabotage/damage that a disgruntled employee could cause. Furthermore, the danger of employee theft over the separation period could be curtailed. The cascading consequences of minimizing sabotage/damage/theft could include upholding customer satisfaction and responsiveness, continuing established quality standards, maintaining internal efficiency, decreasing waste, and minimizing any impending litigation expenses incurred from the prosecution of the employee. The psychological damage that can permeate an organization from employee theft/damage/sabotage can have a longer and more profound effect on the operational climate than just the loss of items and money.

> Any business owner who has experienced theft/sabotage by an employee knows that the sense of betrayal is much worse than the loss of money. Indeed, the main problem with employee theft/sabotage is that it leads business owners to make bad decisions, including deciding to trust no one. (Brodsky, 2002, p. 52)

• The "positive word of mouth" generated internally by this open process could encourage future departing employees to provide the athletic organization with more of a separation notice period (longer than the customary two weeks). Simply put, if employees know that they will be treaded fairly by the organization, they will reciprocate by giving a coach/program administrator ample time to coordinate their departure.

• If an athletic organization acknowledges the fact that employee-generated separations are an unending and proliferating component of all modern business operations, the human resource department can get into a proactive planning mode rather than a reactionary management posture. The human resource department can start to use employment tracking and inventory techniques such as

1. Staffing tables which graphically represent organizational jobs along with the number of employees occupying those jobs now and in the future.
2. Skills inventories which categorize personnel according to education, experience, interests, and skills.

3. Replacement charts which list the current jobholders and persons who are potential replacements if an opening occurs.
4. Markov analysis which tracks the pattern of employee movements through various jobs. (Bohlander, Snell, & Sherman, 2001, p. 133)

With advanced planning, employee separations will have smoother and more expedited employee transitions. This will eliminate "open positions" after employees leave. These "open positions" often place remaining athletic department personnel in precarious and frequently overloaded work situations.

Intangible Operational Benefits

From the outlook of internal intangible benefits provided by a constructive separation process, the principal intangible benefit relates to the influence an amiable employee departure has on the athletic organization's culture. The significance of a positive corporate culture is well documented throughout numerous business/managerial textbooks, articles, and primary research studies. Thompson, Strickland, and Gamble in their graduate text *Crafting and Executing Strategy* sum up the magnitude a positive corporate culture has on strategy execution and productivity by stating

> A culture grounded in strategy-supportive values, practices, and behavioral norms adds significantly to the power and effectiveness of a company's strategy execution efforts . . . conversely, when a company's culture is out of sync with what is needed for strategy success, the culture has to be changed as rapidly as can be managed. (Thompson, Strickland, & Gamble, 2005, pp. 373–374)

Various intangible benefits from a positive employee separation process include the following:

- A positive separation process will consciously take into account the vast power of the informal organization and informal communication inside the traditional athletic organization.

  > Informal communication channels develop outside the formal structure and do not follow a chain of command—they skip management levels and cut across lines of authority . . . the grapevine is the unofficial system of the informal organization . . . it is a network of gossip and rumor of what is called "employee language" . . . it is faster than formal channels . . . it is about 75% accurate . . . people rely on it when they are insecure or face organizational change . . . it is where employees acquire a majority of their on-the-job information. (Kinicki & Williams, 2003, p. 498)

The positive treatment of an employee who is departing will strengthen the informal organization's communication and attitude toward the athletic program. In contrast, a productive employee (who was an emergent leader or popular member of the informal organizational structure) who is treated unfairly and ostracized by the organization's separation process will have tremendous influence on the remaining employees. That individual will potentially become the rallying point to which the continuing employees will gravitate, resulting in a ground swell of negative feelings toward management and the organization. These feeling could cascade into a full-grown organizational insurgency that might be irreparable.

- Coaches/program administrators will experience reduced amounts of chaos and apprehension in dealing with employee-generated separations. If every employee is treated the same, coaches/program administrators can then have a consistent, utilitarian model to work from.
- A supportive, positive separation attitude by athletic administration can promote healthier internal communication for all employees. Superior internal communication enhances employee retention. From a competitive position, any action that can minimize employee turnover must be aggressively pursued.

Environmental Considerations (External)

The assertion that "perception is everything" is truer in today's business environment than ever before. While a positive perception of an athletic organization is not an assurance for developing support, wins, and longevity, a disapproving public assessment of an operation will undoubtedly guarantee decreased support, wins, and longevity (both in the short and long term). Goodwill in the external stakeholder community can have a forceful "domino effect" on all components of athletic operations. Obviously, the image benefits are an undeniable element relating to goodwill. A compelling, positive image can

- position the athletic program in a higher status when customers are taking into consideration purchasing products and services;
- attract the best possible employment recruits to an athletic organization;
- infuse a pride in the program that permeates into a zealous employee commitment and work ethic;
- generate attention from other athletic organizations wanting to have cooperative joint ventures and strategic alliances;
- encourage suppliers and creditors to cooperate and connect with an athletic organization; and
- enlist the surrounding community to become a vested member of the athletic program.

A negative attitude toward an athletic program can (unfortunately) have the inverse effect on an establishment. Customers and potential employees will bear in mind a program's unfavorable image and avoid getting involved with them. Employee self-esteem will be diminished as well as worker exertion, commitment, and ethics. Outside athletic organizations, suppliers, and creditors would be less likely to collaborate with an athletic organization with a negative perception. The surrounding community may avoid contact with the athletic program and, in some cases, may purposefully try to impair operations.

How do these elements of external image and public relations tie into the concept of employee-generated separation? Simply put, your current and former employees are your venture's ambassadors to the outside world. They are characteristically the most visual and vocal component of your operation.

> In many ways, a company's employees (both present and former) should be regarded as high-ranking diplomats representing the firm. Employees should be able to bridge the physical gap between the owner and the firm's clients or customers. Moreover, as they are thoroughly familiar with the company's product or service, philosophy, the state of the industry, and the principles of good practice, they can sell the business again and again, thereby providing a competitive advantage. (Anderson, 1997, p. 96)

While an employee is a part of an athletic organization, he/she (in most circumstances) will censor their unenthusiastic and disapproving comments about the program. However, once an employee initiates the separation process and subsequently departs a program, he/she can (and often does) discuss candidly a program's culture, work atmosphere, management style, and moral principles. Furthermore, because a current/former employee is/was an "insider," his/her conversations about an athletic program often have a more potent public relations force than other groups. The potential outcome with today's advanced technology goes far beyond "word of mouth" dialogue. Leonard, in his article *Cyberventing*, discusses how current and ex-employees can use technology to spread and broadcast their negative organizational message.

> Information technology has created the virtual office, and nearly every aspect of the workplace is now accessible on-line—including the virtual water cooler where workers can gather to complain. . . . Disgruntled employees (present and former) have created web sites, online bulletin boards, and chat rooms where they vent their anger and frustration about work/organization. Griping and moaning formerly confined to hallway conversations and after-work happy hours are now on public display. . . . The comments range from the thoughtful opinions and concerns about their jobs to vitriolic cyberventing. (Leonard, 1999, p. 34)

By providing employees with a hassle-free accommodating separation experience, an athletic program could significantly reduce the external public relations damage an employee could generate or perpetuate. The best-case scenario would have the employee becoming an advocate/spokesperson for the athletic program long after he/she has departed. It must be noted that if an employee's employment tenure has been a trying and poorly managed experience, the amount of negative feelings and ensuing publicity that could be eliminated by having a positive final employment period would, in all probability, be negligible. However, any possible salvaging of the situation is worth the effort.

Employee's Future

The last prominent area that relates to the treatment of employee-generated separation deals with the individual exiting the athletic organization and his/her future contact and influence on the program. It is comfortable to think that a former employee is a non-factor in future operations. However, many times individuals who worked for an athletic organization effect (and sometimes come back to haunt) their past employers.

The primary and most conspicuous reason to have a constructive separation process is that former employees could be athletic organizational rehires in the future.

> Most experts, recruiters and human resource executives, state that returning to former employers is a lot more common than one might expect . . . rehiring the good ones is a common practice . . . a business' best talents may leave for an opportunity and are then rehired at different points in their careers . . . keeping in touch with the best former employees, and getting them back one day, has proven to be good for company morale. Most boomerang (rehire) stories have some common threads; they departed gracefully, stayed in touch with colleagues and genuinely liked the companies they once called home. (Charski, 2005, p. 38)

The human resource advantage from hiring a former employee involves the recapturing of learning curve expenses (positional and organizational) as well as acquiring innovative skills/knowledge/industry information the individual might have attained while working outside the athletic program. Additionally, if the ex-employee has a proven value, rehiring them can reduce the risk of lost value from appointing an unfamiliar new hire. In other words, your athletic organization would take on substantially less risk with a previous employee compared to a new hire; you know from experience the former employee's proficiency and competence compared to a new, unproven employee.

By having a helpful, upbeat separation system in place, an athletic organization could maintain open lines of communication with past employees. Cross and Colella emphasize the importance of networking by stating that "in today's flatter, knowledge based organizations, networks of informal relationships are often more critical to performance and innovation than those formal divisions and units. These networks have a lot to do with productivity, learning, and business success" (Cross & Colella, 2004, p. 101). With open lines of communication, multitudes of networking scenarios with former employees are possible. If the former employee continues in the athletic industry or a directly related industry, he/she could be instrumental in generating significant contacts, new recruits and employees, strategic partnerships and alliances, and additional sales/markets. It must be emphatically stated that all open lines of communication and consequent networking connections have the utmost ethical and legal principles associated with them. A former employee must never be placed into a situation where he/she could compromise his/her current employer's operation and competitive status.

Another salient justification for having a positive separation process is the distinct chance that an ex-employee might one day develop into a prospective employer. While normally this is not an immediate concern, the future has unlimited contingencies. Having a former employee become a future employer (either in an athletic setting or entrepreneurial venture) is not out of the realm of possibility. Furthermore, a past employee who had an encouraging employment and separation experience could be an influential internal reference if one is seeking out an employment position with that particular athletic organization.

Statistics substantiate the fact that one day everyone will be a former employee.

> Not long ago, individuals joined an organization and often stayed with it for their entire working careers . . . however, the concept of organizational loyalty has faded . . . according to current statistics from the U.S. Department of Labor, today's college graduates will, on average, have 8 to 10 jobs and as many as three careers in their lifetimes. Recent data shows that the average person born in the later years of the baby boom held nearly 10 jobs from the ages of 18 to 36. (Byars & Rue, 2006, pp. 199–200)

This data raises a straightforward question: How would you want to be treated if you ever generated an employment separation? Would you want a positive experience that made you preserve the best feelings from years of service with an athletic organization or would you want your last memories to be a stressful, antagonistic experience?

CHAPTER 4

Leadership and Coaching

CHAPTER OUTLINE

CHAPTER 4

OBJECTIVES

- To present the breadth of conceptual definitions for leadership
- To discuss the types of leadership power/influence and their application in athletics
- To explore the concepts of reinforcement
- To stress leadership's commitment and obligation to total quality management
- To identify inept listening tendencies and behaviors
- To impart effective listening habits
- To account for nonverbal communication as it relates to leadership
- To examine various factors of situational leadership

Administrative Tip

As a coach/program administrator, it is essential that one know his/her own leadership style, personality, and abilities. There are countless personality tests available that are both reliable and valid. If possible, self-administer at least three personality/leadership tests to expose one's approach to leadership. Be truthful in all of the answers. Compile the results into a personality/leadership profile.

INTRODUCTION

This section examines the dynamic subject of leadership. The chapter investigates conceptual definitions as well as historical and contemporary concepts of leadership such as communication, listening, and situational leadership. All aspects of business and group leadership are related to the function of coaching and program administration. The chapter concludes with appendix components that highlight numerous theories of leadership and leadership approaches.

CONCEPTUAL DEFINITIONS

The sheer volume of modern literature devoted to the subject of leadership is staggering. In today's business world, leadership is the one dominant characteristic that every organization is trying to identify, cultivate, and retain. It is a subject that has evolved from a single basic concept to one with elaborate models and theoretical definitions. Historically, the classic concept of leadership related to an individual's formal power, which is inherent in the organizational structure. The hierarchical, vertical chain of command structure has one person answering directly to or following orders from a superior. The modern concept of leadership has authority but goes well beyond this to encompass motivation, communication, and situational analysis among others.

Before defining modern leadership, one must determine the factors that should be present for leadership to emerge. There are three conspicuous ingredients that must be present for leadership to emerge. First and most evident, a leader must have subordinates or followers (staff and athletes). Secondly, he or she must have a foundation of applicable power and authority to assert, influence, and control subordinates. Finally, a leader must have a purpose or mission toward which to lead or maneuver the group. Coaches/program administrators maneuver their programs under these three stipulations. In other words, they have the situation and environment for leadership.

The difficulty intrinsic to leadership is that there is no generally accepted definition. It is a dynamic and diverse subject. The following definitions detail the range of insights into the term leadership.

In the 2004 text *Leadership: Theory and Practice*, Northouse defines leadership through components.

> The following components can be identified as central to the phenomenon of leadership: (A) leadership is a process, (B) leadership involves influence, (C) leadership occurs within a group context, and (D) leadership involves goal attainment . . . leadership is a process whereby an individual influences a group of individuals to achieve a common goal. (Northouse, 2004, p. 3)

Another concept of leadership comes from Kouzes and Posner's book *Credibility: How Leaders Gain and Lose It, Why People Demand It*. The authors look at leadership as a give-and-take concept by stating:

> Leadership is a reciprocal relationship between those who choose to lead and those who decide to follow. Any discussion of leadership must attend to the dynamics of this relationship. Strategies, tactics, skills, and practice are empty unless we understand the fundamental human aspirations that connect leaders and their constituents. If there is no underlying need for the relationship, then there is no need for leaders. (Kouzes & Posner, 1993, p. 1)

In the article *How to . . . Lead Leadership Development,* Jenner states that leadership is an individual, introspective concept by asserting that:

> Leadership is complex and lacks a common definition, so it is essential that you have your own definition—ideally based on personal experience and grounded in your own exploration of the leadership field. This does not mean knowing every leadership theory from Collins to Kotter, but it does mean that you are clear in your own mind about whether you believe leadership is born or made, close to the top or distributed, about results or engagements, and so on. Knowing what you mean by leadership will help you embrace the range of perspectives that you meet. (Jenner, 2005, p. 44)

As one can observe from just these three examples, there are abundant definitions for leadership: all different, yet all correct in their own way (or context). The next logical question: To which one do I subscribe? Simply put, all of them apply at one time or another. This is the basic premise behind the concept of situational leadership, which will be examined at the end of this chapter.

LEADERSHIP POWER AND INFLUENCE

In the text *Mastering Leadership*, Williams states that leadership power and influence are derived from the following sources:

Positional Power

- Power of authority, e.g., signing off, giving formal approval (or disapproval), imposing and removing sanctions
- Power to recruit, promote, reward and give formal recognition
- Power to fire, remove from role, demote, reassign and punish

Personal Power

- Power of competence, expertise, knowledge and information
- Power of 'personality', style and charisma, i.e., 'horsepower'

Power of the Transformed Organization

- Power to generate change itself, to recognize, to redesign, restructure, reinvent and re-engineer the organization
- Power to delegate, empower, make responsible and accountable

Moral Power

- The power of personal and professional integrity
- Personal authenticity

Referent power

- Whom you have direct access to and whom you are regularly seen with (Williams, 2006, p. 58)

Williams' five sources of leadership power and influence can be precisely related to coaching and athletic program administration.

Positional Power

As a coach and program administrator, one has prescribed, formal managerial power inherent in his/her positions to "run" the athletic program. The extent of positional (or legitimate) power that the distinct position has relates to the structure of the athletic program and where the coach/program administrator is positioned in the hierarchical chain of command. An imperative aspect of positional power is the lucid, unambiguous awareness of each position's formal authority/power base. A coach/program administrator abdicating positional power to lower/subordinate levels is "opening up" enormous areas of personal and organizational problems. Equally, a coach/program administrator who assumes positional power of a superior is similarly opening him/herself to areas of personal and organizational concern. For the organization to operate efficiently, each position within the organization must maintain positional power/influence boundaries.

Personal Power

For a coach and program administrator to exploit his/her personal power, he/she needs a sound level of sports-specific knowledge as well as an ability to convey/communicate that knowledge. When discussing power and influence, the topic of one's personality and knowledge base can not be understated. No matter how brilliant one's level of sport intelligence, the capability to use one's personality to get that information across is vital. In other words, both components go hand-in-hand.

Power to Transform the Organization

Arguably the greatest power and influence a coach/program administrator has is the potential to alter his/her athletic program (either positively or negatively). For this transformation to be a constructive one, applying the managerial concepts of planning, organization, staffing, leading, and control is essential. An indiscriminate, haphazard, and unskilled attempt to modify, renovate, or completely overhaul an athletic program can have ruinous results. Out of all of the discussed levels of power and influence, the power to transform an organization takes the most premeditated cognitive energy and time.

Moral Power

Another area of influence and power that is essential for long-term athletic program success is a coach/program administrator's moral and ethical standards in dealing with program personnel. Words like integrity, honor, social responsibility, organizational citizenship, empathy, etc. have tremendous impact on the level and extent of one's influence and power. Without these elements in a person's character, a leader could find him/herself without people to lead.

Referent Power

The concept of networking and playing organizational politics has distinct consequences on one's level of influence and power. Developing mentoring relationships with an individual in a superior position in the organization can help support a coach/program administrator's legitimate authority. However, there are some distinct dangers in referent power. The principal hazard is if an individual abuses their personal power network. Abuses can range from harmless "name dropping" to the overt use of a superior's name to get tasks completed. These tactics can (and almost always) come back to damage the individual's influences and power in irreparable ways.

LEADERSHIP AND REINFORCEMENT

The concept of leadership and reinforcement is an indispensable one if a coach/program administrator is to function appropriately as a leader. Reinforcement is segmented into four well-defined elements—positive reinforcement, negative reinforcement, punishment, and extinction. The goals of the four distinct types of reinforcements are the same—to change a subordinate's behavior to desired results. However, each method utilizes very different tactics to achieve those results.

Positive and Negative Reinforcement

Positive reinforcement, by its very nature, is constructive, and enjoyable to the subordinate. The concept of negative reinforcement is frequently misconstrued. The relationship can best be described by the following:

> In positive reinforcement, the frequency of a response increases because that response is followed by a subjectively positive (pleasant) stimulus . . . in negative reinforcement, the frequency of a response increases because that response either removes some subjectively negative (painful or unpleasant) stimuli or enables the individual to avoid it. (Wortman & Loftus, 1988, p. 131)

These modes of reinforcement can be given to subordinates on a continuous (or fixed interval) basis or intermittent (non-scheduled) basis. Positive reinforcements can range from large monetary gifts and other tangible rewards to a small heartfelt thank you. Negative can range from the deletion of a major unpleasant job duty to the elimination of a minor employment factor.

Punishment

Punishment "is involved whenever an otherwise unexpected reward is withheld or any other sanction is applied, with the aim of discouraging a specific behavior" (Child, 2005, p. 139). The distinct danger in the use of punishment relates to the excessive application of this tactic to achieve the desired results and behavior. The statement "less is more" directly applies to punishment. The less a coach or program administrator uses punishment, the more powerful an influential tool it becomes. The ultimate goal is to have an athletic program so strong in its commitment to success that the use of punishment is counter-productive and practically unthinkable.

Extinction

Extinction reinforcement is a concept that is not often applied but is still available to a coach/program administrator.

> With extinction, reinforcements are withheld following undesirable behavior. As a result, the behavior that does not receive reinforcement (is ignored or is not rewarded), may cease . . . extinction not only causes bad behavior to cease but also sometimes causes good behavior to die as a result of lack of attention. (Harris & Hartman, 2002, p. 287)

Another noticeable limitation in the application of extinction is the implication this approach sends to the rest of the subordinates and program as a whole. By ignoring a certain conduct, other program members could see this as an endorsement of that behavior and feel that it is an action they would like to emulate. This could lead to a cascading effect throughout the program and eventually break down the group's cohesiveness and goal motivation.

LEADERSHIP COMMITMENT TO QUALITY: TOTAL QUALITY MANAGEMENT

It is well documented throughout hundreds of managerial texts and writings that one of the most important philosophies in today's business world relates to leadership/management's commitment to the concept of Total Quality Management (TQM). In beginning any discussion of leadership, the element and commitment to quality should be the first and foremost consideration. This concept emphasizes that every action in an organization (e.g., team and program) should have quality as its primary objective. In other words, TQM can be adopted, implemented, and continually enhanced by athletic programs.

What exactly is Total Quality Management and how can coaches (through their team leadership) utilize these principles in their athletic programs? Deming, who was one of the most influential business figures of the 20th century, created a 14-point philosophy on quality management that is universal to all businesses. The following is a summation of his philosophies.

1. Create constancy of purpose—strive for long-term improvements rather than short-term profits.
2. Adopt a new philosophy—don't tolerate delays and mistakes.
3. Cease dependence on mass inspections—build quality into the process on the front end.
4. End the practice of awarding business on the price tag alone—build long-term relationships.
5. Improve constantly and forever the system of production and service—at each stage.
6. Institute training and retraining—continual updating of methods and thinking.
7. Institute leadership—provide the resources needed for effectiveness.
8. Drive out fear—people must believe it is safe to report problems or ask for help.
9. Break down barriers among departments—promote teamwork.
10. Eliminate slogans, exhortations, and arbitrary targets—supply methods, not buzzwords.
11. Eliminate numerical quotas—they are contrary to the idea of continuous improvement.

12. Remove barriers to pride in workmanship—allow autonomy and spontaneity.
13. Institute a vigorous program of education and retraining—people are assets, not commodities.
14. Take action to accomplish the transformation—provide a structure that enables quality. (adapted from Bateman & Snell, 2004, p. 280)

How does a coach/program leader develop these philosophies of quality? Elements such as individual style and persona, communication, and the current situational factors are all critical. However, the first step is to develop an environment that makes quality a priority by doing the following:

1. Do it right the first time to eliminate costly rework and product recalls.
2. Listen to and learn from customers and employees.
3. Make continuous improvement an everyday matter.
4. Build teamwork, trust, and mutual respect. (Kritner & Kinicki, 2007, p. 11)

Without providing these elements, quality would be de-emphasized and the outcomes will be diminished. Additionally, the above environmental factors that lead to quality and enhanced performance will lead to the next definitive question: How does the coach or program administrator provide this type of cooperative, goal-oriented, and progressive feeling environment? The two factors that are critical to determining success are one's communication and listening style and the situational leadership approach.

> There have been some limitations in dealing with TQM concepts. TQM takes a fairly long time to show significant results—very little benefit emerge within the first six months. The long-term payoff of TQM, if it comes, depends heavily on management's success in implanting a culture within which TQM philosophies and practices can thrive. (Thompson, Strickland, & Gamble, 2007, p. 396)

If a coach/program administrator can develop the athletic program environment where there is an unconditional focus and commitment to operational quality, the outcomes can considerably out weigh the time obligation and effort.

LEADERSHIP COMMUNICATION—LISTENING

Being an effective communicator is essential to being a competent leader. Being able to impart critical information and to guide people charismatically is typically the initial characteristic that people associate with leadership communication. The other side, which is perhaps the most overlooked and neglected skill of leadership, is proactive listening. For a program's success, active listening to staff and athletes is often a more critical function of leadership than being a great speaker. Proactive listening can reju-

Administrative Tip

Quality is an upward flowing model that goes from small actions to large program outcomes. If a coach/program administrator can instill quality in every action and thought that program members take (no matter how small the deed may be) then the overall program quality will already be in place. Minor actions combine to produce significant results.

venate interpersonal exchanges, gather imperative information for decision-making, and function as a prerequisite for productivity and rewards.

Ineffectual Listening Habits

There can be many causes of ineffectual listening. Regardless of whether the barriers to competent listening are environmental, physiological, or psychological, the identification and intentional elimination of these listening blocks is critical. Factors of improper and defective listening can encompass:

1. Fact-listening: Dissecting messages only for facts, not intended meanings and denotations.
2. Thinking of an argument: Instead of listening and concentrating on the message, a poor listener diverts his or her attention to rebuttals and counter attacks.
3. Being critical of semantics: Being narrowly focused on semantic (meaning of words) misinterpretations and misuses and concentrating on the technical instrument of communication rather than the themes and ideas being communicated.
4. Dissecting delivery: Focusing attention on the method of delivery (the how) rather than the substance and content of information transmitted (the what).
5. Frozen evaluation: Having a negative preconceived concept of a message and/or speaker will repress information being communicated.
6. Pretending to listen: Faking alertness.
7. Taking detailed notes: Taking and transcribing notes obsessively is detrimental to comprehension because meanings and nuances are lost.
8. Rushing communication: Impatient and often self-centered rushing of the speaker maintains an apathetic, non-conducive communication environment.
9. Hearing, not listening: Hearing and listening are overlapping but different concepts. Hearing is the physical registration of sounds, while listening is the reception, comprehension, and assimilation of information.
10. Daydreaming: Self explanatory.

Effective Listening Habits

The 2002 article titled *Cheers, Ears—How to Listen Well* expounds upon some insightful techniques that will help a coach and athletic program administrator become an effective listener. Good listening tactics that can be adopted include:

Receiver On: Proper listening is active rather than passive. You need to actively decide to give someone a damn good listening to. You

---

Administrative Tip

To become mindful of ineffectual listening habits, consciously observe as many conversations as possible and look for clues of impending communication breakdowns. From those witnessed communication failures, one can become cognizant of one's own conversations and ineffectual habits.

can't do this without setting aside quality time for it. The person you are listening to must know that, for the duration of your conversation, they are your priority. There is nothing more flattering than giving your undivided attention.

Transmitter Off: Strange as it may seem, some people think that it's perfectly possible to listen while carrying on talking continuously . . . you need to put all your thought, concerns, and feelings temporarily to one side and concentrate completely on understanding the thoughts, concerns, and feelings of the other person.

Tune In: When someone talks they will have a host of assumptions—many of which you may not share. You therefore need to use who, what, why, where, when, and how to continually check the meaning of what they're saying.

Volume Up: People will talk about anything given the chance. It's perfectly okay to ask them to talk about what's most on your mind.

Echoing: This is a subtle way of getting someone to tell you more about what you want to hear. Whatever word, phrase or even sentence you repeat, the talker will automatically tell you more about it.

Check Feelings: Ask someone what they think and they'll tell you one thing; ask them what they feel and they'll usually tell you something completely different. If you're looking for the truth, asking for feelings will get you there a lot quicker.

Playback: At the end of the conversation, summarize what the person has just said. If you get it wrong, they'll correct you; if you get it right, they'll feel they've been given a good hearing. (Browning, 2002, p. 106)

Nonverbal Listening

There is another area of listening that does not require verbal interpretation. For a coach to become an even more effective listener-leader, he or she needs to be a decoder of nonverbal communication. How can a coach become an adept observer of nonverbal communication? First and most significantly, an effective leader realizes that nonverbal behaviors are situational, personalized, and not necessarily "on the surface." Strong nonverbal interpreters know that

> people sometimes say one thing and mean something else. So watch as you listen to be sure that the speaker's eyes, body, and face are sending the same message as the verbal message. If something seems out of sync, get it cleared up by asking questions. (Lussier & Achua, 2007, p. 204)

Secondly, deft communicators suppress their own subjective presumptions and feelings while evaluating and interpreting nonverbal/kinetic (body)

Administrative Tip

Listening takes practice and effort. An exercise technique that highlights listening is to see how many times in a conversation with a subordinate one can say "so what you are saying is. . . ." By practicing this method of verbatim message repetition, a coach/program administrator can strengthen his/her listening effectiveness. This constructive listening tactic also reassures the subordinate that they are being listened to and their transmission is important.

language. Finally, all versatile listeners dissect and notice facial expressions and eye movement. There are thousands of illustrative expressions; the possibility for misinterpretation is great. For a leader to become capable of analyzing facial expressions, he or she must realize that it is a personal discipline that must have continual, premeditated practice.

The following list of five items provides a foundation for reading and distinguishing nonverbal behavior.

1. Personal appearance: People's clothing and grooming present insight into their demeanor and their message. As with all nonverbal cues, personal appearances are situational and should be evaluated by their appropriateness in a particular setting.
2. Personal space: An important signal of nonverbal communication is the maintenance of space between speaker and listener. For instance, the distance can indicate comfort and confidence or uneasiness and skepticism (e.g., an *intimate distance* of 1–2 feet, a *personal distance* of 2–5 feet, a *social distance* of 5–10 feet, or a *public distance* of 10 or more feet).
3. Posture: Posture is another profound nonverbal message. For example, if a speaker's posture is brittle and restrictive, it could be concluded that the speaker is uncomfortable. Conversely, if a subordinate's physique is slumped and totally relaxed, boredom or apathy could be transmitted.
4. Appendages: The movement (or lack of movement) in body components such as arms, hands, feet, and legs can broadcast formidable signals. For example, a stationary person with arms folded across the chest could be conveying defensiveness.
5. Timing: The timing of a person's entrance into an interactive setting can disclose consequential nonverbal messages. If one is inexcusably tardy, a message of indifference and animosity could be conveyed, while punctuality could communicate interest and courtesy.

The list of nonverbal cues is endless. The assessment of those elements should be based on the circumstances and the individuals involved. Transforming a coach or program administrator into a person who can benefit from careful attention to both verbal and nonverbal cues is often difficult. It takes a diligent and calculated concentration. However, the payoff for this focused effort is immeasurable. This active technique cultivates staff and athlete retention, as well as enables a coach or administrator to digest all information confidently, which is essential to effective leadership.

SITUATIONAL LEADERSHIP

Because of the dynamic nature of the profession, coaches and program administrators must consciously avoid having a stagnant leadership style. The concept of one style and approach for all circumstances is outdated and

Administrative Tip

Communication is a two-way process. A coach/program administrator should continually observe his/her own nonverbal messages. Throughout the day, periodically stop and dissect non-verbal behavior. Introspectively examine personal appearance, personal spacing, posture, and timing. From the observations, determine if the nonverbal behaviors are appropriate for the situation and communication that is being attempted.

will lead to ineffectual group leadership. Coaches and program administrators need to be situational evaluators of internal and external environments as well as people. In other words, coaches and administrators need to assess situations and choose an appropriate leadership response. That is the underling foundation of situational leadership.

Situational leaders are uniquely flexible in their observation of their surroundings. They look at every person, event, and environment as a distinct, exclusive challenge and understand that the challenges require individual responses instead of formatted reactions. In the simplest terms, for a coach or program administrator to become a situational leader, he or she needs to actively assess his/her surroundings and choose appropriate, definitive responses to maximize the program's potential.

Factors of Situational Leadership

There are some major components to becoming an effective situational leader.

1. Never forget that the coach or program administrator is the leader and decision maker for the team and program. This is easier said than done. Athletics involves emotions that might not be associated with or as intense as business management and leadership. Emotions can cloud decision making and, more importantly, behavior. In most of an athletic program's administrative circumstances, coaches/program administrators usually can control their emotions, which, in turn, can make situational leadership easier. In actual competitive situations, however, emotions can run high, and this makes recognition of the appropriate leadership tactic more difficult. To alleviate emotional debilitation, try to consciously recognize emotional states and use internal speech to reiterate one's leadership role. This will help one assess the situation and choose the right leadership approach.

2. Be true to oneself. Through our backgrounds, everyone has developed personality traits and leadership styles (Appendix 4A delineates dominant styles). Coaches/program administrators must recognize these traits and become consciously aware of them in leadership situations. There are numerous leadership theories and test instruments that can objectively examine one's personality and leadership base. Confirm the findings by asking friends, family, and even athletes and staff if the assumptions and conclusions about one's personality are correct. Once a confirmed dominant style is identified, lock that information away. It will be the leadership base from which one will work.

3. Be true to the athletes and staff. Tell them upfront what type of leadership base one has and how one will handle certain situations.

The fewer number of surprises, the less the apprehension and the greater focus on the message and task. For example, communicate to the staff and athletes that there will be a democratic and participative approach (see Appendix 4A) to setting individual and team goals. Conversely, tell them that in a competitive situation, the adoption of a more autocratic and authoritarian approach will be taken. Also, communicate to the staff and athletes that each situation that arises will be evaluated individually and an appropriate leadership approach chosen accordingly.

4. No matter what the situation or what decision must be made, every leadership action taken must be positive and in-line with the program's pre-established goals and mission (see Chapter 1).

   In the 1997 publication *The Leadership Challenge*, Kouzes and Posner discuss tactics and approaches to leadership. In every instance, the underling theme was optimism and positive actions. For example, one of their major leadership approaches deals with attracting people to a common purpose.

   The common purpose is accomplished through a positive step-by-step process:
   a. Develop a shared sense of destiny
   b. Discover a common purpose
   c. Give life to a vision
   d. Demonstrate personal conviction
   e. Commit to the challenge (Kouzes & Posner, 1997, pp. 123–147)

5. As previously stated, become a good listener. Not only should one listen to people, but one should also listen to the environment in which the program operates.

6. Be equipped to handle a crisis or difficult situation. Whether on the court or off the field, a coach sometimes needs to lead quickly in take-charge situations.

7. Maintain a positive concept of oneself by having self-confidence and truly believing that one can succeed. Self-confidence emanates from a person and is immediately recognized by a group. This, in turn, will have the group believing in its abilities. Use the group's positive concept as an influencer in many situations. The higher the level of one's positive concept, the more accepting of the leadership a group will be. Unfortunately, the opposite is also true. If a coach/program administrator has a lack of self-confidence, his/her leadership will be minimized (or even rejected) and the group will fail to perform.

8. Learn more about leadership. There are countless textbooks, case studies, and self-help books that cover the subject. After developing a knowledge-base of leadership models, look inside our particular

profession to find successful coaches and leaders. Ask questions. Just remember, one must be true to his or her own personality. What might be a successful approach for one person might not work for another in a particular situation.

SUMMARY

Leadership is a perpetually transforming and increasingly essential topic for business managers. These leadership concepts relate clearly to our profession of coaching and program administration. Not only do we as coaches and program administrators need a foundation of theoretical knowledge, we also need to be competent in applying these philosophies in the daily operations of our programs. Concepts such as total quality management, effectual listening, and situational leadership are significant components of everyday operations and should be applied consistently as well as consciously.

KEY TERMS

leadership	autocratic/authoritarian
leadership reinforcement	democratic/participative
leadership power/influence	laissez faire
total quality management	Theory X
communication listening	Theory Y
nonverbal communication	managerial grid
situational leadership	path goal theory
trait theory	situational leadership theory

Review and Discussion Questions

1. What three elements must be present for leaders to emerge?

2. Describe the five sources of leadership power and influence.

3. Define the following: positive reinforcement, negative reinforcement, punishment, extinction.

4. What is TQM?

5. How would a coach or program administrator develop an environment conducive to TQM?

6. What are the benefits of proactive listening?

7. List the 10 factors of ineffective listening and describe each.

8. What are some good listening habits?

9. What are the elements of personal space?

10. What are the factors of situational leadership?

11. What is the underlying premise behind the Trait Theory of Leadership?

12. Define authoritarian or autocratic leadership. Define democratic and participative leadership. Define laissez faire leadership.

13. Describe the five primary management styles in Blake and Mouton's Managerial Grid.

14. List the four theoretical stages of the Hersey/Blanchard Leadership Model.

Appendix 4A

Leadership Theories

Trait Theory

> *Trait theory* is a leadership model constructed on the assumption that leaders possessed unique physical and psychological characteristic that predisposes them to positions of influence . . . leadership studies focused on factors such as height, weight, appearance, intelligence, and disposition. Other studies looked at status, social skills, mobility, popularity, and other social traits in order to determine which of these characteristics were most strongly associated with leadership. (Hackman & Johnson, 2004, p. 65)

This simple method formed the first basis for predicting a leader's effectiveness. In other words, the theory's premise relies on similarity from one person to another. If one person is a successful leader with certain traits, another person with the same traits will also be successful. Even with the theory's subjective nature and obvious drawbacks, it appeals to an intrinsic component of human nature: to investigate a situation or person from the simplest and most straightforward criteria.

The theory examines human traits from both one's physical traits and personal disposition (psyche). Physical traits are the easiest to determine because of their manifested appearance. Historically, our ancestors were often barbaric leaders with tremendous physical strength, size, and agility. As our civilization evolved, the advancements in technology accentuated intellect over anatomical distinctions. From the progression, the trait theory attempts to assemble mannerisms, habits, and idiosyncratic distinctions into systematic categories. Most empirical studies of the trait theory suggest that there are five traits that are commonly shared by most (but not all) successful leaders. These traits are:

1. Drive. Drive refers to a set of characteristics that reflect a high level of effort. Drive includes high need for achievement, constant striving for improvement, ambition, energy, tenacity (persistence in the face of obstacles), and initiative.
2. Leadership motivation. Great leaders not only have drive; they want to lead. They have a high need for power, preferring to be in leadership rather than follower position.
3. Integrity. Integrity is the correspondence between action and words. Honesty and credibility, in addition to being desirable char-

acteristics in their own right, are especially important for leaders because these traits inspire trust in others.

4. Self-confidence. Self-confidence is important for a number of reasons. The leadership role is challenging, and setbacks are inevitable. Self-confidence allows a leader to overcome obstacles, make decisions despite uncertainty, and install confidence in others.

5. Knowledge of the business. Effective leaders have a high level of knowledge about their industries, companies, and technical matters. Leaders must have intelligence to interpret vast quantities of information. (Bateman & Snell, 2004, p. 371)

It should be emphasized that the trait approach is an incomplete leadership theory. Its most serious drawback is its omission of environmental factors, societal values and norms, and other contextual background elements.

Authoritarian/Democratic/Laissez Faire Theory

The most widely known of all leadership theories is based on the behavioral distinctions between of authoritarian, democratic, and laissez faire styles. The following is a breakdown of these three universally standardized styles (also known as *autocratic*, *participative*, and *abdicative*).

Authoritarian/Autocratic

The authoritarian method of leadership is the unbending employment of legitimate power inherent in the position of management (or in our case, coach or program administrator). The flow of decisions is from a top-down hierarchal system in which all administrative decrees and decisions by a leader are absolute and unyielding. The style utilizes straightforward accountability expectations that are clear, logical, and comprehensible. The most common settings for the application of authoritarian leadership are military and medical settings that rely on orders given and carried out.

A distinct downfall of the authoritarian approach is:

Leaders who are consistently authoritarian in style are not usually very popular, although they are prized in an emergency when quick, firm decision are needed . . . in most situations group members do want their voices heard, especially when a decision directly affects them. This is not to say they want prolonged discussion that produces nothing more than "analysis paralysis" or that they don't think their leaders are capable. Rather, most group members just want their opinions heard and respected by their leaders. (Renzetti & Curran, 1998, p. 144)

Conversely, if a leader is respected and has a long track record of success and if the situation is receptive to this technique, the advantages range from timely accomplishment of tasks to the focus of a single vision.

Democratic/Participative

The democratic leadership approach to decision making is diametrically opposite from the authoritarian style. "A democratic leader encourages group discussion and input, works to build group consensus, and tries to explain why members are being rewarded or punished" (Lindsey & Beach, 2000, p. 96). This style accomplishes production and goal achievement through group consensus and acceptance. The most distinguished utilization of the democratic style in our society and culture is through our structured governmental political system.

As with all leadership methodologies, the environment in which a leader is operating will influence the style of leadership. Our society is founded and governed on the philosophical principles of democracy. From this perspective, one could assume that this doctrine is suitable for all facets of our lives. This assumption is invalid. For example, emergencies in our society would have disastrous consequences if the professional involved (whether it be a doctor, firefighter, or policeman) utilized the democratic leadership style. The best example of this would be in the case of an E.R. medical emergency. By the time the doctor finishes polling everyone for their opinion, the patient might have already died. This example can be used via analogy for coaching. By the time the coach gets through polling everyone for their input (staff and players), the game could already be over and lost.

If the situation warrants the use of the democratic method, the benefits are numerous. Some benefits include

- soliciting more input and information from a wider variety of individuals gives a decision maker a different perspective;
- an elevated sense of group morale;
- staff and players having a vested interest in the decisions and outcomes; and
- a rejuvenated organizational focus on goals.

Laissez Faire/Abdicated

The final leadership style of laissez faire/abdicated is best described as a profile of leadership that is "easygoing and makes little attempt to direct and organize a group . . . laissez faire leaders are usually ineffectual in organizational situations because the group lacks directives and tackles problems in a haphazard way" (Robertson, 1987, p. 171). From a coaching or program administration perspective, this leadership philosophy is very irrational, incoherent, and should rarely be exercised. This technique has organizational personnel (staff and players) setting goals, individualizing work ethics, and operational policies. With no direction, staff members and players will set their own agendas, in their own timeframes, and by their own guidelines. The only conceivable circumstance in which this approach could be utilized would be in a sedate, leisurely environment where achieving goals within a given timeframe is not a priority.

McGregor's Theory X and Theory Y

Another widely recognized leadership theory is McGregor's Theory X and Theory Y. McGregor, a student of Maslow (Theory of Hierarchical Needs), probed leadership from two contradictory perspectives. These perspectives examined a manager's opinions, conclusions, and feelings toward his or her subordinates.

His two-pronged theory is as follows:

Theory X argues that:

1. People, by their very nature, do not like work and will avoid it when possible.
2. They have little ambition, tend to shun responsibility, and like to be directed.
3. Above all else, they want security.
4. To get them to attain organizational objectives, it is necessary to use coercion, control, and threats of punishment.

Theory Y argues that:

1. The expenditure of physical and mental effort in work is as natural to people as resting or playing.
2. External control and the threat of punishment are not the only ways of getting people to work toward organizational objectives. If people are committed to objectives, they will exercise self-direction and self-control.
3. Commitment to objectives is determined by the rewards associated with their achievement.
4. Under proper conditions, the average person learns not only to accept but to seek responsibility.
5. The capacity to exercise a relatively high degree of imagination, ingenuity, and creativity in the solution of organizational problems is widely distributed throughout the population.
6. Under conditions of modern industrial life, the intellectual potentialities of the average human being are only partially utilized.

Theories X and Y voice the extremes on the spectrum of leadership thought. The astringent, pessimistic X speculations correlate with the authoritarian style, while the Y theory aligns itself with the employee-centered, democratic approach.

McGregor accentuates the idea that a leader's attitude and disposition toward the employees (staff and players) is the determining factor for their happiness and productivity. If a leader's attitude toward subordinates is that all subordinates are lethargic, lackadaisical, unmotivated, and untrustworthy, the organization's employees will impulsively react precisely to these predetermined notions and expectations. In other words, the leader or coach's attitude and style establish the basis for the subordinates' self-fulfilling prophecy. With this in mind, McGregor focuses a preponderance of his text to the practical application of Theory Y.

McGregor stresses that the best way to integrate Theory Y thinking into the organization is through the creation of conditions such that the members of the organization, group, or team can achieve their own goals best by directing their efforts toward the success of the organization. If the coach or program administrator can prioritize the needs of individuals within the parameters of team goals, Theory Y will be a reality. The benefits of a Theory Y environment include an inspired, goal-oriented team that stresses maximizing of talent and innovation in every player and staff member. The concept is simple, but it has tremendous potential. It should be noted that:

> the acceptance of Theory Y does not imply abdication, soft management, or permissiveness . . . such notions stem from the acceptance of authority as the single means of managerial control. Theory Y assumes that people will exercise self-direction and self-control in the achievement of organizational objectives to the degree that they are committed to those objectives. The theory does not deny the appropriateness of authority, but does deny that authority is appropriate for all circumstances.

(Theories and quotes extrapolated from McGregor & Douglas, 1960, pp. 33–34, 47–48)

Blake and Mouton's Managerial Grid

The managerial grid is a matrix that interprets leadership within two central leadership dimensions. The leadership matrix is structured by a dimension of concern for people and a dimension of concern for production. Each of these directional approaches is divided into nine zones one being the lowest and nine being the highest. Thus the grid yields an 81-point graph surface that is used to illustrate and analyze managerial behavior by the simple philosophy of people oriented, production oriented, or a combination of both.

1. 9,1 Leader, **Authoritarian Obedience of Task Leader** is a task-focused manager who highlights all factors of productivity but distances him/herself from all interpersonal interactions. This type of leader perceives camaraderie with subordinates as counterproductive.
2. 1,9 Leader, **Country Club or Good Neighbor Leader** has little or no interest for end results, productivity, or decision making. He/she is considered a people-centered administrator.
3. 5,5 Leader, **Middle of the Road Leader** embraces compromise be-

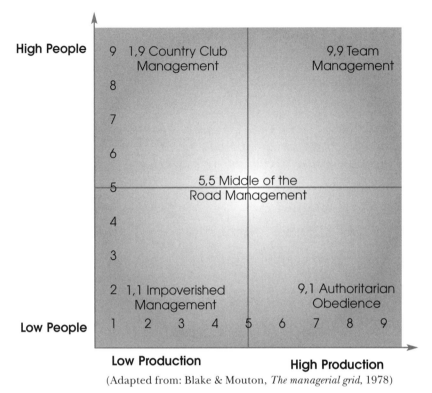

Figure 1. Blake and Mouton's Managerial Grid

tween people and productivity. This approach is consistent and reserved, but lacks innovation and upward motivation.

4. 1,1 Leader, **Impoverished Leader** is, by all definitions, never actually a leader. This manager is non-responsive and apathetic toward people and results.

5. 9,9 Leader, **Team Manager/Leader** is the consummate professional; tenaciously dedicated to the organization and sympathetic and empathetic toward employee concerns.

House/Mitchell's Path-Goal Theory

The Path-Goal Theory of Leadership is similar to previous leadership models in defining certain leadership approaches. House/Mitchell's model differs in that it identifies situations in which one should apply a certain leadership style. The four leadership styles:

Leader Directiveness
- Letting subordinates know what is expected.
- Providing specific guidance as to what should be done and how.
- Making leader's part in group understood.
- Scheduling work to be done.
- Maintaining definite standards of performance.

Leader Supportiveness
- Showing concern for status and well-being of subordinates.

- Doing little things to make work pleasant.
- Treating members as equals.
- Being friendly and approachable.

Leader Achievement-Orientedness
- Setting challenging goals.
- Expecting subordinates to perform at their highest level.
- Showing a high degree of confidence in subordinates.
- Constantly emphasizing excellence in performance.

Leader Participativeness
- Consulting with subordinates.
- Soliciting subordinates suggestions.
- Taking subordinates' suggestions seriously.

(House & Mitchell, 1974, pp. 81–94)

It should be noted that each of the above approaches to managing/leading people is entirely determined on the nature of the task(s), the attributes, effectiveness, and competency of the organization's employees, the urgency and importance of the work, the personality of the individual manager, and the overall environmental condition the organization operates. Each situation will determine which of the four styles should be emphasized. To be a successful leader, each person should have each of these styles in their particular "arsenal" of leadership tools. Knowing which one to apply and when to apply it is the key.

Hersey and Blanchard's Situational Leadership Theory

In the text *Management of Organizational Behavior: Utilizing Human Resources*, Hersey and Blanchard's Situational Leadership Model is founded on the concept that the maturity (time in a program) of the subordinate (whether staff or athlete) will dictate the level of people or task leadership behavior. Within each of the four stages of a subordinate's program matu-

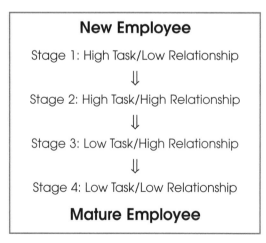

New Employee

Stage 1: High Task/Low Relationship

⇓

Stage 2: High Task/High Relationship

⇓

Stage 3: Low Task/High Relationship

⇓

Stage 4: Low Task/Low Relationship

Mature Employee

Figure 2. Hersey and Blanchard's Situational Leadership Theory

rity, a different combination of task and people relationship behavior should be applied.

Stage 1: High Task/Low Relationship—In this stage, the new subordinate (player or coach) should be initiated into the program's operations by punctuating a high task environment with minimal people- or relationship-oriented leadership. As the coach, one should act in the directive mode employing a one-way communication system that teaches the new subordinate job responsibilities and tasks to be performed. Close supervision and straightforward instructions will be utilized, which, in turn, will eliminate any apprehension from undefined expectations.

Stage 2: High Task/High Relationship—Following the indoctrination of task responsibilities in stage one, stage two emphasizes high task and high relationship. Even though the subordinates are still being directly supervised, the high relationship aspect fosters familiarity, trust, and communication between a coach and his or her player or staff member.

Stage 3: Low Task/High Relationship—In this maturity period, the subordinate has become proficient at his or her position and needs little or no direct task supervision. High relationship-oriented leadership is still employed for the cultivation and fortification of a subordinate's continued performance. This stage manifests an open communication system that will bring innovation and creativity from the subordinate.

Stage 4: Low Task/Low Relationship—The final stage in the model represents the completion of the subordinate's organizational maturity. He/she has mastered assignments and tasks and is capable of exerting self-discipline and motivation. The coach should have absolute confidence in delegating and empowering any previously learned skill. Little or no emotional support is needed.

The key to utilizing the model in a practical application is to become an insightful, receptive coach. One needs to comprehend the subordinate's responsibilities as well as his or her timeframe for transition through the stages. Some subordinates will advance through stages more quickly than others.

Contemporary Leadership Theories

Theory 1

In his 1980 text *The Management Option*, Sudhalter canvasses the idea of leadership from a linear, concrete vantage point. He expounds on 10 distinct qualities that all good leaders are seen to have:

1. To be able to inspire and motivate others.
2. To be able to delegate authority at the right times, to the right people, under the right conditions.

3. To be at least able to see just around the corner, by developing and utilizing the powers of perception.
4. To be able to plan and organize activities of the operation.
5. To have the ability to maintain harmony and equilibrium in an organization.
6. To be able to assume the responsibility for the organization, not only when things go well, but also when they go badly.
7. To be a competent spokesman for the organization's subordinates as well as the entire organization.
8. To be able to negotiate effectively.
9. To be able to manage a crisis calmly.
10. To be able to set reasonable goals that can be accomplished.

Theory 2

From a more philosophical viewpoint, Collier, in his 1992 article *Business Leadership and a Creative Society*, states that the greatest function of leadership is that the leader express, for his or her group, the ideals toward which they all, consciously or unconsciously, strive. What in truth do I seek? What objectives do I have that my employees can also share? On this view, the first task of business leadership is to create an environment that can flourish not only for a single, creative genius, but more importantly, for the collective capacities of all the people in the organization.

Theory 3

Adams, in *Transformational Leadership: From Vision to Results*, scrutinizes the concept of leadership from a strategic action approach. His philosophical position is to suppress our normal tendencies, as leaders, of wanting to . . .

1. Solve problems quickly.
2. Maintain predictability, consistency, and status quo.
3. Reflect on the past, reacting to events after they happen to correct deviations.
4. Think in predominately rational analytical modes.
5. Break situations down into their smallest parts as the means to understanding.
6. Be controlled by external circumstances.

Adams also declares that leadership should be a strategic operation based on the following summarized premises.

Premise One: Leadership is a state of consciousness rather than a personal trait or a set of skills. The leadership state of consciousness sways individuals to

- become self aware;
- live with and value ambiguity;

- create and work with alternative choices, structures, and systems;
- encourage differences and seek the gifts each person has to offer;
- experience the absence of chances as potentially disruptive to high performance;
- reward risks taken in service of vision; and
- develop flexible temporary structures.

Premise Two: A primary role of a leader is to activate, establish, and nurture a focus on vision, purpose, and outcomes. Establishing and holding a vision of desired outcomes greatly increases the possibility of realizing them.

Premise Three: It is cost effective to empower the workforce. Once a vision is shared, the leader needs to remove constraints to inspire performance. A leader must strategically provide conditions that

- create a clear purpose and direction;
- encourage opportunities for innovation;
- seek an individual's potential and gently demand excellence;
- establish and gain commitment to high but attainable standards;
- create challenging, meaningful assignments;
- acknowledge and celebrate success;
- set examples of excellence;
- hold to agreements;
- capitalize on individual differences; and
- allow a wide latitude of self-expression.

Premise Four: A systems perspective is necessary to avoid emphasis on alleviating symptoms. Each functional part of the organization has its own parochial perspective or interpretation of what should be done. What is needed is the coordination of all functions through a systems perspective and shared vision of the whole organization.

Premise Five: Attention to needed support systems is essential to achieving the vision. On the structural level, it is essential that the leader be aware of how adequately various support mechanisms are facilitating desired outcomes. It is not at all unusual to find that a system defeats itself because procedures to get an essential task accomplished are not in place. One of the most frequent reasons why strategic planning does not work is that, as time passes, the accountability for implementing key actions becomes ambiguous, and everyone waits for someone else to initiate them.

Theory 4

Agor expounds on a totally different angle of leadership: intuition. In *Intuition in Organizations*, he stresses that the emphasis, rightly due to strategic, linear, and philosophical positions (as well as other theories) of leadership, should be strongly augmented by an intuitive thought. He states that intuition is becoming more critical in today's organizational context for several reasons:

- There is a high level of uncertainty.
- There tends to be very little precedent.
- Reliable facts are limited or unavailable.
- Time is limited and there is an ever increasing pressure to be right.
- There are several plausible options to choose from, all of which can be supported by factual arguments.

He concludes with the statement that if one hopes to be better prepared for tomorrow, then it only seems logical to pay some attention to the development of intuitive leadership and decision-making skills today.

Theory 5

Conger, in the 1989 publication *The Charismatic Leader*, emphasizes the leadership element of charisma as the most important component of leadership. His four-stage charismatic model of leadership defines leadership as the process of moving an organization from an existing state to some future state.

Theory 6

Through books such as *Tough Minded Management* (1978), *Expectations and Possibilities* (1981), and *Tough Minded Leadership* (1989), Batten has constructed a 12-phase, cyclical leadership theory. Batten's cybernetic circle of leadership is a philosophical declaration that provides fundamental infrastructure for organizational leadership. The 12-phase, cyclical doctrine is as follows:

1. Clarify purpose and direction
2. Ask, listen, and hear
3. Enable involvement and participation
4. Set clear expectations and goals
5. Provide consistent interaction
6. Affirm and optimize strengths
7. Establish measurements
8. Monitor performance
9. Provide developmental counsel

Table 1. Conger's Four-State Charismatic Model

Stage 1

Detect Unexploited Opportunities and Deficiencies in the Present Situation

High Sensitivity to Constituents' Needs

Formulating an Idealized Strategic Vision

Stage 2

Communicating the Vision

Articulating the Status Quo as Unacceptable and the Vision as the Most

Attractive Alternative

Articulate Motivation to Lead the Followers

Stage 3

Build Trust through Success, Expertise, Personal Risk Taking, Self-Sacrifice, and Unconventional Behavior

Stage 4

Demonstrate the Means to Achieve the Vision Though Modeling, Empowerment, and Unconventional Tactics

10. Establish accountability
11. Make tough-minded decisions
12. Expect excellence

Narrative Elaboration:

1. The concept of clarification of operational direction and purpose is to consolidate and focus the organization's personnel toward one collective, unified mission.

2. The leadership objective associated with the function of inquiring, listening, and hearing is the active utilization of the organization's human resource. Through a responsive, two-way communication system, businesses and athletic programs can access a wide variety of potential ideas and impressions from their personnel.

3. Successful leadership energetically solicits the involvement and participation of subordinates. This vantage furnishes pertinent information that, in turn, resolves operational problems and fulfills program goals.

4. Unequivocal, precise expectations give significant clarification to a subordinate.

5. Consistent interaction deals with the beneficial communication process between leaders and subordinates. For a situation and a leader in that situation to be effective, the ongoing and reciprocal exchange of ideas, facts, and data must be transmitted in a logical, understandable fashion.

6. Competent, skillful leadership affirms and employs an organization's strengths.

7. The conclusions of measuring instruments (both qualitative and quantitative) provide subordinates with direction and benchmarks to measure performance.

8. Performance monitoring optimizes personnel motivation and measures operational success.

9. Career advice, professional consultations, and informal subordinate planning are directly related to a leader's interaction capabilities. Unpretentious and down-to-earth leaders will continuously consult employees (staff and athletes) on their progress toward personal and professional goals in a warm and caring manner.

10. Straightforward performance assignments will eradicate the possibility of program miscommunication as well as eliminate apprehension from unclear standards among staff and athletes.

11. Leaders need to make aggressive, accurate decisions. They need to solicit support from subordinates for these decisions whenever possible. Likewise, if the decision is unpopular, a leader must be willing to stand by his/her decision.

12. Anticipation of excellence displays confidence in staff/athletes and standardizes high quality in all actions.

Batten stresses that the cybernetic circle of leadership is a continuous process. For example, after a manager (coach or administrator) has concluded an endeavor, project, or athletic season, he or she will once again begin at step one by re-establishing the organization's mission and direction for the next operational endeavor.

Theory 7

Kouzes and Posner, in their 1999 publication *The Leadership Challenge*, hypothesize that leadership is an indoctrinated, observed function that is attainable by anyone, in any capacity. They feel that if a committed, dedicated individual would emulate their 10 behavioral commitments, this person would become a proactive, successful leader. They have constructed their principles from research surveys of more than 500 contemporary, successful leaders. Success in this context is interpreted as perceived credibility, meeting and surpassing performance expectations, being future oriented, impartial and equitable, imaginative, and broadminded.

Challenge the Process
- Search for Opportunities
- Experiment and Take Risks

Inspire a Shared Vision
- Envision the Future
- Enlist Others and Enable Others to Act
- Foster Collaboration
- Strengthen Others

Model the Way
- Set the Example
- Plan Small Wins

Encourage the Heart
- Recognize Individual Contributions
- Celebrate Contributions

Narrative Elaboration:
1. Search for opportunities: This leadership obligation proactively institutes change. It appraises plausible opportunities and manipulates each opportunity for organizational goal achievement.
2. Experiment and take risks: This behavioral commitment embraces organizational communication channels (internal and external) to envision opportunities; it cultivates and encourages leaders to go beyond personal restraints; it disciplines leaders to learn from each other's mistakes.
3. Envision the future: This leadership perspective observes the future from what is achievable from past tendencies and patterns.
4. Enlist others: This behavioral responsibility embraces open communication channels and accentuates the conviction that no thought or

idea is right or wrong, better or worse; it enlists subordinates through formal one-on-one sessions and collective group brainstorming.

5. Foster collaboration: This leadership tactic is through the development of a participative mission and builds a trust foundation for organizational continuation.

6. Strengthen others: Leaders who nurture a subordinate's strengths will not only provide new opportunities for the group and organization but will earn the long-term commitment of the subordinates.

7. Set the example: Leaders lead by example and should participate in all operational activities (in some capacity). This hands-on demeanor develops teamwork and camaraderie that, in turn, increases productivity.

8. Plan small wins: Leaders should integrate a plan of small program wins. This step-by-step game plan consolidates positive short-term goals into projected organizational missions.

9. Recognize individual contributions: Effective leaders enable others to perform by establishing high but achievable expectations. Performance standards as motivational tools should be associated with tangible rewards (whenever possible). Leaders who provide accolades as performance incentives should actively pursue individuals who are purposeful, tenacious, and exceed performance requirements.

10. Celebrate accomplishment: Leadership behavioral commitments should publicly acknowledge outstanding and timely task achievements.

Theory 8

In his original text *Principles of Technical Management* and in his later 1990 publication *The Art of the Leader*, Cohen provides five straightforward keys to effective leadership problem solving:

1. Always ask the question: Why?
2. Break complicated problems into less-complicated components.
3. Increase the number of alternatives under consideration.
4. Don't try to keep all problem-solving facts in one's head when making decisions.
5. Consider the consequences of each alternative decision.

Narrative Elaboration:

1. Ask "Why?": This crucial question develops a leaders alternatives by confronting every declaration and explanation. A leader who blindly endorses customary answers without interrogation is limiting his or her talents and managerial options.

2. Breakdown of complicated problems into less complicated components: The complexity of some leadership obstacles can overwhelm

a leader and deter actions. The logical dissection of problems into small segments will allow a more sequential, concentrated effort on smaller, simpler components rather than the catch-all approach of aggregate problem solving.

3. Increase the number of alternatives: Increasing alternatives provides leaders with more latitude on deciding which direction tact is the best.

4. Record all factual information: No one individual is flawless and can recollect all minute parts of a situation. The capable application of notes and other recording instruments assures that a leader will not disregard or omit any element in the problem-solving process.

5. Evaluate the consequences: Simply express each alternative under consideration by its ramifications to the organization/program. These results will need to be analyzed as to their probability and operational repercussions.

CHAPTER

Managerial Control and Coaching

CHAPTER OUTLINE

- To define the control function as it interacts with the management process
- To explain reasons for managerial controls in athletic programs
- To appraise the three types of managerial controls: feed forward controls, concurrent controls, and feedback controls
- To define bureaucratic and commitment controls
- To illustrate management by walking around
- To enumerate and describe the four primary steps in the control process
- To present and explain a performance evaluation chart
- To elucidate the advantages and disadvantages of control feedback

INTRODUCTION

This chapter is the last of the five chapters in the section on fundamental management concepts. It examines the depth and application of the managerial function of control and the elements in the control process.

In theory and if done correctly, the first four concepts of management (planning, organizing, human resource management, and leadership) minimize and sometimes preempt the concept of control. In the real world, however, the function of managerial and athletic program control is essential for facilitating operations and accomplishing goals.

CONTROL DEFINED

The word *control* has a unique meaning to each of us. For the most part, the business world has given the functional duty of control a standardized, simple, and step-by-step process (see Control Process section below). The applicable, strategic definition is as follows:

> Strategic managers choose the organizational strategies and structure they hope will allow the organization to use its resources most effectively to pursue its business model and create value and profit. Then they create strategic control systems, tools that allow them to monitor and evaluate whether, in fact, their strategies and structure are working as intended, how they could be improved, and how they should change if they are not working. (Hill & Jones, 2004, p. 411)

From this definition, the importance of the planning process in giving an organization and athletic program focus is accentuated. Without delineated goals and structure there would be nothing to control. This leads to the question, "Why practice managerial controls?"

Administrative Tip

Control is the ultimate step in the management process that leads right back into the first step, planning. In other words, management is a circular progression with no beginning or end.

WHY PRACTICE MANAGERIAL CONTROLS?

Managerial controls are designed to give managers information regarding progress. The manager can use this information to do the following:

1. Prevent crisis—If a manager does not know what is going on, it is easy for small, readily solved problems to turn into crisis.
2. Standardize outputs—Problems and services can be standardized in terms of quality and quantity through the use of good controls.
3. Appraise employee's performances—Proper controls can provide the manager with objective information about employee performance.
4. Update plans—Even the best plans must be updated as environmental and internal changes occur. Controls allow the manager to compare what is happening with what was planned.
5. Protect an organization's assets—Controls can protect assets from inefficiency, waste, and pilferage. (Rue & Byars, 2005, pp. 363–364)

These five major reasons to practice managerial controls can be related to coaching and athletic program administration.

Through proactive planning and control, all coaches should try to avoid crisis management. Because the end product is often the athletic program and athletes' performances, failing to monitor some type of development or control the quality of an athlete's training could lead not only to the athlete failing but also the failure of the entire program. The possible crisis situations in an athletic program are unlimited. However, with strong control systems in place, coaches/program administrators can minimize the possibility of a small problem turning into a major crisis.

Standardizing outputs emphasizes quality control and maximization of resources. As discussed in previous chapters, quality should be a primary goal in all aspects of the athletic program. If the control system and philosophy stress standardized quality, then the program will consistently produce quality outputs and performances.

In appraising employees, control revolves around maximizing an athlete or staff member's skills and capabilities. By their very nature, performance evaluations are direct tools that keep the program's personnel focused, not only on their personal goals but also on the program's goals. The maintenance on this type of control system has a direct effect on productivity and performance.

A business or program plan must foremost be considered a flexible document that can be adapted and revised. In most cases, the only way to determine if an element of the program plan needs adjusting is to examine that element over time. Through good monitoring and controls, one can determine what goals and objectives are still relevant and which targeted plans need to be adjusted (expanded, augmented, minimized, eliminated).

Finally, all programs (no matter how large) have limited resources. Control systems can quickly determine which functions are effectively using program resources (time, money, manpower) and which are not. For example, the program might be utilizing a certain training technique to develop a particular skill or strength. Without proper controls and monitoring, how could one know if this technique is a productive training method or if one could use his/her time/resources/efforts more effectively elsewhere?

TYPES OF CONTROLS

In the text *Essentials of Contemporary Management,* Jones and George illuminate three types of control systems. The three concepts are broken down as follows:

> Feed forward controls—Control that allows managers to anticipate problem before they arise.
>
> Concurrent controls—Control that gives managers immediate feedback on how efficiently inputs are being transformed into outputs so that managers can correct problems as they arise.
>
> Feedback controls—Control that gives managers information about customers' reactions to goods and services so that corrective action can be taken if necessary. (Jones & George, 2004, p. 245–246)

These three types of control systems can be easily adapted to coaching and athletic program administration.

1. Feed forward controls are proactive controls that a coach or program administrator can establish prior to any type of operational work or goal performance. The important consideration in establishing these types of controls is based on the final expected product/performance.

2. Concurrent controls are used to adjust behavior while the program's operations are in progress. This control method keeps the program on track and avoids tangents. A small change early in a process can avoid a large change and restructuring later. Major types of concurrent controls are Yes/No controls. Yes/No controls are essentially go/no-go decisions at selected checkpoints in the program's operations. The key to this type of control process is discovering the points at which to make a go/no-go decision. Typically, these are called the "points of no return" or critical decision junctions. For example, the hardest type of yes/no decisions in the coaching profession relates to the retention or dismissal of athletes. In this scenario, whether one personally determines the "cut-down" date or whether the date is determined by the program's governing body (NCAA, MLB, High School Association, etc.), the coach or program administrator has a program decision . . . does the pro-

Administrative Tip

As a coach/program administrator, imagine control as a continuum. At one end of the continuum is the lack of control and at the other end is micro-management. While the damages of a lack of control philosophy are clearly seen, micro-management is just as perilous to an operation. A good control system and personal philosophy should be to balance these two diametrically opposite positions.

gram go with an athlete or is he or she released? Once again, the control decision is based on the program's goals and mission.

3. Feedback controls are the comparison of actual with projected results after a specific time period has elapsed. This a major premise behind the control process.

Two other distinctions need to be made when talking about types of program controls. They are bureaucratic controls and commitment (or clan) controls. They are defined by the following:

Bureaucratic control—an approach to tactical control that stresses adherence to rules and regulations and is imposed by others.

Commitment (clan) control—an approach to tactical control that emphasizes consensus and shared responsibility for meeting goals. (Black & Porter, 2000, p. 494)

In other words, bureaucratic controls can be described as rigidly enforced controls that are established and outlined in a program's policies and procedure manuals. Clan controls are more of a cooperative, empowered shared vision that provides staff and athletes an opportunity to voice their personal concerns in quality control. In deciding which one an organization should give emphasis to, a sound mixture of both techniques is often prescribed.

The collaborative/clan approach to organizational control can be enhanced by the concept of Management by Walking Around. Management by Walking Around (MBWA) is exactly that. Managers (i.e., coaches and athletic program administrators) observe operations by simply walking around and having open discussions with staff members and athletes. There are some distinct advantages in doing this.

1. MBWA brings control issues to the surface much easier than through bureaucratic channels.
2. MBWA provides immediate awareness to control issues by empirical observation.
3. MBWA has an enormous side benefit of being motivational to employees.
4. MBWA establishes an open culture.
5. MBWA gains information not derived by formal reports and control documents.
6. MBWA breaks down resistance and barriers to control standards.
7. MBWA is a great idea generator and a managerial learning tool.
8. MBWA penetrates the immensely persuasive informal communication channel (know as the grapevine).

THE CONTROL PROCESS

The steps in the control process follow the logic of planning:

"(1) performance standards are set, (2) performance is measured,

(3) performance is compared to standards, and (4) corrective action is taken if needed" (DuBrin, 2003, p. 413).

Before an elaboration of each step is given, it must be emphasized that the control process is not a separate, stand-alone element of the management concept but an integrated feature of management. Furthermore, while the process of control is essentially sequential, the actual variety of applications of the control process inside the program is unlimited. For the process to be effective, it must be an ongoing activity rather than an intermittent and occasional event.

The areas in which a coach and/or athletic program administrator can focus his/her control efforts parallels corporate/business dimensions. Corporate control dimensions are evaluated along the following:

- Quality of product and service
- Quality of management
- Innovativeness
- Long-term investment value
- Financial soundness
- Community and environmental responsibilities
- Use of corporate assets
- Ability to attract, develop, and keep talented people. (Wright, Knoll, & Parnell, 1996, p. 250)

Once again, these corporate operational control essentials can be customized to fit an athletic program administration/control.

- From the perspective of quality of product, coaches can develop quantitative control criteria based on the superiority of their program's outputs (wins/loses, athletes produced for the next level, program reputation, etc.).
- With their pre-established human resource systems, athletic programs can develop control elements for the performance of staff and athletes (policy and procedures, performance evaluation systems, operational manuals, etc.).
- Innovativeness control aspects relate to how well the program "keeps up" with external, contemporary best practices as well as cultivating original internal administrative and coaching techniques.
- Long-term investment controls examine how well current dollars are being used for future program benefit. For example, a current investment in new equipment needs to be continuously inspected as to its potential program payoff in the future.
- Financial controls are essential for all athletic programs. Budgets are established and coaches/program administrators need to have control systems in place to make sure that the budgets are monitored and maintained.

- Because of the visibility of most athletic programs, control systems should be established regulating the number and influence of community concerned activities for both teams and individuals involved in the program.
- Controlling the use of corporate assets in athletics can relate to the capacity utilization of a facility, the amount and value added in program owned transportation, and the use and replacement of equipment.
- Another human resource control system that needs monitoring/controlling relates to the program's staffing system. Questions such as how well is the program recruiting staff and athletes and what is the quality of significant personnel additions need to be scrutinized.

Establish Performance Standards

The first factor in the control process is establishing performance standards.

> Performance standards tell employees—in advance—what level of performance is expected of them. They also measure how well employees meet expectations. . . . There are many ways of developing these standards, such as intuition, past performance, careful measurement of activities, and comparison with other standards or averages. Once standards of performance are set, they should be communicated by means of written policies, rules, procedures, and/or statements of standards to the people responsible for performance. Standards are valuable for stimulating good performance, as well as in locating sources of inefficiencies. (Megginson, Byrd, & Megginson, 2006, pp. 364–365)

The planning aspect of the management process stresses that the program determines specific, tangible, and measurable goals. For example, from an academic standpoint in either high school or college, one of the program goals could be to achieve a team grade point average of 3.0 on a 4.0 scale. To accomplish this, the staff, athletes, and team could determine that the following elements are critical for the athletes and program to reach its academic projected goal:

1. Class attendance and participation.
2. Midterm, finals, and other tests.
3. Term papers and extra credit.

Now establish objective performance standards for each of these targeted performance ingredients. For example:

1. Each athlete must attend at least 90% of all classes and take an active role in all discussions.
2. Each athlete must achieve a score of 75% or higher on all planned exams.

3. Each athlete must achieve a score of 80% or higher on all term papers and all homework assignments must be completed in a timely manner.

Can establishing performance standards be utilized for individuals as well as teams? Absolutely. For example, in the sport of baseball, the coach and athlete can discuss a personal goal of hitting .300 for a season. Both concur that the following performance elements are fundamental in fulfilling that goal:

1. Bat speed must increase.
2. More repetitions/swings must be taken by the player during practice.
3. The player should receive more feedback and instruction on techniques.

Now jointly establish performance standards for each element. For instance:

1. Bat speed must increase by 20%. More intense weight lifting and strength conditioning will be employed.
2. After each practice session, the athlete (along with the coaching staff) hits 50 to 100 extra balls.
3. After each game, the coach and the athlete evaluate game film.

It should be noted that goals and performance standards have to be based on reality. One's mission as a program administrator and leader should be to establish goals and standards that are challenging and achievable rather than discouraging and unrealistic.

Measure Performance

There are two ways to measure performance: one is through quantitative valuation; the other is qualitative, subjective observation. Many business organizations adhere strictly to the philosophy of judging performance according to the "bottom line results." They look meticulously at sales margins and profits. To rely solely on numbers for measuring performance is a monumental mistake for a coach or program administrator. Motivational coaches will augment quantitative measurements with qualitative ones such as desire, intensity, and a concentrated effort to improve and fulfill goals.

Compare Actual Results with Projected Standards

This step in the control process is the easiest to comprehend. The underlying question is, "How does the actual measured performance compare to the projected performance?" The most effective tool for this comparison is a performance evaluation chart. The following performance evaluation chart could be designed from our previous academic example.

Corrective Action

The control process is completed by evaluating the variance column on the

Administrative Tip

When establishing performance standards, use historical data/standards as the starting point but do not finish there. Question what other similar and successful athletic programs have instituted as their performance standards. By merging the competition's standards along with historical foundations, a coach/program administrator can develop specific controls that are rational as well as realistic.

Table 1. Performance Evaluation Chart

Performance Standard

1. Players must attend 90% of all classes and take an active role in class participation.
2. 75% on mid-terms and finals.
3. 80% on term papers and 100% on homework.

Overall Goal: 3.0 GPA

Actual Result

A measured attendance of 86% was recorded. Players' progress reports for class participation were all positive.

Team average of 81% on mid-terms and final. High/low range 72–96%.

64% on term papers, 78% on homework.

Actual: 2.91 GPA

Variance

<4 %>	class variance.
+6%	variance on testing.
<17%>	variance on papers and <22%> on homework.
<.09%>	overall GPA variance.

performance evaluation chart. The evaluation can have one of three possible outcomes:

1. Do nothing—if meeting an acceptable range of variances, then do not adjust control system.
2. Correct deviation—if the variable falls outside acceptable limits, corrective action will be necessary. Positive deviations should be examined for new insights into such successes while negative deviations should be the foundations of learning.
3. Revise standard—after learning that there are certain variances, the revision of performance standards might be necessary. This, in turn, will re-track performance into achievable goals. (Bedeian, 1993, pp. 563–564)

If the individual athlete or the team exceeds standards and goals, readjust the standards to an elevated level yet still make them achievable. If the team, athletes, or staff are not achieving standards:

1. Ask "why?"
2. See if the problem can be fixed.
3. Either maintain standards or readjust them to a more realistic range.

FEEDBACK

Administrative Tip

The first scenario in the appraisal of a program's performance, do nothing, has a potentially perilous long-term ramification associated with it—complacency. If there is ever an option in a managerial control situation, take the challenging choice over the complacency choice, especially in significant operating areas.

The primary advantage of using an organized, participative control system (whether for an individual or a team) is that it provides the basis for feedback. All variances should be discussed whether they are positive or negative. How one handles those variances is a part of one's makeup as a program administrator and leader. In the article *Giving Good Feedback*, McLaughlin discusses seven methods to giving good feedback controls.

1. Ask permission to give feedback—You will not believe the difference in the level of conversation when you ask permission. Asking permission to give feedback sets a positive framework on a situation that could be perceived as negative.
2. Set a tone of energy and optimism—Consciously assume an attitude that embraces both candor and sensitivity.
3. Focus on specifics—When sharing feedback, focus on specific situations and behavior, rather than delving into psychoanalysis.
4. Show appreciation and say thank you—Let them know you value their time as well as their willingness to listen to your feedback.
5. Confront non-performance—Don't wait for the yearly review to tackle this issue.

6. Remember it's a dialogue—Not a monologue. Ask questions and listen attentively to answers. Offer suggestions and support. Jointly consider options.

7. Encourage and energize—Get excited about the changes your direct report can make. Give them examples of how they can improve and show that you're supportive of them making these changes. (McLaughlin, 2007, p. 7)

Conversely, Lindenberger, in her article *Feedback without Fear*, describes some feedback fouls regarding control.

- Doing nothing. Ignoring the problem in hopes it will go away is probably the most common mistake.
- Giving only negative feedback. It is only human to focus on the things that bother you.
- Giving negative feedback months after the fact.
- Criticizing things your staffers don't know how to do better.
- Blaming the need for negative feedback on someone else. Take responsibility for feedback.
- Delivering drive-by feedback.
- Criticizing in public. Besides being humiliating, a public dressing-down hardly encourages the kind of two-way dialogue that leads to improvement.
- Criticizing via voicemail, email, or little notes. (Lindenberger, 2007, pp. 34–38)

A coach or program administrator must communicate to his or her athletes and staff that even though they are ultimately accountable for their own performance results, they are part of a program and the top priority is to help them achieve. If the coach or program administrator can instill this feeling into them and the program, the staff and athletes will look forward to the challenges of higher performance standards rather then dreading them.

SUMMARY

The managerial assignment of control is vital in helping with the smooth flow of program operations as well as the ultimate realization of program goals. Proper control systems isolate and solve problems, ensure quality benchmarks, monitor staff and athlete's performances, and prevent an organization from squandering its limited resources. Through the proactive application of the control process, a coach or program administrator can standardize and measure a staff member or athlete's performance while conveying essential feedback to each for improving and maximizing potential.

Administrative Tip

Throughout all aspects of the management process (and, in fact, all operational activities), aggressively scrutinize other comparable athletic programs. Simply put, if these programs are performing better than one's program, emulate them and even improve on their concepts and operations. The key to emulation is ego. Get rid of ego and stubbornness. If another program's operations are superior, they are superior . . . PERIOD. Learn from them.

control	management by walking around
feed forward controls	control process
concurrent controls	performance standards
feedback controls	performance measurements
bureaucratic controls	performance evaluation chart
commitment/clan controls	feedback

Review and Discussion Questions

1. Why practice managerial controls in an athletic program?

2. Why should a coach or program administrator give a high priority (through planning and control) to avoiding crisis management?

3. What are feed forward controls?

4. What are concurrent controls?

5. What are feedback controls?

6. Define MBWA. What are its advantages?

7. What is the four-step control process?

8. In the control process, what are the three possible scenarios in evaluating variances?

9. What can a coach or program administrator do if his or her program is not achieving standards and goals?

CHAPTER

Budgeting and Travel Administration

CHAPTER OUTLINE

CHAPTER
6
OBJECTIVES

- To provide coaches and program administrators with a practical outline for budgeting
- To distinguish the two types of situational budgeting: entrepreneurial and operating/expense
- To examine the concept of traditional expense budgeting and zero-based budgeting
- To consider budgeting as a function of managerial control
- To explain the essential principles of travel budgeting
- To present a travel spreadsheet template
- To clarify the make-up and calculations behind each categorical section of a travel spreadsheet
- To justify the critical managerial cost control of travel spreadsheets
- To outline the rationale behind constructing a travel itinerary
- To furnish a framework model for the content and design of a comprehensive travel itinerary

INTRODUCTION

Before a discussion of budgeting can commence, it must be emphatically stated that the process of budgeting (in most organizations) is fairly simple to understand. So why does the mere mention of the term evoke extreme mental distress for most program administrators and coaches? Three prominent reasons stand out. The first is that budgets are predictions and predictions deal with uncertainty and ambiguity. The second is that to do them accurately, budgets take time, thought, and effort. If a coach or program administrator is not detail oriented, budgeting can be an arduous process. The third is that budgets customarily deal with a very critical and carefully scrutinized organizational resource—money. Money is the one program resource that elicits immediate attention from all organization stakeholders.

While budgeting is primarily focused on financial resources/money, almost all internal operating resources can (and should be) budgeted. Resources such as personnel and work time, materials and supplies, and facility and equipment usage are just a small amount of the athletic program items that can be budgeted. For our intentions, we will concentrate our dialogue on the internal resource of capital/money.

BUDGETING DEFINED

The most comprehensive use of the term *budgeting* is exemplified by the following definition:

> A budget is simply a forecast of future events . . . budgets perform three basic functions for a firm. First, they indicate the amount

Administrative Tip

If a coach/program administrator has never budgeted before, do not think twice about contacting a colleague with experience to request his/her help. Budgeting takes insight as well as practice. Plunging blindly into the budgeting process can have considerable ramification for the program now and in the future.

and timing of the firm's needs for future financing. Second, they provide the basis for taking corrective action in the event budgeted figures do not match actual or realized figures. Third, budgets provide the basis for performance benchmarks that management can use to evaluate the performance of those responsible for carrying out those plans and, in turn, to control their actions. Thus, budgets are valuable aids in both the planning and controlling aspects of the firm's financial management. (Keown, Martin, Petty, & Scott, 2001, p. 151)

Budgets are for a specific terminal time period (ordinarily a fiscal year). While they are utilized for projecting future resource allocation, they are grounded in historical data. In other words, what is spent in previous budgetary periods will be the foundation for the projections into succeeding budgetary periods.

Budgeting promotes planning and coordination; it enhances performance measurements and corrective actions.

> Planning—The budget formalizes and documents managerial plans, clearly communicating objectives to both superiors and subordinates.
>
> Coordination—The budgetary process forces coordination among departments to promote decisions in the best interest of the company as a whole.
>
> Performance measurement—Budgets are specific, quantitative representations of management's objectives. Comparing actual results to budgeted expectations provides a way to evaluate performance.
>
> Corrective action—Budgeting provides advanced notice of potential shortages, or other weaknesses in operating plans. . . . Budgeting advises managers of potential problems in time for them to carefully devise effective solutions. (Edmonds, Bor-Yi, & Olds, 2008, p. 295)

SITUATIONAL BUDGETING

From coaching and program administration, budgeting can take two different forms. The first and most difficult is that the coach or program administrator is the owner of the club or team. In this case, one must budget extensively and apply detailed accounting procedures to all operations. This circumstance is similar to entrepreneurial and corporate accounting. In this type of operation, it is advisable (unless the coach has a formal accounting and business background) to employ and directly work with an accounting consultant. The consultant will help set up all of the program's financial statements, projected budgets, and year-end fiscal reports. Documents such as cash flow statements, balance sheets, and income statements (both actual and projected) are typically beyond general coaching knowledge.

The second form of budgeting is the one that is relevant for the majority of coaches—operating/expense budgeting. This is a system where the program is a part (or unit) within a whole athletic department or corporate structure. In this case, the process of financial statement generation is completed outside the program. The coach or administrator is provided with specific parameters within which the program must operate. In other words, the program's owner (in a professional setting) or the athletic administration (in a high school, junior, or senior college) stipulates a specific dollar amount for the program to operate. The projected amount can be divided into predetermined line items (recruiting, scholarships, phone, etc.) or it can be an aggregate total. In the latter case, the coach determines the allocation for the individual line items.

TRADITIONAL EXPENSE BUDGETING

Traditional expense budgeting is one that focuses on the disbursement/expense side of the income statement. The first step is to identify all of the program's costs. This concept is not as simple as it seems. A good place to start is with the identification of historical data. Simply put, the expense categories that the program has had in the past and present are the foundations for the future projected categories. However, this is not the end of the process. The program, through planning and goal definition, has a futuristic viewpoint that possibly is very different from its current and historical position. In this instance, discover what new possible expenditures (based on the program's mission, goals, and direction) need to be defined. The coach or program administrator needs to think this step through from every possible angle. Look at the fiscal year completely. While some coaches tend to dissect their in-season expenses, never de-emphasize the off-season projected expenses.

Once the program's expense categories have been determined, enter the dollar amounts that are believed to be accurate. As with budget category definitions, historical data is a good starting point in determining the dollar amount for each line item expense. From that starting point, each expense must be looked at individually to determine operating variables from past years to present. In other words, are operations remaining essentially the same? If so, then the utilization of historical expense information is relevant, applicable, and defendable. If a coach or program administrator has evaluated and subsequently changed any aspect of their operation, then an increase or decrease in a line item might be warranted.

For example, if one's team is traveling to the same locations, with the same travel squad, with the same method of transportation, etc., then historical data can be used with a fairly high degree of confidence to determine the team's travel line item. Any deviations (different travel destinations, a larger or smaller travel squad, etc.) imply that the line item will need to be adjusted accordingly.

Administrative Tip

Consultants (such as lawyers, accountants, medical/trainers, etc.) should be considered a "necessary evil" if the program's operations necessitate their use. They are professional experts in their fields. While these specialists' up-front costs could be considered exorbitant, skillful consultants over the long term can pay for their services many times over. If the program cannot finance consultants on a permanent basis, hire them to set up operational systems that are self-sustaining.

ZERO-BASED BUDGETING

As previously discussed, budgeting is the administrative responsibility that projects and calculates future organizational resource allocations. Budgets provide a tangible framework within which the different components of the athletic program can operate.

> In the traditional approach to budgeting, the manager starts with last year's budget and adds to it (or subtracts from it) according to anticipated needs. . . . Under a zero-based budget, managers are required to justify all budgeted expenditures, not just changes in the budget from the previous year. The baseline is zero rather than last year's budget. (Garrison & Noreen, 2003, p. 380)

From an athletic program outlook, zero-based budgeting is considerably more challenging to develop because of the fact that each expense "line item" is considered a new expense and its projected amounts are derived from original data. In other words, while traditional budgets are considered "rollovers," zero-based budgets stem from primary new budgeting research. If done accurately, zero-based budgets give a truer picture of the financial situation and budgetary projections. A coach/program administrator needs to determine if the additional accuracy of the zero-based budget's primary research warrants the additional time needed to construct. A possible option is to assemble zero-based budgets every other fiscal period to maintain accuracy of the traditional numbers as well as to keep the program using up-to-date primary figures.

BUDGETS AS MANAGERIAL CONTROLS

Budgets, as a managerial control tool, have

> four principle purposes: (1) to fine-tune the strategic plan; (2) to help coordinate the activities of the several parts of the organization; (3) to assign responsibility to managers, to authorize the amounts that they are permitted to spend, and to inform them of the performance that is expected of them; and (4) to obtain a commitment that is a basis for evaluating a manager's actual performance. (Anthony & Govindarajan, 2007, p. 382)

Considering budgets deal with the most critical and limited resource in a program (namely money), all internal stakeholders need to have a guide for operating and spending. For this reason, budgets need to be continuously monitored by the coach/program administrator. A good practice is to keep an expense ledger (either by hand or by computer) that shows a program's individual line items. The line items can be broken down into fiscal budget, actual expenditures, and operational variances. Another ledger technique could be similar to one's personal checkbook where dates and running balances show the remaining funds as well as when expenditures were incurred. Furthermore, if one can accurately maintain encumbrances against running totals, it will give a clear picture of the account. Finally, any major deviations from projected to actual spending should be narratively recorded and explained for budget review clarification at the end of the fiscal year.

Budgeting and Organizational Goals

Because the ultimate ambition of management is goal realization, budgeting and the budgeting process must always have the objectives of the athletic program in mind. In the simplest terms, the budgets established should be a productive tool in the achievement of what the athletic program wants to accomplish. The worst-case scenario in dealing with budgets is that they are a hindrance and a deterrent to achieving goals. "Problems can arise if (1) the budget goal is unachievable (too high), (2) the budget goal is very easy to achieve (too loose), or (3) the budget goals of the business conflict with the objectives of employees (goal conflict)" (Warren, Reeve, & Fess, 2002, p. 820). From a coaching vantage, one's budget must be challenging but achievable to maximize the program's financial resources as well as have everyone's best interest at heart.

TRAVEL ADMINISTRATION INTRODUCTION

This component reviews a primary area of sport management operational budgeting—team travel. The section provides information for the construction of a travel worksheet as well as some general tips on budgeting and team travel. The section concludes with functional uses of travel worksheets as a cost control instrument.

BASIC PRINCIPLES OF TRAVEL BUDGETING

The following are some underlying fundamentals to travel budgeting:

1. As with all types of operational budgeting, in advance, clarify if the organization uses a deductive or inductive budgeting philosophy. Deductive budgeting is deriving conclusions from a known amount. Simply put, there is a certain bottom line dollar amount for the specific budget and the coach or program administrator must work within that amount (backward flow). Inductive budgeting (or zero-based budgeting) is operating forward through each category and line item without targeted bottom line constraints. In other words, inductive, zero-based budgeting would have the coach calculating all of the trips' total expenses and reporting back to the program's administrators what the justified "bottom line" would be for travel.

2. Use actual quotes whenever possible. If quotes are unattainable, use historical price range estimates. It is advisable when using estimates

Administrative Tip

Quotes can be used to get enhanced services at reduced costs. Play travel companies against one another. It is not unscrupulous but a straightforward fact of the competitive market/economy in which all businesses function. If a coach/ program administrator consents to a higher quote without investigating other options, then he/she will have no one to blame when resources at a later point are depreciated. The more money one saves by receiving superior prices (without forfeiting safety and quality), the more money the program will have to disburse in other areas.

to "go high" on all calculations and costs. When getting quotes, remember to ask for all-inclusive prices (i.e., prices that include taxes, fees, etc.). Another sound tip is to get written confirmations whenever possible.

3. Stay consistent with the format and calculations from line item to line item and category to category. Any deviations from the norm must be explained in a supplementary document. Remember, it is substantially easier to justify the numbers if assumptions are applied consistently throughout the travel budget.

4. Personally triple-check all calculations. Then have a program staff member also verify the accuracy of calculations. Remember, it is easier to justify numbers to administrators if they are accurate and stand up to scrutiny.

5. When getting quotes, get three different assessments. If using an outside agent or consultant, insist that they procure three quotes.

6. Standardize the budgetary process by designing and utilizing budget spreadsheets. The design of a budget worksheet will be dictated by the type of information required, the depth of information required, and the durational period of information required.

TRAVEL SPREADSHEETS

The following chart is a traditional travel worksheet. Each category (column) will be briefly explained.

Destination: This line is self-explanatory. In addition to city destination, incorporate actual trip dates. For a more coherent worksheet, keep the program's trips in chronological order from first trip to last.

# of Days: The critical importance of this category is that it will be utilized for other line item calculations. Depending on the budget and monetary circumstance, this category could be broken down into 1/4, 1/2, or whole days. The more detailed the daily breakdown, the more precise (and unfortunately, inflexible) the dollar amounts. Days should be measured from departure time (at point of origin) to projected time of arrival (back at point of origin). For example, the departure time could be noon on Thursday with an estimated arrival time of Sunday at 6 p.m. In this instance, the coach or program administrator could classify this trip as four whole days, 3 1/2 days, or 3 1/4 days.

# of People: Another influential category for other line item calculations is the number of people in the travel squad. A standardized travel squad would simplify the work associated with this item.

Meals: Meals can be computed by using two distinct methods. One could adopt a flat rate method or a per-meal cost. The following are examples:

Destination	#Days	#People	Meals	Lodging	Air	Charter	Van	Gas	Other	Total

Figure 1. Travel Spreadsheets

Flat Rate

3 1/2 days x 20 people x $30.00 per day = $2,100.00 Total Meals

Per Meal

Meals—Breakfast $5.00

Lunch $10.00

Dinner $15.00

In a 3 1/2 day trip, the program could have four team breakfasts, four lunches, and three dinners. The calculations:

Breakfast— $5.00 × 4 total breakfasts × 20 people = $400.00

Lunch— $10.00 × 4 total lunches × 20 people = $800.00

Dinner— $15.00 × 3 total dinners × 20 people = $900.00

Total Meals: $2,100.00

Lodging: The number of rooms needed by the group is solely dependent on the team travel squad and the program's policy on how many players and staff to a room. An example of the room calculation is as follows:

20 people/2 to a room = 10 rooms

10 rooms × $75.00 per room × 3 nights = $2,250.00

Furnish hotels with the travel rooming list as early as possible so they can block rooms in the same general area in the hotel. Furthermore, get confirmations and contractual arrangements in writing. It is strongly recommended to (1) get firm price quotes and (2) subsequent reservations as soon as it is practical in the worksheet process. Most hotels function on the supply and demand principle. Conventions, athletic events, and city functions can decrease availability, which increases price.

The next four categories are directly related to team transportation.

Air: If the program's transportation mandates air travel, then it is a matter of choice whether one uses a travel agent to make the arrangements or does it him/herself. Some essential fundamentals if deciding to engage a travel agent are as follows:

1. Make sure the travel agent is a Certified Travel Counselor (CTC). CTCs are accredited travel agents that have at least five years of experience and have fulfilled all course requirements stipulated by the Institute of Certified Travel Agents.

2. Comparison shop. One method of comparison shopping for travel agents would be to write up the general criteria for airline travel (and other inclusive services such as vans) and then forward it to at least three different travel agents. Some of the travel specifications could include dates and times, places, ground transportation, etc. Select the most competitive, cost-efficient, and time-effective travel service.

3. Once a choice is made of an agency, deal exclusively with one agent. This will eliminate miscommunications, duplications, and omissions.

4. Secure a direct billing system with the travel agent and vendors to expedite payments and ticket distribution.

5. With the travel agent, lock in rates as early as possible. If feasible, keep the travel party's size to 15 people or more to qualify for group rates.

The basic worksheet calculation for air travel is as follows:

# of travelers × ticket price (tax included) = total ticket price

Charter: Any seasoned traveler will testify that not all charter bus lines are the same. If traveling by bus, it is strongly recommended to comparative shop at least five bus line companies. Likewise, get recommendations from other knowledgeable groups or teams that travel by bus.

The distance to be traveled, the size of the bus needed, and days and times of charter service are the three elements that will determine quoted prices. There are three important considerations in acquiring a charter company:

1. While airline tickets represent contractual arrangements between traveler and airline, charter companies deal with nonconforming quotes. Get a written contractual agreement from the bus line that expressly itemizes dates, times, size of vehicle, pickup and drop-off locales, and costs.

2. Specifically inquire if the contractual agreement includes bus driver fees and room costs. Some companies will defray the bus driver's accommodations and miscellaneous expenses, while others will have the coach include them in the program's traveling costs.

3. Most bus line companies operate on a prepaid basis only. However, deposits can hold reservations.

From a worksheet perspective, there are no calculations associated with the charter category.

Vans: There are two instances that necessitate utilizing van transportation; (1) if vans are the program's primary mode of transportation (local trips); and (2) for local around-town transportation if the program has traveled by air. A few salient recommendations concerning van travel. For teams, acquiring 15-passenger vehicles is typically more cost effective and substantially more spacious than other rental vehicles (remember, not only are vans transporting players and staff, but often their bulky luggage). The unfortunate problems associated with 15-passenger vans are their limited availability (especially in smaller markets) and their danger of operation. Van travel for athletic teams and programs over the past few years has come under serious scrutiny (for safety reasons) by governing organizations as well as internal administrators. Once again, secure reservations and subsequent confirmations early in the worksheet process.

Contact major rental companies or car/truck dealerships in destination locales. From a cost standpoint, rental companies operate on

Administrative Tip

In dealing with travel agents/companies (as well as all program vendors), cultivate an intuitive sixth sense. Try to develop a perception for a travel company's professionalism, quality, auxiliary services, collaboration, and timeliness. Remember that in most cases, unless one has a long-term contractual relationship, most travel arrangements can be changed with little or no lead time. However, if the program has a conscientious and high-quality travel company (hotel chain, bus line, CTC, etc.), strive to maintain a good working relationship and productive rapport.

Administrative Tip

As soon as possible, reinforce a positive employer-subordinate relationship with the trip's bus driver. If the driver does not have one, review with him/her the trip's itinerary and targeted timelines. Neglecting to involve a bus driver could have profound travel consequences.

a daily basis with a half hour to an hour grace period. If planning van transportation with this in mind, extra day charges might be avoided. Furthermore, always check for unlimited mileage status on all rentals. Reminder, all drivers must be at least 25 years old. The program must secure all rentals with a major credit card and the optional insurance coverage is solely up to the organization's policy on additional insurance. The coach/program administrator should check state regulations in which they are driving vans and rental vehicles for applicable laws and insurance requirements.

The basic worksheet calculation:

# of vans × # of days x inclusive cost per vehicle = total van costs

An addition to this calculation could be the possibility of excess miles over and above the free rental miles.

Gas: The assessment for gas consumption needs to be consistent throughout the worksheet. Gas costs are estimated from a projected trip mileage vantage. A reasonable rule of thumb for fuel consumption:

Vans—10 miles per gallon

Large Cars—15 miles per gallon

Small Cars—20 miles per gallon

Cost calculation—Total estimated trip mileage/Miles per gallon = Total gas consumption per vehicle

Total gas per vehicle × # of vehicles = Total estimated gas consumption for trip

Total estimated gas consumption for trip × Current market rate = Total Gas Cost

Example—

250 total estimated miles for trip

$3.75 per gallon

2 Vans

250/10 = 25 × 2 = 50 × $3.75 = $185.50 Total Cost

Other: This is the category otherwise known as *miscellaneous funds*. This reserve could be used for any unforeseen and surprise expenses as well as an overflow account to cover any underestimated items throughout spreadsheets. Calculate this amount on a daily basis.

Daily misc. amount x # of days = Total Other

Spreadsheet Summary

Totaling the spreadsheet horizontally will give a per trip cost and vertically a per category cost for the travel season. If the addition is accurate, the bottom right axis calculation should act as the proof for the worksheet.

The worksheet has an ultimate, critical program cost control function. By using a blank worksheet throughout the season, one can record actual, verifiable category expenditures for each trip. When the season is completed, use the actual expenditure worksheet to compare with the original budgeted worksheet to identify and evaluate variances. It is also advisable to use a third worksheet to document each variance. The analysis of these variances will be utilized for corrections on future budgets.

Microsoft Excel Spreadsheet

When designing operational budgets and spreadsheets, the most recognized software is Microsoft Excel. This spreadsheet (which is typically a part of the integrated software package known as Microsoft Office) is capable of numerous functions that can strongly support an athletic program's budgeting. The following is a basic list of its functions:

Worksheets: Worksheets allow you to enter, calculate, manipulate, and analyze data such as numbers and text.

Charts: Charts pictorially represent data. Excel can draw a variety of two-dimensional and three-dimensional charts.

Databases: Databases manage data. For example, once you enter data onto a worksheet, excel can sort the data, search for specific data, and select data that meets a criteria.

Web Support: Web support allows Excel to save workbooks or parts of a workbook in HTML format so they can be viewed and manipulated using a browser. You also can access real-time data using Web queries. (Shelly, Cashman, & Vermaat, 2001, p. e1.6)

With these capabilities (along with being universally known), Microsoft Excel can be a major tool in program operations.

TRAVEL ITINERARIES

The first question that arises when discussing travel itineraries: Why make one? There are numerous, salient reasons to compile the team's travel into a comprehensive travel itinerary packet. The following are just a few reasons:

1. The most important reason for a comprehensive travel itinerary is group contact and accessibility. If an emergency situation occurs and it is imperative that the group be found, a detailed itinerary will accomplish this.
2. It keeps all internal stakeholders (staff and players) on the same page. Never underestimate the importance of team travel organization. A clear and precise travel itinerary will help the group avoid any potential disasters from miscommunication.
3. It keeps external stakeholders (owners, administrators, parents, etc.) informed of all team actions. This, in turn, helps avoid an oth-

erwise endless stream of questions from the program stakeholders about where the program is and what it is doing.

4. It conveys an image of professionalism.

The format and design of the travel itinerary is entirely up to one's own preference. However, the following information should be included no matter what the design.

Trip #: Identify each trip by number. Keep the travel itineraries in numerical order with each trip number corresponding to ascending trip dates. For example, trip number one's dates could be Sept. 1–3; trip number two's dates could be Sept. 10–12; etc.

Trip Dates: Self-explanatory.

Trip Location(s): Each itinerary page should be headed also by trip location(s).

Competition Times and Locations: List all relevant competition times and locations on trip.

Practice Times and Locations: List all relevant practice times and locations on trip.

Departure Time: From point of origin (predetermined site).

Arrival Times: All relevant estimated arrival times throughout trip.

Flight Information: All exact flight information including airline, flight number, flight departure time, gate of departure (if possible), and projected departure and arrival times.

Accommodations: Hotel name, address, phone, and contact name. Additionally, a confirmation number could be included as a precaution against misfiling.

Bus Line: Include the name of the bus line, the contact's name, and phone number.

Miscellaneous Information: Any additional special information that will provide the reader with unusual trip particulars.

SUMMARY

Prior to a coach or program administrator embarking on the process of program budgeting, he or she needs to have a comprehensive understanding of the operational environment in which the organization functions. Entrepreneurial management and independent program budgeting differ significantly from organizational budgeting. Entrepreneurial operations need to generate complex financial statements as well as detailed reporting systems. On the other hand, organizational budgeting is the projection and tracking of expenses within a departmental structure. Organizational budgeting, in which most coaches and program administrators function, deals with a budgeting technique categorized as expense budgeting. Expense budgeting is

1. Identifying program expense categories.
2. Projecting the expense (if possible with a historical perspective).
3. Tracking actual costs for each category. This tracking of expenses must be pursued with diligence and precision.

This three-step process will, in turn, supply the coach or program administrator with a true financial picture of the program.

The significance of proper travel budgeting techniques and travel itineraries can not be overstated. Travel spreadsheets organize the entire array of program travel information from a financial standpoint. Internally, travel spreadsheets furnish a fiscal focus and accountability for the program. Externally, travel spreadsheets convey fiscal responsibility and professionalism. They constitute an outstanding program cost management tool. Itineraries, which are derived from spreadsheets, spell out to all parties the details of all the program's trips. It should be reiterated that travel organization, through travel itineraries, is a considerable component of smooth and safe program operations.

KEY TERMS

budgeting	comparative shop
operation/expense budgeting	direct billing
managerial controls	travel itinerary
deductive budgeting	academic spreadsheets
inductive budgeting	cumulative quality points
quotes	cumulative GPA
travel spreadsheets	scholarship spreadsheets
certified travel consultant (CTC)	

Review and Discussion Questions

1. What are three primary reasons a coach or program administrator would dislike budgeting?

2. Define the term budgeting.

3. What are the two types of situational budgeting? Explain each.

4. What factors should a coach or program administrator examine when defining expense categories and program costs?

5. Why are budgets considered good managerial control tools?

6. Why should a coach or program administrator maintain an expense ledger?

7. What are some common-sense actions a coach or program administrator should use when dealing with price quotes?

8. List the basic travel categories in a standardized travel spreadsheet.

9. Discuss the critical importance for the travel spreadsheet category of *# of days*.

10. What are the five essential ground rules when engaging a travel agent?

11. What are three important considerations when dealing with a charter bus company?

12. How does one calculate a trip's total gas consumption and cost?

13. How can a travel spreadsheet be used as a cost control tool?

14. Why should an athletic program make a comprehensive travel itinerary packet?

15. What categories should always be included in a travel itinerary?

Appendix 6A

Academic Spreadsheets

While academic spreadsheets are not monetary, they are quantitative documents that track academic status and progress. In any sport program that operates under an educational institution, it is imperative that academic progress be monitored and controlled. This spreadsheet is an excellent tool for monitoring scholarly progress. The following is a breakdown of its components:

The top-most section should be for the title of the document. Obviously, program identification and semester or quarter delineation is the first element of the form.

Name: Last name first, then first name followed by middle initial. This section should have the exact spelling of the athlete's name so they can be tracked accurately throughout the program, athletic department, and university or school.

Institution Identification: This column is another tracking element unique to each student athlete. If the program's institution uses a separate and distinct student identification number that is universal throughout the school system, use that number instead.

Year: This column signifies the academic status of the athlete in years. It should be noted that it is possible in some situations to have an incongruous athletic eligibility status in years compared to an academic status in years (e.g., fifth-year seniors).

The next four columns relate to the overall academic condition of each athlete for his or her academic career.

Cumulative Hours Attempted/Cumulative Hours Earned: These two columns show the number of credits (semester, quarter, etc.) taken and successfully completed. Each academic institution will have its own criteria for credits earned.

Cumulative Quality Points/Cumulative Grade Point Average: These two columns represent the total number of grade points earned and an athlete's grade point average. The total number of grade points (or in this case cumulative quality points) is calculated for each course's grade times the number of credits for that course. For example, in a 4.0 grade point system, the following is a breakdown of points per grade:

A = 4 Quality Points— B = 3 Quality Points— C = 2 Quality Points— D = 1 Quality Points— F = 0 Quality Points

Simply take the corresponding quality points earned times the credits for that class. If a student athlete achieved a B in a three-credit course, his or her total quality points earned for that class would be nine. To arrive at the cumulative amount, just add up all of his or her total class quality points. To arrive at a cumulative grade point average, just take the total credit hours earned and divide that into total cumulative quality points.

Semester Hours Attempted/Semester Hours Earned: These two columns deal with the present academic semester.

Semester Quality Points/Semester Grade Point Average: These two columns are a microcosm of the total columns (cumulative quality points and cumulative grade point average). Their calculation formulas are the same as the cumulative columns, but are solely based on the current semester results.

Academic Status: This is a narrative description of the student athlete's progress and status. Descriptions can range from Magna, Summa, Cum Laude as well as good, warning, and dismissal.

Learning Lab Hours: This final column deals with learning lab/study hall hours due for each student athlete. Typically these hours are determined by prior academic performance.

Name	SS#	Yr.	Cum.Hrs. Attemp.	Cum. Hrs. Earned	Cum. Qual. Pts.	Cum. GPA	Sem. Hrs. Attemp.	Sem. Hrs. Earned	Sem. Qual. Pts.	Sem. GPA	Academic Status	Regents R/W	LL Hours

Figure 2. Academic Spreadsheet

Figure provided by Georgia State University Athletic Association Senior Women's Administrator/Senior Associate Athletic Director Carol Cohen

Appendix 6B

Scholarship Spreadsheets

Spreadsheets can be utilized for numerous internal operational items. Their graphic depiction and situational appropriateness is limited only by the program elements being examined. One program element that works well with a spreadsheet is athletic program scholarships. The following chart is an example of how colleges (both two-year and four-year institutions) can utilize this document.

Athlete's Name: List the athlete's full name including middle name if any.

Identification Number: List the institution's identification number for each student athlete (either social security or specific assigned identification number). This will be the tracking record for each student athlete.

Year of Eligibility: Identify the upcoming academic and athletic status year of each athlete.

In State, Out of State, or International: Delineate each student athlete's residential status.

Tuition: List the dollar amount awarded.

On-Campus Housing: List the dollar amount for student athletes living in university housing.

Off-Campus Housing: If the student athletes are allowed to live off-campus, list any cash supplements for off-campus living arrangements.

Meals/Books: Dollar amount awarded.

Total: Individualized totals for each student athlete. These totals are used to cross check any other scholarship documentation.

Comments: Pertinent supplementary information individualized for each student athlete.

Athlete Name	ID Number	Year of Eligibility	In-State/Out of State Intl.	Tuition	On-Campus Housing	Off-Campus Housing	Meals	Books	Misc.	Totals	Comments

Figure 3. Scholarship Spreadsheet

CHAPTER

Marketing Fundamentals for Coaches

CHAPTER OUTLINE

CHAPTER 7 OBJECTIVES

- To present a comprehensive assessment of the marketing concept as it relates to athletic program administration
- To define the concepts of utility and exchange and their significance to marketing
- To elucidate the seven external environmental forces that affect all business organizations as well as athletic programs
- To appraise the breadth of marketing information and research
- To provide an in-depth breakdown of the marketing mix/four Ps of marketing
- To consider sports program product and service development through a structured six-step process
- To convey the central pricing ideas of price elasticity, pricing objectives and goals, and additional pricing considerations
- To furnish the fundamentals of athletic program product and service distribution
- To impart a foundational definition for marketing communication and promotion
- To examine customer behavior through a detailed five-step consumer decision process
- To analyze market segmentation from the perspective of geographic, demographic, psychographic, and behavioristic

Administrative Tip

Marketing college and professional sports is in many ways different from high school and entrepreneurial sport marketing. College and professional marketing is characteristically delegated to an independent marketing director/department while in high school and entrepreneurial sports situations, the coach/program administrator is accountable for all facets of marketing. A viable solution for high school, entrepreneurial clubs, and college and professional athletic programs with insufficient marketing support is the enlistment of college student interns. The financial outlay for these interns is negligible because their pay is college credits earned for work provided. However, this strategy has two inherent problems. The first is that the associations with an intern are customarily as long as the semester lasts (and the credits are earned) and the second drawback is that the degree of work quality can vary greatly from student to student and from school to school.

INTRODUCTION

Marketing is an organizational discipline that interfaces with almost all of the athletic program's functions. Even beyond that, marketing can control a majority of the program's operational components. The term *marketing* is probably one of the most misused and misinterpreted word in today's business world. The first impression that one associates with marketing is advertising. The function of advertising is just one facet of the total concept of marketing. Marketing is also involved with product selection, customer research, distribution of the product, pricing decisions, and numerous other administrative elements.

MARKETING DEFINED

The American Marketing Association (AMA) defines marketing as "the process of planning and executing the conception, pricing, promotion, and distribution of ideas, goods, and services to create exchanges that satisfy individual and organizational objectives" (Marketing News, March 1, 1985, p. 1). This definition has three major elements:

1. Formation of products and services, pricing, distribution, and promotion (also known as the marketing mix or 4 Ps of marketing).

Administrative Tip

The American Marketing Association is a tremendous resource of marketing information and educational options.

2. Behavior and satisfaction of individuals/customers and organizations.

3. Marketing planning process (see Appendix 7A).

The goal of this chapter is to dissect and explain these three primary elements of marketing as they relate to the profession of coaching and athletic program administration.

IMPORTANCE OF MARKETING

The significance of the marketing function for all business enterprises (including athletic programs) can not be stressed enough. Marketing produces customer value, satisfaction, and relationship development through the model of utility.

> Utility is the satisfaction, value, and usefulness a user receives from a good or service in relation to the users wants . . . marketing function creates place, time, and possession utility. . . . Place utility is the value added to goods and services as a result of having them available where the customers want to buy them. . . . Time utility is the value added to goods and services by having them available when the customer wants to buy them. . . . Possession utility is the value added to goods and services that comes about as a result of the passage of legal title to the buyer through sales transactions. (Schoell & Guiltman, 1990, p. 7)

In addition to utility, marketing presents the organization with elements such as information on the external operating environment (which can facilitate long- and short-term strategic decisions), details on the make-up of the organization's customer base (which can concentrate and conserve operational resources), details on the make-up of the organization's competitors (which is an indispensable component of survival), and a logical process to developing new products, pricing options, where to place products/services, and promotional considerations.

OVERALL MARKETING ENVIRONMENT

An assessment of the program's overall marketing environment must precede the three focal components of the AMA's definition. Essentially, the practical application of business marketing consists of taking the program's internal product or service and selling it externally. In other words, marketing facilitates exchanges between the organization and its current and potential clientele. However, prior to engaging in an exchange, one will need to become familiar with how the marketing environment will affect that exchange.

Figure 1 is an illustration of the marketing concept and how outside environmental factors affect it.

A generalized clarification of the illustration follows.

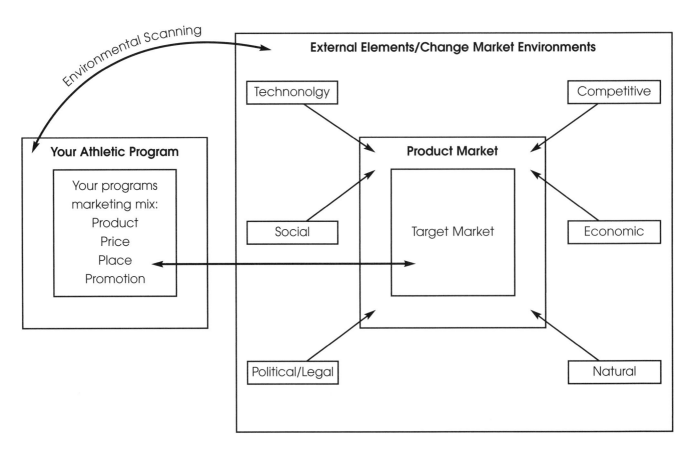

Figure 1. Marketing Concept and the Environment (adapted broadly from Lamb, Hair, McDaniel, 2003, p. 30)

Athletic Program's Operation and Marketing Mix

The far left boxes denote the particular sports program and the product that it produces for an exchange. The marketing mix (4 Ps) details how the coach/program administrator is going to conceive, price, distribute, and promote the product that the program produces.

Exchanges

Exchanges can best be defined by the following:

> Marketing occurs when people decide to satisfy needs and wants through exchanges. Exchange is the act of obtaining a desired object from someone by offering something in return . . . exchange is the core concept of the discipline of marketing. For a voluntary exchange to take place, five conditions must be satisfied:
>
> 1. There are at least two parties.
> 2. Each party has something that may be of value to the other party.
> 3. Each party is capable of communication and delivery.
> 4. Each party is free to accept or reject the other parties offer.
> 5. Each party believes it is appropriate or desirable to deal with the other party. (Kotler, 2003, p. 12)

To reiterate, the model of exchanges is at the heart of all business actions. Exchanges deal with benefits and perceptions. In other words, does the consumer experience a positive benefit (tangible, social, personal, or sensory) and did that exchange provide a "value for value" trade? If so, the consumer will seek out that exchange again. If not, then the service or product in need will be purchased elsewhere. The job of coaches and program administrators is to provide the most value to their customers so they will develop a strong need that, in turn, will promote future exchanges.

Product and Target Markets

A market is "a group of individuals, organizations, or both that have needs for products in a given category and that have the ability, willingness, and authority to purchase such products" (Pride, Hughes, & Kapoor, 1993, p. 333). A target market is merely a group of people inside a market with even more explicit attributes in which a business (athletic program) converges all of its marketing effort. For example, the all-encompassing market for athletic programs is entertainment. One can then break down the broad market classification of entertainment into the more detailed (but still sizeable) category of sports entertainment. From there, dissect the sports entertainment market into the precise target market of sports entertainment customers for a specific sport, in a particular geographic area, with a distinct income level, etc. The more clear-cut the athletic program's target market, the more systematic and coherent the program's marketing efforts. This topic will be elaborated on in the discussion of market segmentation later in this chapter.

Environmental Scanning

The seven external environmental factors that must be continuously monitored by an athletic program are technology, competition, natural, social, economic, political/legal, and demographic. These seven factors will affect how the product (sports program entertainment) is perceived, accepted, and desired by the program's target market. The seven factors are discussed below.

Technology Factor

The first environmental factor that the coach or program administrator should examine is technology. There is virtually no business that is not profoundly affected by the accelerating volume of technology. Sports programs are no exception. Computerization, cell phones, advanced training systems, and the Internet are just a small number of technological advancements that need consideration. The technological investigation should focus not only on currently available technology but on how projected technological advancements may affect the program's operations in the future.

Competition Factor

Another influential external environmental factor that needs monitoring is competition. To do this, the coach or program administrator must assemble what in the business world is called a competitive analysis. In their 2006 text *Essentials of Marketing*, Perreault and McCarthy design an effective framework for competitive analysis. The subsequent table presents an adaptation of their concept.

An elaboration of the chart follows.

Columns—The first column is the program's unique competitive position and strategy while the next two columns are the direct competitors' positions. Each section going down the column is centered on the perception of a tactic or plan as a strategic strength (+) or a weakness (-).

Rows—There are seven separate areas (rows) in which to register what the program is doing (strength/weakness) and what the competition is doing (strength/weakness).

- *Target market* is who the program and its competition are focusing marketing efforts on.
- *Product, price, place, promotion* describe how the program and its competition are internally conceiving, pricing, distributing, and promoting that product.

	Firm's Current or Planned Strategy	Competitor 1 Strengths and Weaknesses	Competitor 2 Strengths and Weaknesses
Target Market			
Product			
Price			
Place			
Promotion			
Competitive Barriers			
Competitive Responses			

Figure 2. **Framework for Competitive Analysis (structure adapted from Perreault & McCarthy, 2006, p. 86)**

- *Competitive barriers* "are conditions that make it difficult, or even impossible, for a program or the program's competition to compete in a market. Such barriers may limit your own plans or, alternatively, block competitor's responses to an innovative strategy" (Perreault & McCarthy, 2006, p. 86).

- *Competitive response* category is what the projected strategies and tactics the program and its competition will take to counterbalance each other's strengths and weaknesses.

Nature Factor

For most sports programs, the natural environment might not be as consequential an environmental factor to scrutinize as the other six external factors. Obviously sports programs that are outdoors need to address geographical weather patterns, pollution, and other possible natural/nature concerns that could affect marketing activities.

Social Factors

The factor of the social environment is defined as

> the people in a society and their values, beliefs, and behaviors. . . . Marketers describe this environment in terms of who the people are (their ages, incomes, hometowns, and so forth) and the characteristics of their culture. (Churchill & Peter, 1998, p. 38)

From this designation, the leading questions that surface for sports programs are

1. How does society view our sport and program?
2. What marketing opportunities are possible from this perspective?
3. Are some subcultures more interested in our sport and program than others?
4. Does society expect our sport and program to act in a socially responsible way?

Economic Factor

The economic environment deals with a region/nation's purchasing power and its discretionary income. An economic environment that is stable or growing has stronger purchasing power. The stronger the purchasing power, the higher the discretionary spending. This presents numerous marketing opportunities. Conversely, the more financially deprived the economic situation in a city, region, or nation, the less the purchasing power and discretionary spending in that area. A climate of economic downturn and recession presents significant marketing concerns for sports programs whose "life blood" is based on unencumbered discretionary spending.

Political/Legal Factor

The political/legal factor in environmental scanning is the legislation affecting one's program operation. From a sports standpoint, athletic programs have two tiers of legislation to identify and monitor. The first is U.S. governmental legislation that all businesses have to recognize and comply with. Examples of this can range from the IRS to the INS to the EEOC. The second

---

tier is the particular sport's governing body and its regulatory legislation. The concentration and intensity of regulations, bylaws, and directives is sport specific as well as level specific (e.g., NCAA, NAIA, professional).

Demographics

The final external environmental element a coach/program administrator needs to survey relates to the demographic characteristics of both the overall, comprehensive market and the program's target market segment. Demographic forces are

> the characteristics of a population, such as age, gender, ethnic origin, race, sexual orientation, and social class. Like other forces in the general environment, demographic forces present managers with opportunities and threats and can have major implications for organizations. (Jones & George, 2006, p. 204)

By understanding demographic characteristics, a coach/program administrator can uncover details on the make-up of the existing market as well as predict changes in the future market. From a current perspective, demographic analysis is the foundation for constructing a customer profile. Customer profiles are managerial instruments that definitively catalog all of the relevant demographic characteristics of an organization's target market. With the profile, athletic program's can concentrate (sometimes limited) resources directly on that precise customer base. From a futuristic standpoint, demographic knowledge can help an athletic program predict/strategize the best course of action for its future customers. Simply put, customers transform and change. By knowing the athletic program's current customers, a coach/program administrator can forecast what they will be like in the future.

MARKETING INFORMATION AND RESEARCH

Learning how to plan, organize, implement, and analyze marketing research goes far beyond a chapter in a textbook or a course in college. Marketing research is a lifetime profession that takes years of theoretical knowledge and practical application to master. However, from a coaching/program administration viewpoint, marketing research can impart vital information that can assist a coach/program administrator's decision making. The question then becomes . . . how can a coach/program administrator solve the conundrum of obtaining critical information to support decision making while knowing that marketing research is beyond their typical life experience and education? The answer relates to the delineation of primary research versus secondary research.

"Primary research is data gathered and assembled specifically for the research project at hand. Secondary data is data that has been previously collected for some project other than the one at hand" (Zikmund, 2000, p. 58).

Administrative Tip

Always maintain the most recent sport-specific legislative materials for referencing. Maintain a file of legislative changes by the sport's lawmaking body throughout the year.

In other words, primary research is conducted by the coach/program/organization for an exclusive need or problem. Secondary research is conducted buy someone else to solve a particular need or problem.

To conduct primary research, a coach/program administrator would require substantial resources, time, and research experience. The benefit from performing primary research study is obvious; the information accumulated (if done correctly) is going to be focused on the athletic program's explicit needs. The decision a coach/program administrator has in performing a primary research study is a cost benefit analysis one . . . is the information gathered from an internal primary research investigation worth the time and expenditures associated with this type of study?

Secondary research has noteworthy advantages and disadvantages in relation to primary research. The advantages are predominantly in expense and time. Secondary research just needs to be uncovered rather than conducted. In some cases the time and outlay saving is enormous. The disadvantages of secondary research include three elements:

1. Problem to fit—does the secondary research fit the program's special need or problem.
2. Outdated information—since the research was done in the past, how obsolete/archaic has it become.
3. Confidence in research—was the research completed by credible researchers who where objective and dispassionate.

If the coach/program administrator can answer that the secondary research fits the program's situation, it is timely, and was prepared by a trustworthy source, then secondary data is tremendously valuable.

The following is a list of possible avenues to pursue secondary data:

- Library (both public and academic)
- E-Library/Commercial Sources
- Periodicals/Journals/Magazines
- Electronic Sources/Internet/Search Engines
- United States Governmental Sources
- Directories/Trade Association Publications

In conducting secondary research, there is one resource that is indispensable—librarians. Clearly stated, librarians are remarkable when it comes to resolving informational needs. They can help define research problems, direct one to sources that will correspond to the athletic program's needs, and can assist in the follow-through to solve one's data collection obstacles.

THE MARKETING MIX: 4 Ps OF MARKETING

After the external marketing environmental scanning, a coach or program administrator should consider the internal marketing process known as the marketing mix or 4 Ps of marketing. In the business world, the marketing mix is defined as:

the proper blending of the basic elements of product, price, promotion and place into an integrated marketing program . . . the right product for the target market must be developed. Place refers to the channels of distribution. Promotion refers to any method that communicates to the target market. The right price should be set to attract customers and make a profit. (Megginson, Byrd, & Megginson, 2006, p. 187)

Kotler analyzes the 4 Ps in further detail. Figure 3 is an adaptation of his concepts.

All four of these marketing elements play a role in sports programs. However, sports programs produce services that have entertainment value rather than actual tangible products. "Services have four unique characteristics that distinguish them from goods; intangibility, inseparability, heterogeneity, and perishability" (Lamb, Hair, & McDaniel, 2003, p. 267).

As stated earlier, sports programs are in the entertainment market. Athletic programs are commodities that are consumed via spectator participation and fan involvement. They do not generate a tangible product. The inseparability of a service refers to the concept that the consumer is using a service at the same time as he/she pays for the service. In other words, the fan is present during the delivery of the entertainment. The characteristic of heterogeneity refers to the fact that while products can be very similar (if not precisely alike), services such as sports performance are distinct and dynamic. Finally, services such as sport entertainment are perishable because they are time specific. Once a performance is over, a consumer can never see it again in present time. With this distinction between services and products given, we can definitively adapt the marketing mix concept to athletic programs.

Marketing Mix

Product	Price
Product Variety	List Price
Design	Discounts
Quality	Allowances
Features	Payments
Brand Name	Credit Terms
Packaging	
Sizes	
Services	
Warranties	
Returns	

Target Market

Place	Promotion
Channels	Sales Promos
Coverage	Advertising
Assortment	Sales Force
Locations	Public Relations
Inventory	Direct Marketing

Figure 3. The Four Ps of Marketing (adapted from Kotler, 2003, p. 16)

Product/Service/Output/Performance

As a program administrator, the primary concern is with the product (in the case of this text, athletic performance). Inside that theme, there should be an unconditional single-mindedness on quality and value. Quality can relate to an athletic program's performance, presentation, facilities, operational administration, and any other aspects that directly or indirectly influence its output. Without quality, marketing and promotions break down.

Another product/service issue relates to the uniqueness of one's athletic program. Uniqueness is used to separate the program from its competition and to confirm and sustain the image (also known as branding) of the program in the mind of the customers and supporters. Uniqueness is the strategic concept of differentiation that is reviewed in Chapter 12.

Another major marketing product/service consideration that affects sports programs is the selection of the type of products and services the program is currently offering and which products and services it is going to accentuate in the future. Some programs may be at a given point in time restricted to emphasizing base products or services. Lack of resources, inadequate staffing, and insufficient stakeholder cooperation are a few of the reasons to contemplate a single service marketing strategy. However, in most cases, programs have capabilities to mature beyond the base product of performance and competition. Expanding the service into instruction, merchandising, and new athletic endeavors are just some of the ways to diversify.

To develop new products/services, one should follow a step-by-step process that generates ideas and appraises their feasibility. The New Product Development Process is as follows:

1. Idea Generation
2. Idea Screening
3. Business Analysis
4. Product Development
5. Test Marketing
6. Commercialization (Churchill & Peter, 1998, p. 260)

Step 1: Idea Generation

Idea generation is the origination of new, relevant ideas for expanding, improving, or developing new products and services. Idea generation can be through various avenues such as formal requests, informal conversations, brainstorming, etc. A key to idea generation is to get as many internal and external stakeholders involved in the process as possible.

Step 2: Idea Screening

This stage takes the aggregate list of new ideas from Step 1 and "weeds out" all the notions, thoughts, and conceptions that are inappropriate for the program. Idea Screening, like Idea Generation, is typically qualitative and subjective in nature. The coach or program administrator and the program staff's expert opinions are customarily the determining factors. In a formal or informal setting, the coach and staff will "talk through" each new product idea to gage its merits and appropriateness for the program now, and more notably, in the future.

Step 3: Business Analysis

This phase involves a more quantitative analysis of the program's capabilities and resources. The analysis is performed in order to determine the feasibility of an idea. Resources include the program's capital and financial

Administrative Tip

When attempting to conceive a new program product and service, at all costs avoid gimmicks and publicity stunts that will damage the integrity of the athletic program. While these marketing techniques will direct short-term attention to the product/program, their long term effects could be irreparable. Uniqueness with a high-class reputation will bring extended growth.

situation, building and facilities, and other tangible assets that it possesses and can utilize to help realize new product idea. Capabilities include the program members' intangible skills and knowledge. These are some of the questions asked in the business analysis stage:

- Does the idea fit our program's overall mission?
- Do we have the finances to pursue this new service or product idea?
- In the future, will we have the finances (or potential to raise the funds) to pursue this new service or product?
- Does our current building or facility have the ability to support this new idea?
- Does the idea have the potential to generate profits?
- Will there be additional labor associated with the new idea? If so, how will that affect our current personnel structure and budget?
- Do we have the technical and logistical knowledge to pursue and realize this idea?

The list of questions is extensive. Logically, the more detailed the questions asked and the more that is and becomes known about the proposed idea, the less chance of poorer decisions and failure.

Step 4: Product Development

After an idea has been probed and scrutinized and determined to be desirable and feasible, the next phase is product development. For tangible products, this step necessitates that engineering and production experts come up with a prototype of the product. Unfortunately, with the exception of merchandising, sports programs deal with intangible services so the best that a coach or program administrator can do is to put together a comprehensive plan for the new sports service. In essence, the service plan is a complete step-by-step written amplification of what the new service (instructional camp, athletic endeavor, etc.) is about. It must be reiterated that since we are unable to visualize and hold this intangible service, the service plan must be as comprehensive and as carefully delineated as possible. The service plan is at the core of the next step—test marketing.

Step 5: Test Marketing

Test marketing

> is an experimental procedure that provides an opportunity to measure sales or profit potential for a new product or to test a new marketing plan under realistic marketing conditions . . . the major advantage to test marketing is that no other form of research can beat the real world when it comes to testing actual purchasing behavior and consumer acceptance of a product. (Zikmund, 2003, p. 217)

From a sports program vantage, testing out a new service concept has notable advantages. Test marketing allows program members to observe

Administrative Tip

In the preliminary stage for idea screening, it is always critical to keep current and potential supporters in mind. Their enthusiasm is a notable predictor of whether a new product and service will work. In others words, ask if the idea will generate value and benefits for present supporters and future projected supporters.

how the consumers react to a new idea or concept in authentic, real-world situations.

Such real-world testing is critical to determine

- whether an alteration in the sport's service is necessary;
- whether modifications are needed to make the new program product or service more desirable for customers and fans; and
- whether a new idea should be scrapped rather than moved into full production.

Testing should be done on a cost sensitive and timely basis. Additionally, open discussions or surveys of customers should be employed in conjunction with customer participation and sales testing efforts.

Step 6: Commercialization

The final section in the new product development process is commercialization. Plainly stated, this is the "go for it" stage where one has appraised and tested the idea and found it to be a sound proposition. At this point, commit the program's allotted resources to producing this new service. Effective utilization of steps 1–5 will decrease the possibility of concept failure. Will it remove the possibility of failure completely? No. However, implementing the stages will give the program the optimum opportunity of launching a new and successful sports product/service.

Pricing

Now that there is a viable, desired product or service (whether a recognized, conventional one or an innovative concept), one will need to price it for maximization of profits while still maintaining and increasing the program's customer base.

> Price is the amount of money a seller is willing to accept in exchange for a product at a given time and under given circumstances . . . no matter how well a product is designed, it can not help an organization achieve its goals if it is priced incorrectly. Few people will purchase the product with too high a price, and a product with too low a price will earn little or no profit. Somewhere between too high and too low there is a "proper" effective price for each product. (Pride, Hughes, & Kapoor, 2003, p. 399)

Once again, comprehending the intricacies of pricing a product (sports service) is beyond the scope of this book. However, by understanding the central concepts of pricing, a program administrator or coach can be more conscious, in general, of pricing decisions and how they can affect the sports program.

Price Elasticity

Price elasticity is a concept that connects changes in price with changes in demand. Specifically, price elasticity reveals how sensitive the change in demand for a service is when there is a change in price for the service. If the service is elastic, then adjustments in price produce radical swings in the number of people who want it. For example, assume that the price being charged to attend one of the program's sporting events is $5.00 per ticket. Assume further at the $5.00 level the attendance is at 1,000 fans. The price would be considered elastic if an increase in the cost by $1.00 is associated with the program losing 500 fans. In this case, a 20% increase in price yields a 50% decrease in attendance. This example shows high price elasticity. Using the same example, once again the ticket price is increased from $5.00 to $6.00 but the decrease in fans was from 1,000 to 950. This situation is known as inelastic demand. A 20% change in price only resulted in a 5% decrease in fans. There is also a premise known as unitary demand. This is when a percentage change in price furnishes an exact percentage change in demand. This is illustrated from the above example by changing the price from $5.00 to $6.00 and the attendance decreases from 1,000 to 800 (a 20% change in price has a 20% change in demand). Whatever service offered (e.g., attendance at an event, merchandise, instructional camps), it is indispensable to know the elasticity of the item, which, in turn, will show what flexibility one has in pricing it.

Pricing Objectives and Goals

Once a coach or program administrator has a picture of the price elasticity of the sports service, he or she will need to generate the pricing objectives and goals for that service. One should price the program's services to keep them in harmony with the program's overall goals. These objectives should be straightforward and easily understandable. An objective fixed on survival is essentially an emergency approach to pricing that is designed to "keep the program afloat." The only consideration is to situate the price at whatever level makes it possible just to keep the business enterprise or athletic program going. Pricing for a targeted/predetermined return is principally done by establishing a desired profit over and above the estimated costs and working the price to achieve the projected amount. Strengthening/enlarging market share and maintaining competitive position is basing the price on not only what the competition is doing but on how one can aggressively establish and acquire more customers.

Additional Pricing Considerations

Three Methods of Pricing: To price a sport's products and services, three distinctive facets must be considered—cost, competition, and value. From a cost viewpoint, prices must be established to "cover" expenditures associated with the product/service as well as additional fixed program operating costs. A coach/program administrator must formulate a breakeven analysis (which is a breakdown of costs associated with projected revenue) to know when the program's outlays/expenses are covered at a certain price level. The second factor to research relates to the market and a comparison of competitor's prices. Clearly stated, how competitors price out their similar products and services will directly affect the foundation of how the athletic program prices out its products and services. The final component of pricing deals with the value customers put on the athletic program's products and services. The more value (and subsequent demand) the customer places on the program's offerings, the more price control a coach/program administrator has over the product and services.

It should be stated that each of these can be used separately to devise a program's price structure. However, a blending of all three methods (cost, competition, and value) will give a more precise and realistic representation of what the price configuration of the athletic program is.

Price Skimming versus Price Penetration: The concept of price skimming versus price penetration corresponds to the pricing philosophy of new offerings (products and/or services) in an athletic program. Price skimming is introducing a new product/service into the market with a high price. The core rationale for doing this type of pricing strategy is to recapture as much initial developmental costs as possible with limited sales. Price penetration is introducing a new product at a minimal cost to gain as many new customers as possible. The prime incentive for this type of pricing approach is to get as much of the overall market share as immediately as possible.

Psychological Pricing: Pricing an athletic program's products and services can have a psychological influence on current and prospective customers. A product/service with a high price can convey superior quality (whether quality exists or not). This type of psychological pricing is known as prestige pricing. Conversely, pricing a product low could communicate a lack of quality (whether quality exists or not). Another psychological pricing technique is odd-even pricing. Odd-even pricing is when a price is established that makes a customer think that the price is lower than it really is. For example, $19.99 is essentially $20.00, while customers will often acknowledge the price as $19.00. Bundle pricing can also be a psychological pricing tactic. By combining a set of products and services together, a coach/program administrator can increase sales of multiple items, increase offerings, and utilize psychological perceptions of a better overall package price.

There are six additional considerations when instituting prices for an athletic program's products/services/performances.

1. What should be the balance between costs, the competition, and customer when arriving at a price?
2. Will the deal be a once-only transaction or the beginning of a relationship with potential long-term benefits?
3. Is the price to be a fixed number (or schedule) or something that will be negotiated, bargained for, and possibly changed over time?
4. Are we dealing with a single customer, guest, or buyer or with a group of people?
5. Which parties to the deal have sufficient power to influence the outcome of a negotiation and what is the source of this power?

6. Does the price in question require pricing a single, specific service or does it involve a full schedule of prices? (Lazer & Layton, 1999, p. 291)

Discounts

In addition to the six considerations when pricing, discounting is utilized when a program wants to stimulate sales in a condensed timeframe. In other words, discounting an established price is a short-term solution that can only be applied for limited periods. If it is discovered that the price level established is elastic at a certain level, the possible reevaluation of the service price rather than repeatedly discounting should be examined. The variety of discounts can encompass:

- Quantity discounts—provide customers with discounts proportional to the amount they purchase.
- Seasonal discounts—used to balance out cyclical fluctuation in sales.
- Early payment discounts—used to encourage faster payments, decreases in accounts payable, and increases in cash flow.
- Special event discounts—promote a program's special event and increase awareness.
- Repeat business discounts—special discounts provided to repeat customers.

Administrative Tip

Discounting can take on countless forms. Whichever technique one uses, remember that discounting is a short-term solution to stimulate sales and support. Their abuse can depreciate the overall worth and distinctiveness of a program.

Place/Distribution of Sports Services

The elementary difference between a tangible product and an intangible service (sport service) is most evident when discussing distribution. There are two ways to dispense sports services: either the customers come to the program's location or one must take the program's service to them. The key to making a good choice between these two is accessibility. Ask which approach has the greatest potential to get the sports service the largest number of customers? For example, if one's sport program is extremely visible, in a heavily populated area, and is easily accessible, the program's service distribution would undeniably be to have the customers come to the program. However, if the program is in a remote location with inadequate exposure, creative distribution might be required. The coach may need to take the sport service to an auxiliary locale to maximize customer interaction and sales.

Promotion of Sports Services

Promotion is the fourth and final component of the marketing mix.

> Promotion is communicating information between sellers and potential buyers to influence attitudes and behaviors. . . . The main promotional job is to tell targeted customers that the right product is available, at the right price, at the right place. . . . What the marketer communicates is determined by customer needs and at-

titudes. . . . How the message is delivered depends on what blend of various promotional methods the marketing communicator chooses. (Perreault & McCarthy, 2006, pp. 318–319)

Promotion and advertising will be examined at length in the next chapter.

CUSTOMER BEHAVIOR AND SATISFACTION

The indispensable means to successfully implementing the program's marketing mix relates to the most important statement in business: *The customer is everything.* The number one priority should be to have this philosophy in mind no matter what the circumstance, activity, goal, or direction. Appreciating and satisfying the customers' needs and wants is vital in developing, maintaining, and increasing support.

Identifying how the consumer makes his or her purchase determinations is crucial to understanding how to cultivate and retain customers. A substantial portion of practically every marketing text published today is dedicated to the fundamental consumer decision process.

The five-step consumer decision process is as follows:

Step 1: Problem Recognition

Step 2: Information Search

Step 3: Evaluation of Alternatives

Step 4: Purchase Decision

Step 5: Post Purchase Behavior (Griffin & Ebert, 2004, p. 293)

Every single purchase made by a consumer (no matter how large or small the purchase) goes through this five-step process. Sometimes the process can happen in literally a split second and, in other cases, it can take hours, days, or longer.

Step 1: Problem Recognition

We all have needs. They are the instinctual elements that provide each of us with the tools to survive, socialize, and achieve esteem. Maslow, in his historic, groundbreaking book *Motivation and Personality*, contends that needs are hierarchal in nature and that the only way to attain higher, more luxurious desires is to make sure that our critical physiological and safety needs are satisfied first. The following is his graphic depiction of the hierarchy of needs (in ascending form).

From a coaching perspective, discernment of human needs is the basis for identifying the program's target market and what the customers in that target market are looking for in a product or service. For example, an individual who is looking to satisfy the bottom level of needs in Maslow's Hierarchy model (physiological and safety) would not be concerned, at that point in time, with attending a sporting event. For target market identification, sports and entertainment focuses on groups who want to fulfill higher needs of belonging, esteem, and self-actualization. In the most direct terms, our product of sports entertainment is vying to meet the needs of people with discretionary income over and above their survival and safety needs. The practical application of this theory narrows the market substantially.

Step 2: Information Search

Once people (or targeted groups) acknowledge a need that they must or would like to satisfy, they proceed to gather information about it.

> The information search
>
> may be internal, *retrieving knowledge from memory or perhaps genetic tendencies*, or it may be external, *collecting information from peers, family, and the marketplace.* Sometimes consumers search passively by simply becoming more receptive to information around them, whereas at other times they engage in active search behavior, such as researching consumer publications, paying attention to ads, searching the internet, or venturing to shopping malls and other retail outlets. . . .The length and depth of search is determined by variables such as personality, social class, income, size of purchase, past experiences, prior brand perceptions, and customer satisfaction. If customers are delighted with the brand of product they currently use, they may repurchase the brand with little if any search behavior, making it more difficult for competitive products to catch their attention. That's why victorious firms place high priority on keeping customers satisfied. When customers are unhappy with current products or brands, search expands to include other alternatives. (Blackwell, Miniard, & Engel, 2001, pp. 73–74)

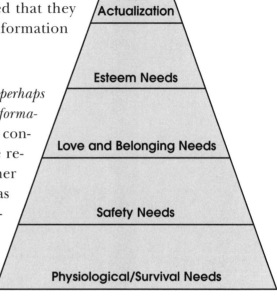

Figure 4. Hierarchy of Needs (adapted from Maslow, 1954)

The category of product or service will typically determine the extent to which individuals will seek out information for it. Products and services are typically classified as follows:

Convenience Products/Services: Little time and mental effort put into information search, low cost relative to customer base, everyday common purchases.

Shopping Products/Services: Moderate amount of time and mental effort exerted for information searching, substantial (but not consequential) cost, and infrequent purchases.

Specialty Products/Services: Extensive amount of information search, "big ticket" and high cost purchases for customer base, very infrequent and rare purchases.

Sports entertainment products and services need to be understood in terms of the type of product (convenience, shopping, or specialty) they represent to the customers. Each program has to verify its product classification as this will guide the marketing efforts and determine how much information the customer will demand.

For example, if a consumer is considering purchasing skybox tickets (or the entire box itself) for a professional sports season, he or she might consider that a specialty purchase. The professional team selling the tickets will furnish the customer with extensive information, focus its selling methods on a more personal level, and realize that since this is a specialty purchase and big cost item, they will need to furnish the consumer with the best options and services available. Conversely, if a consumer is considering purchasing tickets for a local high school sport, the purchase might be deemed more of a convenience purchase. For this type of sale, information will be supplied generally to a wide group (market), selling methods will be impersonal and open, and services will be limited.

Step 3: Alternative Evaluation

This is the point in the process that the consumer, after gathering all the significant information needed, looks at all of his/her choices. In other words, the consumer is comparing all of the possible alternatives that might satisfy his/her needs.

> Once consumers feel that they possess enough information, they will compare purchase alternatives using criteria they deem important. These criteria can be objective (e.g. price and service) or subjective (e.g. image) . . . the alternative selection will depend on which is less expensive, requires less time, and does the best job . . . at this stage of the purchasing process, sales people can be influential by introducing additional criteria and by relating how their products and services satisfy important buyer themes. (Marks, 1997, p. 91)

Consumer alternative evaluations can be effected by

- personal background factors such as education, family influences/ childhood experiences, income level, peer groups, social status, etc.;
- geographical factors such as rural versus urban, metropolis versus small town, north versus south, etc.;
- knowledge factors such as exposure to literature/media influences, past usage (directly or through other's experiences), sampling, etc.; and
- attitudinal and motivational elements such as introspective feelings and opinions, evaluation processes, psychographics/lifestyles, etc.

These primary factors are what the program's advertising/promotional campaign should target. The desire is to have the consumer perceive that the program's product (athletic entertainment) is the finest option to fulfill his/her needs.

Administrative Tip

A coach/program administrator's job is to impart as much quality information as possible to current and potential supporters. The key is to find out the best and easiest avenues to convey the program information. This is done by understanding what information the program's supporters will use and then formatting information to fit their needs.

Step 4: Purchase Decision

> When a sufficient number of alternatives have been identified, the decision maker must evaluate them and make a choice. This evaluation can be accomplished in one of two ways. Either the decision maker can compare each alternative to every other alternative, or the decision maker can compare each alternative to the desired goal. (Northcraft & Neale, 1994, p. 145)

From a program standpoint, one straightforward directive is associated with the action of purchasing: make it as simple and painless as possible. The worst thing that a program administrator can do is to make the purchase experience for the consumer complex and bewildering.

Step 5: Post-Purchase Behavior

The final step in the decision-making process relates to the consumer's satisfaction with the service purchased, as this will influence how he/she will choose and behave the next time the same need surfaces. There is one noticeable phenomenon that takes place in this stage that a coach/program administrator needs to attach importance to and concentrate on—cognitive dissonance or buyer remorse.

> Cognitive dissonance occurs
>
> in situations where there is high involvement, a socially visible purchasing experience, or if the product or service is expensive . . . consumers often experience doubt after purchases . . . because of the investment in time, money, and ego, it is natural for a consumer to question a decision. (Clow & Baack, 2002, p. 163)

An outstanding way to minimize buyer remorse is to provide the customer with a quality product (quality entertainment experience). The more costly the product, the more one needs to concentrate on cognitive dissonance. Follow-up contacts, personal notes, special promotions, and other related "perks" are all ways to ease buyer remorse.

MARKET SEGMENTATION

Now that coaches and program administrators have an underlying insight into the consumer decision-making process, they should concentrate on the market, how to divide it up and, subsequently, which "piece of the pie" the program is going to target.

In Ross' article *Segmenting Sports Fans Using Brand Association: A Cluster Analysis*, sports market segmentation's importance is delineated by the following passage:

> The practice of pinpointing groups within the current fan base is necessary for success, because a sports organization cannot gain a strong foothold within the market place if these individuals are not identified and managed appropriately. As a way of optimally meeting the needs of all fans and establishing a strong position

in the sports marketplace, an organization should not only identify the distinct groups of members, but also develop marketing strategies that are tailored to these different groups. This process of identifying well-defined clusters of consumers is knows as segmentation, and a wide variety of strategies have been used to achieve organizational goals. (Ross, 2007, pp. 15–24)

Once again, from a coaching and program administration perspective, an athletic program's inclusive market falls under the broad umbrella of entertainment. From there, one can narrow down the overall entertainment market to the smaller (but still substantial) sports entertainment market. The market of sports entertainment is the one coaches/program administrators need to analyze, examine for niche opportunities, and approach in a manner that capitalizes on the program's superior competitive position. Moreover, from the definition of marketing segmentation, to commit all of the program's existing resources to the correct target market segment, a coach/program administrator must:

1. Categorize and segment the market into clear-cut, defined segments.
2. Select the most appropriate piece (or pieces) to focus the marketing mix—4 Ps.

In identifying segments, a marketer needs to research all of the possible bases for segmentation. One needs to investigate how the market is broken down into precise, identifiable groups. The potential ways to break down a market into distinct segments are presented below.

Geographic Features: global location/country, financial level of geographic area, urban/rural, population concentration, geographic environmental elements (temperature, terrain, etc.)

Demographic Features: male/female, maturity level/age, earning potential, household factors (spouse, children, relatives, etc.), profession, educational degree, religious convictions, ethnic group, social caste

Psychographic Features: standard of living, activities, qualities, interests

Behavioristic Features: patterns of consumption, capacity, previous encounters, allegiance to a product/service, consumer preference

Demographics are associated with population characteristics; geographic criteria relate to locations; psychographics are lifestyle choices; behavioral features are an individual and/or group's use of the product or service.

To get all-inclusive and accurate market segmentation, each category and subcategory must be dissected for its relevance to the sports entertainment market. By questioning a market's demographics, geographics, and purchasing behavior, one is developing segmentation profiles of individuals and groups. For example, some categories might not have a significant effect on how a market is segmented. In sports entertainment, typically city size and density is not applicable for sports fans that come from all diverse city sizes and densities.

Administrative Tip

When determining which target markets are appropriate for the program, do not dismiss any potential groups solely on the basis of opinion. Get concrete information. It is very possible that some of the program's most ardent supporters could be profile groups that, on the surface, one would reject. For example, some senior citizen demographic groups could on the surface be easily written off as potential supporters. Yet if secured as one of the program's target markets, they could be a powerful support and financial group.

The most useful application of this chart is for identifying the program's specific target market. With one's particular sport in mind, go through each category and develop a specific profile of the target market group. Ask the following questions:

1. Who are they? Go through the demographic and psychographics subcategories.
2. Where are they? Go through the geographic subcategories.
3. When will they buy? How will they buy? Why will they buy? Go through the behavioral subcategories.

A few salient points on identifying target market segments:

- Each sport, at each level of competition, will have its own distinctive segment (or, as the definition describes, niches).
- Is it feasible to have more than one target market segment? Absolutely. One might come up with several target market segments in which the group profile is ideal for one's sport.

In selecting the target market(s), a coach/program administrator should consider the following criteria:

- Measurable. Can you quantify the segment?
- Accessible. Do you have access to the market?
- Substantial. Is the segment of sufficient size to warrant attention as a segment? Further, is the segment declining, maturing, or growing?
- Profitable. Does concentrating on the segment provide sufficient profitability to make it worthwhile?
- Compatible with competition. To what extent do your major competitors have an interest in segment? Is it an active interest or of negligible concern to you competition?
- Effectiveness. Does your organization have sufficient skills and resources to serve the segment effectively?
- Defendable. Does your firm have the capability to defend itself against the attack of a major competitor? (Paley, 2000, p. 163)

To reiterate and clarify, segment size and growth relate to sales, growth rate, and anticipated profitability of a segment. Segment structural attractiveness defines the potency of the competition's ability to go after a given market segment. Availability or possibilities of substitute products that can make customers switch affect a segment's attractiveness. The stronger each of these alternatives are, the less attractive the segment. Program objectives and resources must always form the backdrop to determine if the segment is in line with the program's goals and whether the program posses the capabilities, assets, and capital needed to take advantage of that segment.

If one can verify that the segment being evaluated is in an attractive group that presents an opportunity, that it has good profitability and growth potential, and is in line with the program's mission and resources, then it is an exemplary segment to pursue.

Administrative Tip

In selecting target markets, know the program's resource boundaries and limitations. For small athletic programs, a niche/focus strategy can present a strong competitive advantage. If the target market niche is successfully captured by the program first, the program will be identified with that niche and be on the ground floor of future increased support. The key is finding a niche group that can sustain the program currently that also shows long-term growth potential.

SUMMARY

Marketing is the business function that facilitates exchanges in a corporate enterprise (in the case of this text, an athletic program). Externally, it helps coaches and program administrators

- delineate outside environmental factors that influence a program;
- analyze consumer behavior and their decision-making process; and
- evaluate the overall market of sports entertainment and the segmentation of that market. In addition, segmentation will identify niche opportunities that give a program a defined target market in which to exert it efforts.

Internally, athletic program marketing

- examines product selection and development;
- provides foundations for pricing a program's service;
- elucidates the choices of distribution of a program's service; and
- communicates the benefits to potential consumers of the program's service.

The practical application of marketing by a coach/program administrator will escalate the program's exposure as well as increase revenues. It creates desires and action in program supporters and, if utilized correctly, it can transport a program to another operational level and competitive position.

KEY TERMS	
marketing mix (4 Ps of marketing)	price
utility	place/distribution
marketing research	promotion
primary research	price elasticity
secondary research	pricing objectives
marketing environment	price skimming
exchanges	price penetration
target market	prestige pricing
environmental scanning	customer behavior and satisfaction
technology	consumer decision process
competition	hierarchy of needs
natural	cognitive dissonance/buyer remorse
social	market segmentation
economic	geographic
political/legal	demographic
demographic	psychographic
competitive analysis	behavioristic
competitive barriers	marketing plan
product	

Review and Discussion Questions

1. What is the AMA's definition of marketing?

2. What five conditions must be present for an exchange?

3. How can a coach or program administrator derive his or her target market from the all-encompassing market of entertainment?

4. List the seven external environmental elements in which a coach or program administrator must always monitor.

5. When analyzing the external social environment, a coach or program administrator should ask what questions?

6. Describe the four components of a marketing mix.

7. What are the six steps in the new product development process?

8. What are some problematic questions that should be addressed in the business development stage of the new product development process?

9. What is price elasticity? Define elastic, inelastic, and unitary demand.

10. What is the basic premise behind the distribution of sports services?

11. Explain the statement "The customer is everything."

12. List the five steps in the consumer decision-making process.

13. What are the three classifications of a product?

14. Define sports market segmentation.

15. What are some ways a coach or program administrator can break a market into precise, identifiable groups?

Appendix 7A

Marketing Plan Outline

The marketing plan is a microdesign of the program's operational plan (Chapter 1). In other words, it is a "plan within a plan." Its mission, objectives, and strategies all emanate from the comprehensive program operational plan. It principally focuses on the marketing aspect of the program and how it will help accomplish the program's overall goals and mission.

The following is an outline of the marketing planning process. Note the close resemblance between marketing planning and organizational/ program planning. Additionally, the concept of SWOT will be detailed in Chapter 12.

Step 10: Evaluation
Step 9: Execution
Step 8: Marketing Plan Budget and Calendar
Step 7: Tactical Marketing Mix Tools
Step 6: Communication Goal
Step 5: Plan Strategies
Step 4: Target Market and Marketing Objectives
Step 3: Sales Objectives
Step 2: Problems/Opportunities
Step 1: Business Review

Figure 5. Marketing Planning Process (adapted from Hiebing & Cooper, 1997, p. xxvii)

CHAPTER

8

Athletic Program Promotion and Marketing Communication

CHAPTER OUTLINE

CHAPTER 8 OBJECTIVES

- To clarify the promotional communication concept and the promotional mix of advertising, direct marketing, sales promotion, personal selling, and publicity
- To present the major strategic goals of marketing communication
- To illustrate advertising avenues to coaches and program administrators
- To familiarize coaches and program administrators with the advantages and disadvantages of the six major media outlets for advertising
- To elucidate the promotional concept of A.I.D.A.
- To present the concept of direct marketing
- To investigate sales promotion techniques
- To acquaint coaches and program administrators with the personal selling process
- To expound on the concepts of strategic marketing communication alliances and marketing communication budgeting

INTRODUCTION

The essential importance of Chapter 7, *Marketing Fundamentals for Coaches*, cannot be stressed enough when discussing the role of promotion and marketing communication. To blindly jump into advertising and promotion without consciously knowing the fundamentals of marketing would be at best a "hit or miss" proposition. These prerequisites provide focus to the program's marketing communication and promotion. Understanding market communication and promotion requires understanding of

- the marketing mix (product, pricing, distribution, and promotion) and how advertising is an interrelated component;
- how to distinguish and segment the market;
- how to choose a portion or segment to target the program's resources;
- how customers go through the purchasing process; and
- how to construct a comprehensive marketing plan.

PROMOTIONAL TOOLS

As previously clarified in Chapter 7, the fourth P in the marketing mix is *promotion*. Promotion is, in fact, marketing communication. Marketing communication consists of five major tools:

Advertising—any paid form of non-personal communication, by paid announcements in the print, broadcast, or electronic media, designed to gain acceptance of the advertiser's message.

Direct Marketing—selling directly to customers, rather than via a mass medium. It includes methods such as direct mail and telemarketing.

Administrative Tip

Positive word of mouth is the ultimate aspiration of any marketing communication. If one can get the program's supporters talking about the program's product/service/team in an optimistic (and maybe even enthusiastic) fashion, they will generate a "snowball" effect that can take the program beyond all expectations. A critical fringe advantage of positive word of mouth generation is that one will need to spend fewer resources on marketing communication in the future.

Sales Promotion—selling aids, often at point-of-purchase, which reinforce other types of promotion. (Shim, 2006, pp. 11, 122, 344)

Personal Selling—a form of person-to-person communication in which a salesperson works with prospective buyers and attempts to influence their purchase needs in the direction of their company's products and services.

Public Relations—identifies, establishes, and maintains mutually beneficial relationships between sports organizations and the various publics. (Shank, 2005, p. 316, 324)

MARKETING COMMUNICATION GOALS

Prior to discussing these five promotional and communication tools, a coach or program administrator will need to succinctly examine strategic goals pertaining to marketing communication:

1. Create Awareness: Inform markets about products, brands, stores, or organizations.
2. Build Positive Images: Build positive evaluations in people's minds about the product, brand, store, or organization.
3. Identify Prospects: Find out names, addresses, and possible needs of potential buyers.
4. Build Relationships: Increase cooperation among stakeholders (internal and external).
5. Retain Customers: Create value for customers, satisfy their wants and needs, and earn their loyalty. (Churchill & Peter, 1998, pp. 445–446)

As a program administrator or coach, map out the program's objectives for a promotional communication campaign. Can one undertake and achieve multiple goals with a single campaign? Absolutely. In other words, can a coach put together a promotional communication strategy (by using advertising, direct marketing, sales promotions, public relations, and personal selling or a combination of these) that not only generates recognition for the program but also fosters positive perceptions and relationships while retaining and even increasing the program's customer bases? Yes. It is more complicated to have multiple goals but if one is imaginative and can think the campaign through, there are no limits.

After conceiving and defining the goals for the program's promotion, examine the communication tools of advertising, direct marketing, sales promotion, public relations/publicity, and personal selling. Once again, it should be noted that a close examination of each of these tools is well beyond the scope of this book. In fact, each of these areas offers opportunity for study and is a specialized career. Thus, it is not the purpose of this text to enable each reader to become an authority on these tools and their use. It is the purpose of this book to enable the reader to gain a working knowledge that will allow each of these tools to be adapted and utilized with purpose within the specific athletic program or team.

Administrative Tip

It is advisable to align certain marketing communication goals with selected marketing communication tools. For example, the goal of one's athletic program could be to create awareness for the program. This might be best accomplished through advertising techniques in the operational area.

ADVERTISING

The prime promotional communication tool at a coach's or program administrator's disposal is advertising. Advertising is

> a non-personal sales presentation communicated through media or non-media forms to influence a large number of consumers . . . it is a common method for promoting products and services. Although advertising is generally more expensive than other methods, it can reach many consumers. . . . Brand advertising is a non-personal sales presentation about a specific brand. . . . Comparative advertising is intended to persuade customers to purchase a specific product by demonstrating a brand's superiority by comparison with other competing brands. . . . Reminder advertising is intended to remind consumers of a product's existence. . . . Institutional advertising is a non-personal sales presentation about a specific institution. . . . Industry advertising is a non-personal presentation about a specific industry. (Madura, 2007, p. 529)

Administrative Tip

The vital key to any paid advertising campaign is reaching the target market and then impacting the target market. Within budget constraints, ask which advertising tools will have the most influence on the projected audience. Typically, quantity of messages communicated is not as important as quality of messages communicated. Think which advertising tools will provide the program with the highest quality powerful message that will reach the target market efficiently.

Media Advertising
Newspapers
Magazines
Trade Journals
Specialized Publications

Brochure Advertising
Media Guides
Game Day Programs
Specialized Literature

Broadcast Media
Television (local, regional, national)
Radio (local, regional, national)

Exhibitions
Special Events
Trade Show Displays

Internet
Web Pages
Banners

Video/Film
Promotional Videos/DVDs and Films

Outdoor
Posters
Point of Purchase Displays
Billboards
Transit/Transportation Advertising
Signage Arena and Sports Facilities
Special Events
Aerial Advertising
Mobile Billboards
Movie Theatre Advertising

Figure 1. **Advertising Media**

From this list, the coach or program administrator can begin to uncover which advertising communication tool is desirable. In the 2003 text *Principles of Marketing*, Lamb, Hair, and McDaniel expound on the advantages and disadvantages for each type of advertising/media communication tool. The following is an extrapolation of their impressions.

Newspapers:

- Advantages—Geographic selectivity and flexibility, short-term advertiser commitments, year-round readership, high individual market coverage, short lead time.
- Disadvantages—Little demographic sensitivity, limited color capabilities, low pass-along rate, may be expensive.

Magazines:

- Advantages—Good reproduction, color, demographic selectivity, regional selectivity, local market selectivity, relatively long advertising life.
- Disadvantages—Long-term commitments, slow audience buildup, lack of urgency, long lead time.

Radio:

- Advantages—Low cost, immediacy of message, can be scheduled on short notice, highly portable, short-term commitments, entertainment carryover.
- Disadvantages—No visual treatment, short advertising life, high frequency required to generate comprehension, background sound.

Television:

- Advantages—Ability to reach a wide, diverse audience, low cost per thousand, creative opportunities, immediacy of message, entertainment carryover.
- Disadvantages—Short life of message, skepticism about claims, high campaign costs, long-term advertiser commitments, long lead times required for production.

Outdoor Media:

- Advantages—Repetition, moderate cost, flexibility, geographic sensitivity.
- Disadvantages—Short message, lack of demographic selectivity, high "noise" level distracting audience.

Internet:

- Advantages—Fastest growing medium, reach narrow target audience, short lead time required for creating Web-based advertising, moderate cost.
- Disadvantages—Difficult to measure ad effectiveness and return on investment, ad exposure relies on "click through" from banner ads, not all consumers have access to the Internet. (Lamb, Hair, & McDaniel, 2003, p. 449)

After researching each type of advertising communication tool for its germane advantages and disadvantages, the ultimate criteria for selecting an advertising mix (which is a package of tools to promote the athletic program) is financial. The advertising goal from a financial standpoint is simple and uncomplicated. Which advertising tool (or tools) should the program employ to amplify its target market exposure and get the most from its limited advertising dollars? This is where the previously discussed subject of program marketing comes into play and affects advertising communication. Knowing the customers (and prospective customers) is the salient key. Through market segmentation and subsequent target market selection, a program administrator or coach can get a well-defined profile of current and potential supporters. This segment profile will furnish answers to questions such as the following:

- Who are they?
- Where are they?
- What type of people are they?
- What are there demographics? Psychographics? Geographic? Lifestyles?
- When is the best time to communicate with them?
- How often do they need promotional communication?

With these customer profile questions answered (through marketing planning), the question of how to contact and persuade the customer becomes easier. In the simplest terms, one must know the current and potential customers before one can promote and communicate with them. After determining who the customer is, match the financial resources up with the most effective advertising tools the program can afford. Hopefully the program's financial budget will support those tools.

Once connected with the program's potential customers, the concept of creativity comes into play. Marketing communication should follow the AIDA concept. The acronym is explained below.

Attention: The advertising tools utilized must first secure the customers' attention. In a majority of all advertising, one has a precious few seconds to achieve this. Since people are saturated with a continued bombardment of advertising, if one does not "catch and grab" the prospective customer's *attention* instantaneously, he or she will move on.

Interest: After successfully getting customers' attention, the advertising communication must seize their *interest*. In other words, once they are *grabbed* they must be *held* until the message is delivered.

Desire: Subsequent to getting prospective customers' attention and interest, one must get them to *desire* the program's product (or in the case of this text, entertainment service). If the advertising is imaginative and directed toward the program's target market, developing the desire for the service is the next progressive step in the AIDA progression.

Action: This is the final stage. If A, I, and D are fulfilled, getting the customer to purchase and to support the program should fall in line.

Administrative Tip

Because advertising is using the most valued organizational resource—money— conduct extensive research to provide a distinct supporter profile. Quantify as much of the program's research as possible. Knowing the supporters is the first step in reaching them.

In today's world, the concept of creativity in advertising is crucial. If one wants to achieve AIDA, the creative advertising work must be focused on what the customers are interested in. Actual inspiration and generation of ideas typically comes from non-structured techniques such as brainstorming and free association methods.

DIRECT MARKETING

Direct marketing is

> the use of consumer-directed (CD) channels to reach and deliver goods and services to customers without using marketing middlemen. These channels include direct mail, catalogs, telemarketing, interactive TV, kiosks, Web sites, and mobile devises. Direct marketing is one of the fastest growing avenues for service customers. Direct marketers seek measurable response, typically customer order. This is sometimes called direct-order marketing. Today, many direct marketers use direct marketing to build long-term relationships with the customer (customer relationship marketing). (Kotler, 2003, p. 620)

The key to contacting large volumes of individual prospects though direct marketing techniques comes from advances in technology and is known in business as mass customization. Mass customization enables mass-produced products (or in this case, advertising and promotion) to be customized for each individual.

Another important aspect of direct marketing is the development of a substantial database of qualified target market customers. The operative word in the last sentence is *qualified*. While a phone book may be a viable database of potential customers, it probably would not be a qualified database for sports programs. How does one find a suitable database to use for direct marketing purposes? Such a database should come from the market segmentation process discussed in Chapter 7.

To review:

1. Identify the program's overall operational market.
2. Break down the market into segments of people with similar needs, wants, characteristics, and purchasing behavior.
3. Select the most appropriate segment on which to focus organizational efforts.
4. Profile the selected segment to find the most efficient way to contact prospects through one of the aforementioned direct marketing techniques.

As mentioned, direct marketing techniques are managed through databases. There are two ways to gain access to a database. The first and more difficult way is to construct one's own. To do so, find potential supporters, design the system of data retrieval and use, and then catalog and computerize the list. The second option is to utilize a database that already exists. The sources of databases that already exist are plentiful and, through the ever-growing power of computers, the number of relevant lists available is continuously increasing. Whether it is a geographic, demographic, psychographic, or behavioral database, never forget that the program's segment profile will determine which one (or ones) to utilize.

As with all forms of communication, direct marketing involves extensive planning and research as well as creativity tactics, cohesion of concepts, target market appeal, AIDA, and production and distribution systems. Whatever direct marketing techniques are selected to reach the target market segment, one must know the marketing concepts behind each technique.

It would serve a coach or program administrator well to do a cost-benefit analysis to evaluate if direct marketing is warranted and financially feasible. The investment of time and money in putting together a direct marketing plan is extensive. Once again, the ultimate determinant of whether to utilize any promotional tools is the customer. Through analysis, if direct marketing is proven to be effective and the financial resources of the program can support a direct marketing campaign, then it is a powerful and focused promotional instrument.

Administrative Tip

A conspicuous danger in direct mailing is saturation. Temper and monitor the amount of direct contacts the program has with its supporters. If the program exceeds tolerable direct contacts with its support groups, not only will the message be disregarded but it might instill a negative perception of the program in the eyes of the supporters.

SALES PROMOTION

Sales promotion is defined as

> Non-personal marketing activities other than advertising, personal selling, and public relations that stimulate consumer purchasing and dealer effectiveness . . . sales promotion has emerged as an integral part of the promotional mix. Promotion now accounts for close to half as many marketing dollars as are spent on advertising and promotional spending is rising faster than ad spending. Sales promotion consists of forms of promotion such as coupons, product samples, and rebates that support advertising and personal selling. (Boone & Kurtz, 2006, p. 463)

These nonrecurring techniques are used to create awareness and to stimulate sales. Some of the possible sales promotion techniques include rebates, coupons, samples, etc. From a sports administrative perspective, the creativity that goes into sales promotion techniques can be rich and rewarding.

The following lists sales promotion techniques along with their relative cost and time considerations.

Sales Promotional Techniques

Free samples are especially useful in generating a trial of the product. They can be distributed in the mail, passed out at points of purchase or other high traffic areas, or made available upon request from a potential buyer.

Price oriented program which seeks to reduce the consumer's real cost per unit in some way, e.g.,: (a) *cents-off coupons* . . . (b) *mail-in refunds or rebates.*

Premiums—another item is given away or offered at an attractive price if a certain number of units are purchased.

Tie-Ins—similar to premiums, but involves joint promotion of two items. . . . Typically, the two parties share the cost of the promotion.

Continuity Program—a reward is given in recognition of continuing relationships.

Contest/Sweepstakes—used to generate excitement about product. (Lal, Quelch, & Rangan, 2005, p. 267)

Once again, it must be emphasized that while relative cost and time are important considerations in choosing a sales promotion, the most critical choice factor is the program's target market and the market's receptivity to a certain sales promotion technique. No matter how time and cost effective a sales promotional method could be, if it does not stimulate or support sales, it is inappropriate and will squander program resources.

PERSONAL SELLING

Personal selling is one-on-one, face-to-face interaction between a coach or program administrator (or program representative) and a prospective supporter. The benefits of a successful sales call can be immeasurable. Not only can a personal sales call close an immediate sale, it also establishes a personal rapport for future encounters. This, in turn, can lead to "positive word of mouth" networking that creates more sales. Virtually every marketing and advertising text goes through a step-by-step procedure to make a sales presentation (or to close a personal sale). While there are slight variations in the stages, content, and sequencing, in order to be successful, each sales person must have certain general traits.

While no ideal set of characteristics has been found to guarantee success, a number of factors are strongly related to performance: hard work, working smart, the ability to set goals, maturity, a good appearance, communicative ability, dependability, honesty, and integrity. In some cases, the individual may possess these traits instinctively, but in all cases, these characteristics can be developed through thought and careful practice. (Marks, 1997, p.55)

The following is one of the many step-by-step procedures that can be used in making a sales presentation and closing a sale.

Step 1: Prospecting for new customers

Step 2: Set effort priorities

Step 3: Select target customer: Identify who influences purchase decision and/or who is involved in buyer-seller relationship

Administrative Tip

The concept of AIDA is pertinent with all communication tools, especially sales promotions. Sales promotions, to be valuable, must concentrate totally on the support group and its tendencies. If one truly knows who the program supporters are, think through what sales promotion techniques will grab their attention and get them to take action.

Step 4: Preplan sales call and presentation: Prepare presentation

Step 5: Make sales presentation: Create interest, overcome problems/objectives, arouse desire

Step 6: Close sale: Get action

Step 7: Follow up after the sales call to establish relationship and follow up after the purchase to maintain and enhance relationship

(Perreault & McCarthy, 2006, p. 360)

Personal selling goes beyond a generic communication tool. Personal selling has been referred to as a business skill or science that takes hard work and extensive experience to master. It is composed of

- building relationships both short term and long term;
- providing adept demonstrations;
- interpersonal recommendations;
- showmanship and presentation dynamics;
- tactical negotiation;
- networking and campaigning; and
- role playing and performing for affect.

For a coach or program administrator to exploit this methodology in program promotion and communication, one must set aside the time to appreciate and understand the process as well as rehearse and practice its use.

STRATEGIC ALLIANCES IN MARKETING COMMUNICATION

A potential solution to athletic program marketing communication deals with the concept of strategic alliances.

Many strategic alliances take the form of marketing alliances. These fall into four major categories.

1. Product or service alliance: One company licenses another to produce its product or two companies jointly market their complementary products or a new product.

2. Promotional alliances: One company agrees to carry a promotion for another company's product or service.

3. Logistical alliances: One company offers logistical services for another company's product.

4. Pricing collaborations: One or more companies join in a special pricing collaboration. (Kotler, 2003, pp. 108–109)

A coach/program administrator has two additional marketing strategic alliance options:

The athletic program could "piggy back" on a marketing communication plan of another organization. The significance to this type of alliance is having a mutually beneficial relationship. Simply put, by working together on cooperative marketing/promotional activities, the athletic program and outside organization are both profiting from the joint promotion. Shared promotions devices can encompass alliances in advertising, sales promotions, special events, sponsorships, and public relations.

The second form of strategic alliance deals with having an external marketing agency supply all of (or a portion of) the athletic program's marketing communication/promotional activities for something of value the athletic program could provide in return. The key to this strategic alliance is the value-for-value trade-off between the athletic program and the external marketing agency.

MARKETING COMMUNICATION BUDGETING

As discussed in Chapter 6, budgeting is the control function that assists a coach/program administrator in establishing and maintaining guidelines for spending. When constructed accurately, these benchmarking tools help forecast needs and describe circumstances through quantitative parameters. However, budgeting money for marketing communications/promotion is as much a philosophical issue as it is financial. In other words, an athletic program's way of thinking toward designating money to the function of marketing communication will often influence the extent to which that "line item" is financed. Some coaches/program administrators possess the attitude that marketing communication is a luxury and whatever is available at the end of the financing/budgeting process is what gets apportioned to marketing communication. More progressive coaches/program administrators are realizing the indispensable worth of marketing communication and have prioritized its budgeting/financing.

Specific techniques associated with the "nuts and bolts" of marketing communication budgeting can include the following methods:

Arbitrary Allocation—The simplest, yet most unsystematic, approach to determining promotional budgeting is called arbitrary allocation. Using this method, sports marketers set the budget in isolation of other critical factors . . . promotional budgets are established after the organization's other costs are considered.

Competitive Parity—Setting promotional budgets based on what competitors are spending (competitive parity) is often used for certain product categories in sports marketing.

Percentage of sales—The percentage of sales method of promotional budget allocation is based on determining some standard percentage of promotional spending and applying this proportion to either past of forecasted sales to arrive at the amount to be spent . . . it has a number of shortcomings. . . . With sales declining, it may be more appropriate to increase (rather than decrease) promotional spending. A second major shortcoming of using this method is the notion that budgeting is very loosely, if at all, tied to the promotional objective.

Objective and Task Method—Objective and task method could be characterized as the most logical and systematic. The objective and task method identifies the promotional objectives, defines the communication tools and tasks needed to meet those objectives, and then adds up the cost of the planned activities. (Shank, 2005, pp. 290–291)

One final point on marketing communication budgeting: there are clear dangers in under-funding a program's marketing communication and promotional activities. Under-funding restricts the effectiveness of communication tactics and limits a program's projected exposure. Conversely, over-funding marketing communication strategies is just as detrimental to an athletic program. Precious resources (money) will be wasted and other strategies the program might want to pursue will be missed due to the lack of funds. The key to a good marketing communication budget is knowing the funds needed to accomplish communication goals and dispersing the exact capital to achieve those objectives.

SUMMARY

Marketing communication encompasses five primary promotional elements: advertising, direct marketing, sales promotion, personal selling, and public relations (Chapter 9). The promotional mix of these devices is through a planned process that takes into account goals, budgets, and, ultimately, the program's target market. The effectual combination of these tools can maximize a program's exposure, image, and support. However, it should be reiterated that marketing communication is a part of the whole concept of marketing. By itself and without the proper background concepts of the marketing mix, it will inescapably fail to achieve it intentions.

KEY TERMS	
marketing communication	media
promotion	mass communication
advertising	database
direct marketing	AIDA
sales promotions	reach
public relations	frequency
publicity	sales presentations
personal selling	

Review and Discussion Questions

1. What are the five tools of marketing communication? Briefly describe each.

2. What are the five goals of marketing communication?

3. What are some of the major advertising avenues a coach or program administrator can pursue?

4. List the advantages and disadvantages of radio advertising.

5. Which advertising tool (or tools) should the program employ to amplify its target market exposure and get the most from its limited advertising dollars?

6. The AIDA concept of creativity consists of what components? Briefly describe each.

7. What are the two ways to access a direct marketing database?

8. What are the seven steps in a personal sales presentation?

Appendix 8A

Creating a Print Advertisement

The following appendix is adapted from the textbook *Advertising Procedures* by Russel and Lane (pp. 464–468).

Guidelines for Creating an Ad

1. **Keep It Simple, Stupid.** The KISS principle, as this is called, has no better application than in advertising, yet it is probably the most abused principle of all . . . advertising needs to catch the eye quickly, and allow the reader to leave as quickly as possible.

2. **You're Not Selling the Product; You're Selling the Benefit of the Product.** If an advertiser does not answer the reader's implicit question—What's in it for me?—the ad is unlikely to attract any real interest. . . . But the best ads directly address the problems that the product or service solves and suggests how that solution makes life better for the potential consumer.

3. **When Appropriate, Spice It up with Sex.** It should be emphasized that sexy ads tend to be simple ads.

4. **Use Celebrities.** Celebrities may not be believable, but they are very effective at attracting readers' attention, the first job of any advertisement.

5. **Exploit the Potential of Color.** Print advertising has the potential to contend with television . . . print's ability to generate astonishing, eye-catching colors is substantial.

6. **Go with the Flow.** Every ad has flow to it, and the flow is determined by the position of the various creative elements. Ads with good flow send the reader's eye around the page to take in all the important elements: the illustration, headline, body copy, and brand name.

7. **Avoid Ambiguity.** Americans have little tolerance for advertising that does not offer clear and distinct message.

8. **Heighten the Contrast.** We live in a visual culture, and one thing that delights the eye is contrast. So advertisers would do well to employ what might be called "visual irony" in their advertising.

9. **Use Children and Animals.** Almost any advertising can succeed with an appeal to the emotions, and children and animals appeal to all but the most hard-hearted.

10. **When an Ad Has a Good Deal of Copy, Make It as Inviting as Possible.** The best written, wittiest, and most powerful copy will be overlooked unless it is well spaced and sufficiently large and clear to invite the reader.

Appendix 8B

Internet Technology and Athletic Program Marketing Communication

The following lists illuminate the magnitude and importance of internet/web technology, the marketing communication applications for athletic programs, and the possible dangers associated with internet/web operation.

Importance of the Internet Medium

- Accessibility to the internet is becoming commonplace and strongly desired by consumers 24/7. From an athletic program vantage, this ease of use can affect image, productivity, and support.
- Internet/web page technology is informative beyond all other marketing communication techniques. A well designed web page can be the "centerpiece" of an athletic department's marketing communication. Internet/web technology can assimilate all promotional mix elements (advertising, sales promotion, public relations, personal selling).
- Costs associated with internet use is "leveling the playing field" between smaller athletic programs and sizeable athletic programs. In other words, the medium is affordable to all athletic programs.
- The scope of the internet is global. No other marketing communication technique has this much wide-spread impact on an athletic program's operations.

Internet Marketing Communication Uses for Athletic Programs

- With the newest hardware and software improvements, athletic program web sites can make profound and dynamic statements about the athletic program's quality.
- Web pages have become a key recruiting tool for athletic programs.
- Internet technology has mass customization and direct marketing capabilities at a fraction of the cost of other techniques. The internet furnishes athletic programs with the capability to contact unlimited individual supporters while tailoring the message for each.
- Web pages can be constructed for an extensive variety of informational capabilities. Scores, schedules, program information, athlete information, bios, etc., are just some of the athletic program benefits.
- Internet technology has the internal ability to measure (quantitatively) its own effectiveness.
- If an athletic program has tangible products, they can be sold and distributed directly to supporters.

- An athletic program's incorporation of its web page into powerful search engines can increase exposure tremendously.
- With future technological advances, creativity options for web page design are unlimited.

Dangers

- Complacency in updating and revising an athletic program's web page can substantially affect marketing communication.
- Web pages are becoming heavily scrutinized by external stakeholders. Athletic programs are now being compared by internet web appeal.
- The most important danger in dealing with internet technology and web pages for athletic programs is the risk of underestimating their exponentially increasing importance in the athletic industry.

CHAPTER

9

Public Relations
for Coaches

CHAPTER OUTLINE

- To introduce and describe the concepts of public relations and publicity
- To distinguish between internal and external publics
- To explain the distinction between a public relations campaign and perpetual public relations program/ system
- To examine the stages in a public relations campaign
- To assess perpetual public relations systems
- To illuminate tactics in handling a public relations crisis
- To present the concept of issues management
- To elucidate the basic concepts of budgeting public relations
- To list the possible media and communication avenues for public relations

INTRODUCTION

Coaches and program administrators have the capacity to be the most significant individuals in how the public perceives and identifies their program, sport, and industry. Coaches can develop cooperative relationships with prominent individuals, groups, and the overall community through the deployment of publicity and public relation systems. These collective relationships foster program goodwill, an optimistic perception of the program, and receptive communication channels between internal and external stakeholders. While the development of these relationships may seem unsystematic and governed by informal styles, the concept of public relations and publicity is conceived, developed, and implemented through tangible, coordinated procedures.

While the creation of a positive image is an important goal of publicity and public relations, it must be emphasized that the primary intention of public relations is to be a part of the athletic program's inclusive marketing concept (see Chapters 7 and 8). Marketing communication techniques such as advertising, direct marketing, sales promotion, and personal selling are all applied in harmony with public relations. Simply stated, public relations, as a marketing tool, directly and indirectly helps facilitate sales and exchanges.

PUBLIC RELATIONS AND PUBLICITY DEFINED

From an academic standpoint, the concepts of public relations and publicity have numerous definitions that vary in substance and structure. For the purpose of this book, the following description encompasses the fundamental nature of publicity and public relations for sports programs.

Publicity—Promotional tool in which information about a company or product is transmitted by general mass media . . . publicity is free.

Marketers usually have little control over publicity, but because it is presented in a news format, consumers often regard it as objective.

Public Relations—Company-influenced publicity directed at building goodwill with the public or dealing with unfavorable events. . . . A firm will try to establish goodwill with customers (and potential customers) by performing and publicizing its public-service activities. (Griffin & Ebert, 2004, p. 379)

A core consideration that these definitions underscore is the need to develop and preserve a highly regarded public image. This corporate identity (in this case, athletic program identity) is the context not only for the way people think of the program now, but also for the way they imagine the athletic program in the future. If the athletic program's impression is one that elicits upbeat, positive feelings, the program's public relations foundation is formidable and can support the operation. If the current program image has little or no response (neither positive nor negative) associated with it, one can look at this situation from a "clean slate" viewpoint and the program's public relations outlook is an opportunity for growth. Finally, and regrettably, if the athletic program's image provokes negative connotations, one will need to stem the tide of disapproving opinion and start the lengthy process of building an optimistic picture for the program.

As with most business applications, public relations and publicity need a formal proactive plan. For athletic programs it should be clarified that public relations have two distinct elements. The first is known as *campaign public relations* and the second is *perpetual public relations*. The difference between the two is captured by the factors of frequency and duration. Public relations campaigns are one-time projects with a fixed, terminal timeframe. Perpetual public relations is a continual process set up (through a public relations system) to operate as long as the program is functioning. Campaigns are associated with intensive development efforts and attempts to reach identified goals, while perpetual public relations systems are characterized by long-term maintenance and consistency.

INTERNAL AND EXTERNAL PUBLICS

An athletic organization has two major sub-groups for public relations—internal and external publics. Internal publics are all athletic department members and stakeholders (staff, administrators, athletes, coaches, support personnel, etc.) who are on the "inside" of the program while external publics are outside athletic program operations (communities, supporters, customers, suppliers, etc.). Conventional public relations focus communication on the external publics while underestimating the importance of internal communication/public relations. "The function of internal communication is to let employees know what management is thinking and to let management know what employees are thinking" (Moore & Kalupa, 1985, p. 86). Without sound

Administrative Tip

Always be mindful of the program's public relations image. A coach/program administrator should in no way allow the program's public image to be compromised. If that happens, it requires the most strenuous operational effort to rectify the problem.

internal communication, an athletic program could experience dissent, dysfunction, gossip and innuendo, and reduced productivity.

The following bullet points elaborate on the importance of both external and internal publics as well as some of the inherent problems in communicating with each group.

Internal Public Relations

- There is reluctance in management to be candid with internal communication. This internal public relations philosophy is ingrained from years of confrontational "in-fighting" between management (coaches/program administrators) and employees (staff, athletes).
- Internal communication/public relations has to assertively battle the unofficial in-house communication channel commonly know as the "grapevine." Inside disinformation from the grapevine can be exceptionally destructive to any athletic program. Coaches/program administrators need to have internal public relation and communication systems in place to negate disinformation.
- Time-honored internal communication has been a top-down process. New internal public relation systems need to accept a continuous flow of information (both up and down) from all levels. The public relations benefit will enhance an athletic program's operations appreciably.
- The commitment to have an internal public relations system is considerable. Time, resources, planning, organizing, and controlling the system are just a few areas a coach/program administrator must consider when establishing the public relations communication structure. However, the positive aspect of having an internal public relations/communication system in place far outweighs the "up-front" expenditures. Most operational problems can be circumvented or avoided outright with good internal communication.
- The selection of techniques to communicate to an internal group is critical. Whether it is through oral, written, electronic, or in-house publications, the choice of the right mode is vital if the athletic program's message is received correctly or not.
- Strong internal communication/public relations have a direct influence on external communications/public relations. If an athletic program's internal public relations are superior, there will be a resilient correlation to positive external public relations. Regrettably, the converse is also true.

External Public Relations

- The public is distrustful of external public relations programs and "spin doctors." An athletic organization will need to cultivate relationships with its external public before it can see positive results. These interactions will take time and careful planning.

- As our population and society grows, there will be new external sub-groups that will need personalized public relations communication. A coach/program administrator will need to categorize each sub-group and work toward communicating with them independently. This will take listening to an eclectic variety of opinions and interests.

- External public relations take targeting community "opinion makers" and getting the correct transmissions to them. The difficulty arises because each opinion maker will have his/her own agenda with the athletic program.

- What to disclose and what not to disclose is a major question when dealing with external public relations. Releasing too little can have the appearance that the athletic program is trying to "hide something" and divulge too much could damage the image and the message of the program.

PUBLIC RELATIONS CAMPAIGNS

The listing below identifies the stages in a public relations campaign.

- Situational Analysis
- Problem Statement
- Goal Statement
- Targeted Publics
- Tentative Strategies
- Statement of Limitations
- Management Liaison (generated from Kendall, 1996, text concept)

Situational Analysis

The initiating phase in a public relations campaign, situational analysis, is known as a "where are we now" perspective. A situation analysis

> is the unabridged collection of all that is known about the situation, its history, forces operating on it, and those involved or affected internally and externally. A situation analysis contains all the background information needed to expand upon and to illustrate in detail the meaning of a problem statement . . . a situation analysis begins with a thorough and searching review of perceptions and actions of key actors in the organization, structures and processes of organizational units relevant to the problem and the history of the organization's involvement. . . . The internal situation analysis also includes a "communication audit"—a systematic documentation of an organization's communication for the purpose of understanding how it communicates with its publics . . . an analysis focuses on the external factors, both positive and

negative. The starting point may be a systematic review of the history of the problem situation outside the organization. (Cutlip, Center, & Broom, 2000, pp. 347–348)

Additionally, during this current-time analysis, conduct a preliminary public relations SWOT investigation. To be discussed later in Chapter 12 of this text, SWOT analysis involves a thorough evaluation of the program's internal strengths and weaknesses along with its external opportunities and threats. A SWOT study is appropriate for all business functions within a program, especially public relations.

Problem Statement

While the phrase *problem statement* has a pessimistic connotation, it does not have to be negative in context. With the help of a SWOT analysis, the coach/program administrator may have discovered encouraging opportunities and notable strengths. The problem statement should be as clear-cut and concise as possible. Clarity is essential since the public relations campaign, whatever it is designed to achieve, will emanate from this declaration.

Goal Statement

A goal statement

> should be evaluated by asking (1) does it really address the situation? (2) is it realistic and achievable? and (3) can success be measured in meaningful terms? Public relations basically have two kinds of goals: informational and motivational. Informational objectives are goals designed primarily to expose audiences to information and create awareness . . . the difficulty with an informational objective is in measuring how well the objective has been achieved . . . motivational objectives try to change attitudes and influence behavior . . . because they are bottom-line oriented, they are based on measurable results that can be clearly quantified. (Wilcox, Ault, Agee, & Cameron, 1998, p. 148)

From a sports program viewpoint, an informational public relations goal could be to provide a website for fans and supporters to access data about the program's players and staff. A motivational public relations objective could be to inform and energize the target market (through various media) about upcoming events. The quantifiable measurement to see if this goal was accomplished could simply be by tickets sold and/or stands filled. Once again, it is essential to understand that whatever type of objective one chooses, the objective should be in line with the program's public relation problem statement, which is directly aligned with the marketing mission statement, which, in turn, closely reflects the program's mission statement.

Administrative Tip

As with all introspective program investigations, the public relations situational analysis must be as unemotional and as dispassionate as possible. A truthful assessment is the key to a thriving campaign.

Administrative Tip

Dig deep to expose the program's true public relation problem, not just its symptoms. Even though the symptoms might initially seem like they are the bona fide predicament, they are more than likely superficial signs of something more profound.

Targeted Publics

The idea of *targeted public relations segments* corresponds with the marketing concept of *target markets*. In other words, a coach/program administrator should find the targeted public relation groups the same way that one established (and exploited) the target market group(s). Look at the public as a whole, segment it into groups with similar wants, needs, characteristics, and perceptions, and then select the target groups on which the program will concentrate its available resources. Will the public relations target group be the same as the marketing target group? Possibly, perhaps even likely, but not always. It depends on the goals, the situation, and what one is attempting to achieve. From a bottom line approach, motivational goals will produce very comparable public relations and marketing targets. Inspirational goals might be broader in nature because they are trying to create awareness in a larger population.

Tentative Strategies

Tentative strategies in the planning process are exactly that: preliminary strategies to achieve the program's public relations goals. From targeting, the coach/program administrator knows whom he or she is going to attempt to reach. This stage answers questions like the following:

- How am I going to reach them?
- What type of media would best get their attention?
- What message do I develop? What story do I want told?
- What type of creativity should I employ?
- How frequently do the targeted groups need to be exposed to the message?
- When should I reach them?
- Is my P.R. message ethical? Legal? Factual?
- If they get our message, when should we see results?
- Ultimately, will the P.R. strategy work?

As one goes through the inventory of strategic questions, each specific tactic will have its own distinct set of issues. The more thoroughly these types of questions are asked, the higher the likelihood that the chosen tactic will work and the public relations goal will be realized.

Statement of Limitation

The statement of limitation is principally the "W" (weaknesses internally in the program) of the SWOT investigation. In other words, what internal deficiencies (lack of skills and/or resources) does the athletic program have that might affect its projected public relations strategies and goals? Skills can relate to managerial abilities, knowledge base, and technical know-how, among others. Resources directly relate to personnel, time resources, and, ultimately, financial constraints.

Management Liaison

The concluding step in the public relations campaign process, management liaison, might not pertain to all sports programs. If the program is considered autonomous and thus functions without peripheral, external influences, the managerial liaison phase is not applicable. However, if the program operates as one unit within a larger department or if it has a controlling board, owner, or committee, then, as the program administrator, one must act as the managerial liaison. The managing group will need to (in some cases) authorize the program's public relations plan, sanction it through funding, provide its input and insight, etc. Each situation and program will have different reporting criteria.

PERPETUAL PUBLIC RELATIONS

Perpetual public relations are how, on a permanent and continuous basis, a coach/program administrator enlightens, informs, and communicates with the media and the public. Public relations relates to the business concepts of operating systems, policies, and procedures. The public relations system, in which the program communicates externally, is the way staff members interact and who is specifically responsible for them. Public relations policies and procedures within established systems are more specific rules and step-by-step "how to's."

Before developing and implementing a perpetual public relations system, it is crucial that one both define what a system is and delineate its components. While the system concept in the 2003 text *Management: A Practical Introduction* is geared toward administrative/managerial applications in organizations, the authors do provide the structural definition and essential ingredients to describe any system. The following is an abridged explanation of the system concept and its functions:

> **A system is a set of interrelated parts that operate together to achieve a common purpose . . . the *systems viewpoint* regards the organization as a system of interrelated parts**. By adopting this point of view, you can look at your organization both as (1) a collection of *subsystems*—**parts making up the whole system**—and (2) a part of the larger environment. The four parts of a system are:
> 1. *Inputs* **are the people, money, information, equipment, and materials required to produce an organization's goods and services**
> 2. *Outputs* **are the products, services, profits, losses, employee satisfaction or discontent, and the like that are produced by the organization.**
> 3. *Transformation* **processes are the organization's capabilities in management and technology that are applied to converting inputs into outputs.**

Administrative Tip

In the capacity of managerial liaison, a coach/program administrator must understand that to be successful, he/she must maintain open lines of communication with all relevant program stakeholders. Keeping everyone continually informed throughout all aspects of the campaign is an essential point. Conversely, one needs to balance the amount of information given so as not to inundate people with trivial information.

Administrative Tip

Perpetual public relations systems require time to cultivate key media relationships and feedback. As the program's visible leader, spend time developing positive relations with key media personnel. Goodwill and trust are earned, so be patient and persistent.

4. *Feedback* **is information about the reaction of the environment to the outputs that affects the inputs.** (Kinicki & Williams, 2003, pp. 48–49)

From this description of systems, a coach/program administrator can develop a program's public relation system and procedures. Ask the following supporting questions to systemize the program's public relations. These questions are nonspecific and in no particular order. The organization's operating environment will dictate the precise questions.

Inputs/Resources

- What type of equipment will the program need to have for a professional, proficient public relations communication system?
- What type of human resource needs will the public relations system demand?
- What individual qualifications and expertise will be needed on the program's public relations staff?
- What type of printing service is available? Postal services? Email and database availability?
- What access does the program have to internal organizational staff that could be utilized for speaking engagements and interviews?
- For athletic programs that rely on statistics, what type of statistical tracking software is considered necessary?

Processing: Converting Inputs to Outputs

- Who is accountable for
  — press releases
  — compiling statistics
  — assembling press kits
  — securing interviews
  — speaking engagements
  — public relations events
- What are the step-by-step actions for constructing the above public relations items?
- Who is responsible for scheduling, organizing, and operating public relations functions?
- Are the program's conversion processing activities computerized? If so, are these procedures the most up-to-date for efficiency?

Outputs/Final Product

- Is the final public relations product professional?
- Is it factual and accurate?

- Is it relevant to the reader/listener?
- Does it "tell the story" that one would like?
- Is it reaching the media in an opportune, timely manner?
- Is the produced output targeted toward appropriate sources?

Two other components that are of great consequence to a high-quality public relations system are feedback and control. Questions that will refine the program's public relation system that deal with these two components are as follows:

Feedback/Reverse Communication

- What was the external reaction and opinion to the public relations communication?
- Is the program getting the public relations exposure expected?
- Is the public relations output the same as the public relations media coverage given?

Control/Adjustments to the System

- Is the program attaining its public relations goals?
- If not, how can the coach or program administrator modify the program's inputs, processes, and outputs to improve results?

To reiterate, the key to putting together a well-designed public relations systems is to establish successful procedures and to monitor the overall process.

CRISIS PUBLIC RELATIONS

No matter what business or sports program one operates, the subject of crisis public relations is not only important but, sadly, a fact of life. Accidents can happen at any moment. People make unforeseen mistakes. Program communications can be misconstrued from their original intention. How one handles events and public relation "nightmares" could be the difference in the program surviving or one having a career. Is it better to have a plan for potential problems? Absolutely.

It is impossible for an organization to prepare for every crisis eventuality. However, there is a checklist that could be used to assist a coach/program administrator when a public relations predicament occurs.

Do the Following

- Get out your prepared crisis management steering committee, call in experts to help analyze and explain the crisis, and open the lines of communication.
- Notify top management and refer them to the crisis plan.

Administrative Tip

When putting together a public relations system, remember that it will not happen overnight. Public relation systems take far-reaching thought and planning. Front-end thinking will eliminate backside mistakes when it comes to public relations.

Administrative Tip

Think proactively when embroiled in any public relations crisis. Get out in front of the situation to manage as much of it as possible. Never forget that taking a defensive, non-committal attitude encourages aggressive offensive tactics by the media.

- Channel all inquires to the designated spokesperson who was selected and trained in advance as part of the crisis planning preparation.
- Set up a news center for media and begin providing information as quickly as it becomes available.
- Be open and tell the full story. Demonstrate the organization's concern for what is happening and for the people who are involved and affected.
- Have someone on-call 24 hours a day and stay with the story as long as the media are interested.
- Reconvene the crisis management team afterwards to summarize what happened, to review and evaluate how the plan worked, and to recommend improvements in the crisis plan.

On the Other Hand

- Do not speculate publicly about what you do not know to be fact.
- Do not minimize the problem or try to underplay a serious situation.
- Do not let the story dribble out bit by bit.
- Do not release information about people if it will violate their privacy or if it blames anyone for anything.
- Do not say "no comment" or make off-the-record comments.
- Do not play favorites among the media or reporters.
- Do not try to capitalize on media attention and interest by trying to promote the organization, cause, products, or services. (Cutlip, Center, & Broom, 2000, p. 392)

Some important lessons can be derived from the above bullet points. First and foremost, never take a "defensive stance" in a public relations emergency. This posture will only provoke an aggressive response from supporters and media. Additionally, once the athletic program (and coach/program administrator) adopts an "it's-not-our-fault" mindset, it is virtually impossible to turn around and reverse that position. Another lesson that can be derived from the bullet points is *to think*. In other words, think through all aspects first (think before speaking). Comments made in haste and without proper judgment can actually compound and, in some cases, accelerate the crisis. Lying to curtail problems will, in fact, exponentially increase the crisis as soon as the lie is discovered (and they almost always will be exposed). Finally, it is necessary to have good communication both internally and externally throughout the crisis. The choice of the right spokesperson is imperative. Spokespersons must be able to monitor and curtail their emotions, communicate the story that the program wants told, and only answer questions for which the answers are substantiated. Their most central characteristic should be that they do not get rattled and are "unflappable" under pressure. A display of panic can discredit the speaker and the message being communicated.

ISSUE PUBLIC RELATIONS

Issue management/public relations is not crisis management/public relations. Issues management is the proactive handling of an identified and acknowledged organizational issue (either now or in the near future) that necessitates reliable public relations to communicate the athletic program's message about the issue. Issues management is typically terminal in nature with definitive time frames. Each concern will need its own specific public relation plans.

Issue management process involves five steps:

1. Issue identification
2. Issue analysis
3. Issue change strategy options
4. Issue action program
5. Evaluation of results.

(Caywood, 1997, p. 174)

From an athletic program perspective, issue management can take on the following:

Issue Identification—For athletic programs with limited resources, it is important that a coach/program administrator isolate the true issue to be managed. In other words, knowing which issues may now or in the future need to be addressed is an essential first step in the process.

Issue Analysis—Once an issue is identified, that topic will need to be dissected as to its influence and projected impact on the athletic program now and in the future. The bigger the issue, the more cognitive analysis it will need.

Issue Change Strategy Options—This is the stage in issue management where ultimate actions are determined and documented. Strategic options can range from simple tactics to complex, multifarious stratagem.

Issue Action Programming—This is the implementation of issue management strategies. Implementation must be timely, have accountability, and be evaluated continuously throughout the execution.

Evaluation of Results—Once the strategy plan has been implement, an overall evaluation of the way the issue was managed should be conducted. The purpose for this stage is to enhance processes in future issue-related P.R. situations.

BUDGETING PUBLIC RELATIONS

By definition, public relations is free marketing. That statement, while in theory is accurate, in practicality is not necessarily the truth. A publicity campaign is not an advertising campaign. Besides the added credibility of a publicity-driven story's appearing in the media (and in the public's acceptance that your message is so worthwhile that you don't have to pay to have it carried), there is in fact a typical lower cost to P.R. than advertising. But "lower cost" does not mean free. Many companies, service groups, and trade associations that have a P.R. agency or consultant on retainer for amounts in the area of $20,000 per month or more may spend less that that on trade or community advertising. There are also the costs of media kits, photos, literature, premiums, banners, and other related expenses to be considered. . . . It may be *cheaper*, but it is definitely not *cheap*. (Marconi, 1999, p. 32)

As with all athletic program budgeting, the goals and targeted objectives are always the starting point for the delineation of resources. However, money should not be the "sticking point" to public relations. There are many cost savings methods of communication that can be utilized by even the smallest athletic programs.

TYPES OF MEDIA AND AVENUES OF PUBLIC RELATIONS COMMUNICATION

The following Figure is a listing of possible media and communication avenues for public relations communication.

It should be noted that the ultimate goal of selecting the right media and communication techniques is to generate positive word of mouth for the athletic program.

Electronic/Technological	Traditional Methods
Internet "Blogs"	Public Relations Community Events/Sponsorships
Newsletters	Public Appearances (top internal personnel)
Industry-Wide Electronic Publications	Press Releases and Press Kits
Direct Electronic Communication	Correspondence Inserts/Billing Inserts
Athletic Program Web Pages	Traditional Advertising Media (TV, radio, periodicals, direct mailing, etc.)
Chat Rooms/Discussion Boards	News Stories
Search Engines	Interviews
Video Teleconferencing	TV and Press Conferences
E-Conferencing	Brochures and Internal Fliers
	Paraphernalia (cups, hats, t-shirts, pens, etc.)

Figure 1. **P.R. Media and Communication Avenues**

SUMMARY

The potential for the use of public relations campaigns for sports programs is considerable. The most salient point is that the expenditures associated with public relations are, in comparison to other promotional and marketing communication techniques, minimal. For sports programs with nominal funding, public relations can be a compelling, cost effective tool. Another significant aspect of public relations is it is perceived by the public as more reliable and convincing in comparison with paid promotional approaches. Other promotional techniques, such as advertising, are seen as manipulative while public relations articles and editorials are taken as more accurate and sincere. Finally, public relations is proactive in nature. If continually used, even when the program is encountering little or no public instability and disapproving opinion, it can build up positive points for the time when there is a crisis situation involving the program. If a publicity predicament never occurs (which is doubtful in any organization), then the constructive benefits still remain.

KEY TERMS

public relations	communication audit
publicity	SWOT
program identity	perpetual public relations
public relations campaign	systems
publicity image	inputs
situational analysis	processing
problem statement	outputs
goal statement	feedback
tentative strategies	control
targeted publics	crisis public relations
statement of limitations	press releases
management liaison	

Review and Discussion Questions

1. What effect does a coach or program administrator have on public relations?

2. What is a core consideration when defining publicity? What are the three possible scenarios for program identities?

3. What are the seven steps in a public relations campaign?

4. What is a situational audit?

5. How does the concept of targeted public relation segments correlate to the marketing concept of target markets?

6. What type of questions should be asked when developing tentative strategies for a public relations campaign?

7. Define *perpetual public relations.* Define *public relations systems.*

8. What are the five components of a system?

9. What are some major considerations of crisis public relations?

Appendix 9A
News Releases

The following section provides sports administrators and coaches with fundamental information in constructing press releases. The concepts are extrapolated from Beckwith's 2003 text titled the *Complete Publicity Plans: How to Create Publicity That Will Spark Media Exposure and Excitement*.

CONTACT INFORMATION

Who should the reporter or customer contact for more information after reading your press release? Place contact name, phone number, and e-mail address at the top of the first page, on the right side.

CATCHY HEADLINE

When writing headlines use an active voice—"introduces" rather than "plans to introduce"—and colorful or energetic words. Make it exciting, but don't exaggerate.

ATTENTION-GETTING LEAD

Craft an attention-getting lead—your first one or two release sentences—without worrying about including all the details. When the subject lends itself, use a clever lead.

MAKE YOUR PRESS RELEASE STAND OUT

Use statistics and facts: When possible and appropriate, use statistics and facts to support the premise of your press release.

Include a Quote: A quote from a company leader or expert is appropriate for most press releases. The quote can amplify information already presented, or express an opinion, but it should add to the story.

Use Number List or Tips: In general, when your release needs to make several consecutive points, use bullets for readability.

Include a Paragraph About Your Company: Always conclude your release with a paragraph that describes your company without hype or exaggeration.

REMEMBER THE FIVE Ws AND ONE H

Work to get the Five Ws and One H—who, what, where, when, why, and how—into the first two paragraphs.

- Avoid complicated language
- Keep your release short
- Make it clear and complete
- Fact check, proofread, and check again

For the actual structure and format of a press release, a variety of textbooks and periodicals have format examples.

CHAPTER

10

Athletic Program Fundraising

CHAPTER OUTLINE

CHAPTER

10

OBJECTIVES

- To describe program fundraising and clarify the major areas of fundraising for athletic programs
- To distinguish the underlying difference between annual and capital fundraising
- To offer and explain possible athletic program fundraising special events
- To offer and explain possible athletic program fundraising activities
- To present the essential rights of all athletic program patrons/donors
- To delineate several underlying rules to fundraising

INTRODUCTION

This chapter conveys concrete techniques for the athletic program function of fundraising. The importance of fundraising is determined by the financial position of the organization. If the existing monetary status of the program warrants fundraising, the athletic program's uses for the augmented contributions, gifts, and donations can be unlimited. Fundraising can supplement salaries, furnish the means to procure additional equipment, expand travel regions, and amplify promotional activities. Whatever the uses, to generate supplemental program finances, a coach or program administrator must apply the systematic foundations of management (Chapters 1–5: *Planning, Organizing, Human Resources, Leadership*, and *Control*) as they relate to and are focused on the endeavor of fundraising.

FUNDRAISING DEFINED

Merriam-Webster's Online Dictionary characterizes fundraising as "the organized activity of raising funds (as for an institution or political cause)" and fundraisers as "a person employed to raise funds . . . a social event (as a cocktail party) held for the purpose of raising funds." To be a lucrative fundraiser, a systematic leadership approach should be developed, tested, and implemented.

The first step in recruiting outstanding fundraising leadership is to describe the qualities you want for your organization. . . . A partial list could include:

1. Integrity
2. Humility
3. Ability to think on the spot
4. Willingness to listen and learn
5. Willingness to grow and stretch
6. Trust in the group process
7. Ability to develop new people
8. A goal-oriented nature
9. A sense of humor (Flanagan, 1993, pp. 35–36)

Administrative Tip

The financial needs of the athletic program will dictate the fundraising plan that one should choose. Additionally, the choice of fundraising activities can also relate to the long-term growth potential of some fundraising programs. Some fundraising programs take multiple applications, over years of use, to reach their maximum financial potential. Once these types of multiple programs "get rolling," they typically accumulate far greater capability of making dollars for the program.

In most cases this undertaking of fund solicitation falls to the coach or program administrator.

ANNUAL AND CAPITAL FUNDRAISING

There are two distinct and separate categories of fundraising. The first and most consequential is annual fundraising. The ultimate objective of an annual program is the maintenance and fortification of ongoing operations for the current season and fiscal year. Annual fundraising programs should fill the deficit between revenues generated and expenditures incurred. If the existing program is functioning at a net income (surplus funds or "in the black"), the prime utility of an annual program may be to upgrade and diversify services to the staff and players as well as to enlarge the volume of spectators through increased promotion.

In most not-for-profit/nonprofit ventures, annual fundraising is used to underscore sizable endowment campaigns. This fundraising effort concentrates on large philanthropic donations from a small number of individuals. While this approach is the most straightforward to track, it is also a tremendous gamble. For example, if a program has five principal benefactors and one or two of these individuals or organizations are unable to match their annual projected contributions, the program could immediately experience up to a 20–40% reduction in operational funds. From a risk averse prospective, a program that cultivates a broad base of donors and fundraising activities will experience far less financial impairment from smaller abstaining donations. This is not to argue in support of abandoning the large donors and sponsors, but rather to stress the monetary stability of a broad-based fundraising philosophy.

The principal difference between capital and annual fundraising is that the former is considered more of a perpetual, unending activity while the latter is an assignment-specific endeavor. Because of this element, the bigger the "one-time" donation, the better. Most capital fundraising programs have multimillion dollar goals, characteristically within two to five years.

FUNDRAISING EVENTS AND PROGRAMS/ACTIVITIES

The sections below clarify each fundraising event/program/activity's distinct advantages and disadvantages. They do so relying on or using a fairly

Administrative Tip

Obviously, a coach/program administrator needs to select the most lucrative annual and capital fundraising activities for the athletic program. However, one must appraise the limitations of the program as a guiding element in choosing a fundraising activity. The worst-case scenario is a coach/program administrator who chooses too many fundraising programs and does not complete any of them. Utilize fundraising activities that have the greatest promise within the resource restrictions of the program. Any other tactic will exhaust resources rather than augment them.

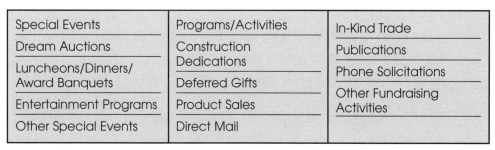

Special Events	Programs/Activities	In-Kind Trade
Dream Auctions	Construction Dedications	Publications
Luncheons/Dinners/Award Banquets	Deferred Gifts	Phone Solicitations
Entertainment Programs	Product Sales	Other Fundraising Activities
Other Special Events	Direct Mail	

Figure 1. **Fundraising Events and Activities**

abstract conceptual format. For the program's precise development and execution, fundraising ideas require open discussion by the coaches and staff to determine their operational feasibility.

SPECIAL EVENTS

A nonprofit special event is a unique fund-raising program that strengthens the nonprofit's image in the community and recruits and involves volunteers; it raises money as well as friends . . . special events should be a part of a nonprofit's overall development program . . .

Seven Goals for a Successful Special Event

1. Raise Money
2. Update the Mission Statement to Educate Your Constituency
3. Motivate Board Members and Major Givers
4. Recruit Volunteers and Future Board Members
5. Expand the Organization's Network
6. Market the Organization
7. Solicit Endorsements (Wendroff, 1999, p. 2)

The following are just a few of the possible special fund-raising events an athletic program could adopt and operate.

Dream Auction (Annual/Capital)

Dream auctions are fundraising programs that are solo events that can be administered as one time capital projects or annual events. Because of the amount of preparation required, dream auctions are not suited as a recurrent fundraising endeavor. The program's basic structure is as follows:

1. The fundraising staff and volunteers solicit charitable gifts and services from local, regional, or national businesses and corporations. For example, a local business or restaurant may donate a dinner for two or a hair salon may contribute a free hair cut. Rewards for the corporations and business entities that award products and services are beneficial, positive publicity. Additionally, all donations are at cost and tax deductible. It should be distinguished for future reference that businesses are more likely to donate products rather than cash because products are valued at retail but have cash cost value at substantially lower amounts. Additionally, during the recruiting process, the developmental staff should inaugurate an intense promotional campaign to publicize the event. All "blue chip" donations of products and services should be tied into promotion to gain interest and attendance at the event.
2. The affair, through a public auction format, barters and sells these gifts and services for auctioned values. For large auctions, it would be advisable to enlist the aid of a professional auctioneer to facilitate

Administrative Tip

There are some complexities in dealing with generous philanthropic donations and the individuals who bestow them. While these altruistic people are valuable to a program's funding, a coach/program administrator needs to take into account the desires and motivations behind their gifts. If their needs and motives are benevolent and sincere, work with these people to maintain their contributions and assistance. If a donator's purpose and needs are not compatible with the program's operating philosophies, no matter how much money and backing is being offered, never sell the program's integrity.

the program. Another alternative is the concept of silent/blind auctions where items are displayed and people bid on them in on open format. Each item will have a starting bid displayed and the participants could either tender offers through a lock box or via an exposed document list.

The realizable income from a prosperous dream auction is tremendous. The two functions of product or service solicitation and event promotion must be coordinated through the coach or program administrator. The promotional mix for this type of event can incorporate media advertising (e.g., newspapers, television, radio), direct target mailings, and personal invitations. The event should have a meticulous itinerary and an itemized catalog of products and services to be auctioned. A pre-event reception (formal cocktail reception for distinguished programs or casual receptions for community-wide programs) is also recommended so patrons can browse and look at tangible items.

Luncheons/Dinners/Award Banquets (Annual/Capital)

Award banquets are fundraisers that are geared toward philanthropic recognition and appreciation as well as future charitable contributions. The foremost fundraising objectives are as follows:

1. For a first-time event, the honoring of a cherished individual, program, or holiday that can stimulate community enthusiasm and collaboration is imperative. Someone who is an affluent, steadfast supporter of the athletic program could be a recipient of an annual award. It is noteworthy to single out an event conscientiously without community overlap and antagonism.
2. A per plate price is established. The price determination is based solely on the occasion and the value to the community. Benchmarking similar events by other organizations is a good starting point.
3. If possible, the event, which could be a yearly program or one-time activity, should be a black tie affair involving prominent community and nationally renowned speakers.

There are dangerous financial prospects associated with award banquets as fundraisers. First and foremost are the initial expenditures absorbed (up-front costs). Facility rental, music, food costs, and personnel can be exorbitant. Secondly, the event must be timed for maximum community participation. And finally, RSVP responses need to be tracked accurately and prioritized. One possible solution that could alleviate the inherent up-front monetary vulnerability of an awards banquet could be to have the projected expenses underwritten by a local or national corporation. For their participation, the company (or companies) will be the signature sponsor and receive numerous publicity opportunities arising from the event.

Entertainment (Annual)

Entertainment benefits as fundraising activities can incorporate an extensive variety of programs and applications. Because athletic programs are by definition entertainment, coaches and program administrators can concentrate their attention on something that they know quite well. From an athletic program standpoint, sponsoring instructional camps and clinics, indoor and outdoor tournaments, and pro and Olympic exhibitions are just a handful of the program-specific events that can be utilized as fundraisers. Non-athletic entertainment can encompass musical groups or singers, comedians, satirists, and featured speakers and lecturers.

Following are some fundraising guidelines for this type of endeavor:

1. The development director must secure a suitable entertainer. Obviously, the more fashionable and popular the entertainer or entertainment, the easier it will be to acquire sponsorship and promotion. The entertainment should be (if possible) contracted by a net profit percentage. This will eliminate initial expenditures. Other costs could include advertising, facility rental, and event employees.

2. Advertising for this category of fundraising should be dynamic and intensive while at the same time community oriented. The acquisition of media coverage (through public relations, which is non-paid advertising) should be optimized.

3. The realizable income is not only contingent on the entertainment, but the organization's commitment to the program. As with similar fundraisers, the predominant downside is the initial overhead costs and the risk of sparse attendance.

Other Special Events

Celebrity Signings/Team Signings (Annual)

Because of the ever-increasing popularity of autographs, autographed sports items (uniforms, bats, balls, hats, etc.), and autographed paraphernalia (posters, magazines, books, pictures, etc.), an excellent fundraising program is a celebrity and/or team autograph day. A couple of salient keys to consider:

- The celebrity/team must be a known quantity in the community in which the event is taking place.
- The media should be invited (and courted) to cover the event.
- If the athletic program's team is the enticement for the autographing event, the occasion should be scheduled/programmed as close as possible to the start of the team's season for the benefit of ticket sales and additional support.
- The autograph date could incorporate other fundraising activities such as games, speakers, and information about the program.

Administrative Tip

For athletic programs with long histories, a Hall of Fame banquet/ceremony can achieve two enormously notable fundraising purposes. First, the Hall of Fame event could be a profitable function within itself. Secondly, the individuals that are nominated and accepted into the Hall of Fame will then be vested members of the athletic program and become likely future donors.

Administrative Tip

Before scheduling an entertainment fundraising event (as well as any other one time specific fundraising event), a coach/program administrator should triple check all possible community calendars to avoid overlapping events. This will minimize a loss of support and attendance as well as friction from other event organizations.

- It is strongly recommended that a formal contractual arrangement be made with any/all celebrities participating in the event.

Game-day Events (Annual)

A popular fundraising model is game-day events for supporters/boosters of the athletic program. Pre-game meals, youth contests, preliminary competitions (in conjunction with the main contest), and pre-game entertainment are some of the potential cooperative events. Not only will these activities raise money, they will also develop community awareness and athletic program goodwill. The pre-game events should in no way impinge on the coaches or athletes. They will need to focus their cognitive and physical preparation for their competition.

Skills Contests (Annual)

Another way for an athletic program to involve community members in the program as well as raise funds/resources is to have sport-specific skill contests. Obviously, the athletic program's sport will be the foundation of the proficiency challenge. These contests/skills tests could be used with other fundraising events or in concert with the athletic program's competition. The value and quality of prizes can fluctuate with the level and costs incurred by the program. If the program elects to have a considerable prize, insurance can be purchased to guarantee and secure the prize (e.g., million dollar hole-in-one). A per attempt fee can be charged and less significant prizes could be presented to maintain interest. Some of the feasible skills contests could include:

- Golf—Hole-in-one contest
- Baseball/Softball—Throwing through target or hitting homerun
- Basketball—Half-court shot
- Volleyball/Tennis—Serving into target
- Football—Punt, pass, or kick skills
- Hockey/Soccer/Lacrosse—Shot on goal contest
- Bowling—Three strikes contest

A coach/program administrator must balance contest creativity, fan appeal, and achievability in constructing a skills contest.

Carnivals/Community Celebrations (Annual/Capital)

Carnivals and community celebrations are exceptional vehicles for increasing funding for an athletic program. If the community and athletic program supporters attend the events, their profitability as fundraisers and builders of goodwill is substantial. However, there are some clear dangers in their adoption. These day-long events take extensive planning, substantial upfront resources, a sizeable volunteer pool, and far-reaching promotion. Their use for smaller programs is very limited. Nevertheless, if an athletic department or an assemblage of multiple athletic programs could merge together for the event, the risk would be spread out and minimized.

Golf Tournaments (Annual/Capital)

The attractiveness of golf tournaments (either celebrity or general) is a major factor in their popularity as legitimate fundraising events. Golf tournaments can supply supporters with a pleasurable activity that has a definite tangibility to it. While they take considerable planning, a superior golf tournament can develop into an enormous resource generator. Tournament golfing can be supplemented by banquets, media coverage, and other related activities. Fees charged can be for individuals, foursomes, or organizations. The location of the event as well as its promotion is a critical component to its success.

PROGRAMS/ACTIVITIES

Construction/Brick Dedication (Capital)

For an enterprise (athletic program) that is constructing or has impending future facility construction or renovation, the brick dedication fundraising program is an exceptional, high-potential fundraising activity. The operation conditions are as follows:

1. For a predetermined price (usually in the range of $50.00–$100.00 per brick), the fund-raising committee solicits donations by selling bricks for the new or renovated facility. The program's paramount selling point is that each brick will have the donor's name (or tribute name) inscribed on it and it will be a permanent, visual component of the structure. The unit cost per brick with etching can be a minimal $5–10.00 per brick (depending on the construction type and quality).

2. For large donations, the contributor will have the opportunity to erect a facility plaque or a sectional dedication. Because this dedication has more logistical work associated with it, it is advisable to place a $500.00–$1,000.00 minimum on this type of solicitation.

3. An extensive promotional program for this type of capital undertaking is a prerequisite. Community involvement is most important. Publicity and sales should be instituted at least two years in advance of ground breaking.

4. All sales have to be registered and mapped for future reference by donors. These maps should be as clear-cut as possible to locate any and all dedications.

It should be noted that a vital first step before the program is implemented is getting a definitive maximum number of bricks from the construction engineer that can be retailed. All public areas should be exactly measured and bricks to be used quantified.

The dimensions of capital funds raised by this fundraising strategy are only constrained by the size and the number of new or renovated facilities and the consolidated effort put into selling the bricks. For every new potential building, walkway, or public area under construction, a new brick dedication fundraising program could be instituted. However, brick dedication projects should be selected strategically to avoid potential fundraising saturation which, in turn, could minimize their importance.

Deferred Gifts, Wills, and Bequests—Long-Term Fundraising (Capital)

Deferred gifts and endowments are more comparable to "planned gifts" rather than special events and activities. Their goal is to transfer monetary gifts and pledged assets to an organization or program through fiduciary trusts, wills and endowments, insurance policies, and annuities. While this idea might seem a bit radical for a small athletic program, the long-term benefits of such solicitations are tremendously alluring. For example, endowed scholarships are directly related to wins and losses. They provide the athletes the program needs to compete. It should be noted that all types of deferred donations should be in conjunction with both party's legal counsel and advisors.

Product Sales (Annual)

Product sales are worthwhile fundraising activities for annual operations but are typically impractical for capital programs because of their limited financial potential. Underlying principles of product sales are as follows:

1. The fundraising director will contact a contingency sale/fundraising company. Articles to be sold can comprise clothing, candy, business paraphernalia, and personalized athletic items.
2. Because the sales are contingency supported, the program bears no liability for unsold products.
3. The sales force can be composed of designated internal stakeholders and selected external stakeholders. A targeted goal should be specified for each individual involved in the sales program. Sale incentives and awards can be employed to intensify participation and targeted goal achievement.

The principal disadvantages to contingency product sales are that they are fairly limited as fundraising activities (due to the fact that most items being sold have a low retail value), the sales force is not trained in professional selling techniques, and the commitment factor necessary for success is extensive. A profitable sales campaign involving 20 people could reach a peak of approximately $3,000–5,000.00. However, product sales are a creditable, rapid source of funds for program operations and are a way to harvest middle to lower socio-economic community members.

Administrative Tip

Brick dedication fundraising programs can be connected with other fundraising activities such as banquets and receptions. The size of the ceremony depends on the magnitude of the "grand opening" of the new project/building. For example, the opening of a new core building that had brick sales would warrant a major function with receptions, food, and speakers.

Direct Mail (Annual)

Direct mail is a superior mechanism for laying the groundwork for other fundraising tools and programs. But because of the low response rates associated with its operation (characteristically 3–5% on general mailings), it should not be retained as the athletic program's only organizational fundraising appliance. Its chief justifications and objectives are as follows:

1. The prime rationale for direct mailing is to indoctrinate and inform community members about program successes and fundraising goals. The solicitation of substantial funds is quite limited even with extensive volume mailing.

2. Each individual direct mailing must have a cost-benefit analysis done to determine its effectiveness in relation to its substantive costs. The cost elements of direct mailing are becoming a major ingredient in the utilization of this fundraising methodology. In other words, because of the continual increasing cost of postage, print work, and design, the athletic program must forecast the realizable earnings and evaluate if the mailer is justified and cost sensible.

3. Products and materials for a bulk mailing must be engineered to be community relevant, successful at communicating the significance of the program and its fundraising considerations, straightforward and comprehensible, rationally appealing, creative, and easy to respond to.

Direct mailers are typically time consuming in their production and entail having sizable mailing lists. Mailing lists, which can be from internal or external sources, are the most important component of direct mailing. A centralized, targeted listing can facilitate fundraising success. An unsuitable and outdated list will lead to costly resource wasting and fundraising failure.

Other Fundraising Activities

In-Kind Trade (Annual)

In-kind trade relies on an exchange of goods/services. The organization or program trades its product, service, or exposure opportunity for another organization's product or service. An example of an in-kind trade and exchange is an exchange of season tickets and advertising space in return for an automobile dealer vehicle. All trades should be value-for-value.

Publications (Annual/Capital)

If the athletic program creates and distributes a media guide or visiting team travel guide, the sale of space inside these publications is a viable way to raise external funds. Businesses are reluctant to pay for advertising space. In-kind products for advertising space are a value-for-value bargain that will benefit both parties. This technique for raising funds can also apply to athletic program web pages.

Administrative Tip

Because of the volume of direct mail received by potential and current supporters, the program's direct mailing undertaking must be as distinctive and engaging as possible. Quality is typically the best way to differentiate the program's direct mail from other organization solicitations. Quality in direct mailing can be achieved via such components as writing, construction, artwork, and assembly. If financially feasible, direct mail something of value to the prospective supporter. This tactic, while having a higher upfront cost associated with it, can drastically boost the response rate of the mailing.

Administrative Tip

When soliciting in-kind trades, underscore the fact that all in-kind trades are valued at retail but cost the donating organization purchased value. Also accentuate the possibility of substantial tax implications of retailed valued gifts.

Phone Campaigns (Annual)

As with direct mail campaigns, phone campaigns are limited fundraising activities due to the sheer number of phone solicitations individuals receive daily. Additionally, cold calling will have a much lower success rate compared to phone solicitations to a targeted, vested stakeholder group. Phone volunteers should work from a drafted script and should always remember that they are representatives of the program.

Miscellaneous Fundraising Activities

Walk/Bowl/Swim-A-Thons (Annual)—Fundraising activities based on pledged dollar amounts to volunteers for their realization/accomplishment of targeted goals.

Holiday Sales (Annual)—Product sales (on consignment) of holiday specific items; products can be related to athletic program, holiday distinct, or a combination of both.

Corporate Sponsorship (Annual/Capital)—Solicitation of corporate backing/finances through one-on-one contacts; this wine-and-dine skill should be executed by prominent athletic program personnel.

Day with Team/Guest Travel (Annual/Capital)—For a specified level of financial backing, an athletic program booster can spend a competition day with the team, coaches, and program personnel; the contributor can be designated as an honorary team captain. Note: As with all fundraising, please verify athletic governing body regulations regarding guests/boosters.

Credit Card Strategic Alliances (Annual/Capital)—Large athletic programs/teams can enter into strategic alliances with credit card companies. Credit cards will be tailored toward the athletic program and reward benefits will be distributed back to the athletic program for every purchase made on that card.

Dog/Car Washes (Annual)—A standard, but confined, program fundraising activity.

BASIC GUIDELINES TO FUNDRAISING EVENTS AND PROGRAMS/ACTIVITIES

A special note relating to all fundraising activities, whether they are annual or capital in nature: There are indispensable guiding principles that must be imparted to anyone associated with the program's fundraising.

1. No amount is too small. A minor contributor today could be a generous benefactor tomorrow.

2. Always personalize the "thank you" for the donation. The thank you should present the accomplishments of the event or activity/program as well as reiterate the individual's worth in reaching the athletic program's fundraising objectives. Thank you notes should continuously be sent to all volunteers, donors, key players, board

members, and community officials. The intrinsic reward realized by each of the individuals receiving a thank you note is immeasurable.

3. The fundraising activity needs to be selected based on its capacity to correspond with the organization's goals, target market, image, and inclusive operation. The choice of an inappropriate fundraising event/program/activity could have enduring damage to the athletic program.

4. The athletic program's donor list needs to be persistently updated. Data on steadfast program supporters and new patrons should be as accurate as possible.

5. If an athletic program is smaller and unable to put resources into its own independent/autonomous program, the opportunity of "piggybacking" on another organization's fundraising is a distinct possibility. The key to this arrangement is cooperation between the athletic program and the external organization. Both parties must experience a mutually beneficial relationship and, in no way, encounter a conflict of interest.

6. Contingency planning is imperative in all special event fundraising. A backup plan for inclement weather, community conflicts, and other possible circumstances is critical for fundraising endeavors.

7. Once again, all athletic program fundraising should be approved through the program's athletic administration and the particular sport's governing body regulations. The avoidance of any impropriety and regulatory violations should be paramount. Additionally, detailed financial records must be maintained for review by all parties involved in the organization.

SUMMARY

The aggregate number of fundraising programs accessible to an athletic program is restricted only by the resourcefulness and enthusiasm of the people involved. If the coach as the program leader and fundraising director has "bought into" the fundraising program and is committed, the rest of the staff will be committed. While fundraising activities can be difficult and a tremendous amount of hard work, they can have both extrinsic and intrinsic rewards. The extrinsic rewards from fundraising are simple—increased cash flow and operational funds. The intrinsic rewards from a successful fundraiser can range from providing others with enjoyment to the satisfaction of knowing that the program is being funded.

KEY TERMS

fundraising	banquets
fundraiser/developmental leader	deferred gifts
annual fundraising	direct mail
capital fundraising	in-kind trade
non-/not-for-profit	phone solicitations
philanthropic	entertainment programs
dream auctions	product sales
construction dedications	publications

Review and Discussion Questions

1. Describe *annual fundraising*.

2. What is the difference between capital and annual fundraising campaigns?

3. What is the major premise behind dream auctions?

4. Why should a fundraiser map out brick sales in a construction/brick dedication fundraising program?

5. What are the dangers associated with luncheons, dinners, and awards banquets?

6. Describe *deferred gifts*.

7. What are the two primary disadvantages of contingency product sales?

8. Why are phone solicitation campaigns considered limited fundraising activities?

9. List the basic guidelines to fundraising events and programs/activities.

Appendix 10A

Donor's Bill of Rights

(Mutz, Murray, 2000, p. 39 and the NSFRE)

1. To be informed of the organization's mission, of the way the organization intends to use donated resources, and of its capacity to use donations effectively for their intended purposes.
2. To be informed of the identity of those serving on the organization's governing board, and to expect the board to exercise prudent judgment in its stewardship responsibilities.
3. To have access to the organization's most recent financial statements.
4. To be assured their gifts will be used for the purposes for which they were given.
5. To receive appropriate acknowledgement and recognition.
6. To be assured that the information about their donations is handled with respect and with confidentiality to the extent provided by the law.
7. To expect that all relationships with individuals representing organizations of interest to the donor will be professional in nature.
8. To be informed whether those seeking donations are volunteers, employees of the organization, or hired solicitors.
9. To have the opportunity for their names to be deleted from mailing lists that an organization may intend to share.
10. To feel free to ask questions when making a donation and to receive prompt, truthful, and forthright answers.

CHAPTER

Fundamentals of Risk Management for Coaches

CHAPTER OUTLINE

CHAPTER 11

OBJECTIVES

- To highlight the magnitude of risk management for coaches and program administrators
- To analyze the four major areas of sports risk management
- To investigate facility and equipment risk management from a procedural and sensory perspective
- To examine personnel risks
- To assess the conditions for contractual agreements as well as areas of athletic program operation which necessitate contractual agreements
- To appraise external risks from an insurance perspective
- To provide a step-by-step process in handling accidents/injuries
- To underscore other safety and risk management considerations

INTRODUCTION

The issue of risk management in athletic programs is an enormously detailed and specialized legal and financial field. Therefore, it is not the intention of this chapter to instantly make a coach or administrator a certified expert in risk management. However, it is an aspect of business about which program managers should be cognizant and have a fundamental working knowledge. Coaches and program administrators work with people in a service industry that is exceedingly physical and dynamic. Extensive travel is involved, numerous facilities are utilized, and athletic programs typically have a wide range of support staff that require supervision. It is necessary to persistently evaluate the athletic program's environment and make the appropriate judgments to reduce the chance of risk and loss.

RISK AND RISK MANAGEMENT DEFINED

The most reasonable explanation of risk and risk management is as follows:

> Risk needs to be understood across a continuum from those events that present the potential for damage to the business strategy, to those that compose uncertainties implicit in the execution of that strategy, to those that must be embraced in order to achieve the goals of the organization. Expanding this definition of risk management in this manner has the potential to engage the entire organization . . . and assess the risks that are not only to be avoided but also embraced in the service of achieving the goals of an organization. (Sharon, 2006, pp. 62–63)

Administrative Tip

When dealing with risk and risk management, never take for granted that all parties involved with the program know the precarious consequences of risk management. Assumptions are dangerous in any business situation, especially in the realm of sports program risk.

Another key element in risk and risk management relates to the word *losses*. From the word *losses*, one might think of litigation through gross negligence. However, lawsuits can transpire over the slightest and most improbable incidences. Let's be honest in assessing our culture by stating that we exist in a "sue happy" society. Outrageous legal court settlements (whether warranted or not) are commonplace and coaches are as vulnerable as anyone.

The concept of risk management goes beyond gross negligence. Throughout her text, *Sports Business Management*, Miller categorizes risks into the following environmental segments:

1. Facility Risks/Equipment Risk
2. Personnel Risk
3. Contract Related Risk
4. External Risk (Miller, 1997, text concept)

If coaches adopt her classifications and fashion them toward their individual sport, it will give them the basis for instituting a game plan of approaching and reducing program and personal liabilities. Will risk ever be eliminated? No. Risk is a concept of uncertainty. However, the objective should be to influence and manage as many variables as possible so that the likelihood of a detrimental and liable occurrence is diminished.

FACILITY AND EQUIPMENT RISK

In reviewing conceivable facility and equipment risks, a coach or program administrator must first think of all the worst-case scenarios and, around them, all potential problems. The question that one must always ask is, "What is the most catastrophic scenario?" In other words, a coach or program administrator must be a consistent and intentional observer of potential disasters. Facilities and equipment deal with the physical aspects of athletic programs. They are tangible objects that one's senses (seeing, hearing, touching, and smelling) can examine and evaluate. When assessing the condition, layout, and safety of existing (or potential) facilities and equipment, it is advisable to set aside separate, unencumbered time prior to facility and/or equipment usage that distinctively utilizes one's senses to evaluate the situation. Once a scheduled activity begins, a coach's heightened attention is more on that activity than the surroundings. As a result, the facility/equipment walk-through should be completed considerably in advance to circumvent any other distractions. For example, before commencing preseason training, set the gym, field, or facility up according to the precise practice requirements a day before starting. With the program's staff, do a safety walk-through. Use the five human senses and ask questions:

- How does the ground (floor) feel? Is it clean of miscellaneous items or does it need more attention?
- Is the light adequate enough to conduct practice?

- What is the facility temperature? Is there proper circulation?
- Is there proper spacing around the participation areas? If not, are the walls or boundaries padded to avoid injury?
- What is the condition of the operational equipment? Is it in good working order?
- What is the condition of the locker rooms? Is there an unhealthy smell? Is the locker rooms area secure?
- Does the current design of the field (court, gym) minimize the chance for injury?
- Where will the athletes obtain water? Could there unintentionally be a hazardous situation caused by its placement and distribution?

Dougherty and Bonanno, in their text *Management Principles in Sport and Leisure Services*, delineate an outstanding outline for proactively examining most facility and equipment risks. Their specific guidelines for the provision of a safe environment include:

I. Develop and implement regular inspection and maintenance schedules for all facilities and equipment.
   A. Assign individual responsibilities.
   B. Establish procedures for correcting deficiencies.
II. Be sure any new facility exceeds all applicable safety standards. Give great attention to such details as surfacing, free area around courts and fields, lighting, and the presence of obstacles or dangerous protrusions on walls.
III. Be sure all equipment meets or exceeds applicable safety standards and is designed properly for the purpose in which it will be used.
IV. When equipment must be installed, give careful attention to the question of who will do the installing. The use of local staff in the installation process often voids any guarantee that may exist and, in certain instances, may absolve the manufacture of liability in the event of product failure.
V. Provide safety equipment for all participants and require its use. Post reminders for staff and for the participants to guarantee their awareness of the importance of protective equipment.

Dougherty and Bonanno go on to say

> Administrators must guarantee the safety and appropriateness of the area in which the activity takes place and also the safety of any equipment used . . . there is a clear obligation to eliminate any environmental conditions that may interfere with the safety of the participants. (Dougherty & Bonanno, 1985, p. 136)

The aggregate number of questions to be asked will be based on the condition of the operational equipment or facility and the coaching staff's sensitivity to risk. Obviously, the newer the facility or equipment, the less one

Administrative Tip

Retain all maintenance records (in chronological order) when it comes to facility and equipment repairs. If physically possible, have the repair companies itemize all work completed as fully as possible. If applicable, copy all program supervisors on all work completed.

should worry about its structural condition rather than its continual up-keep. Even the newest facilities become hazardous without appropriate maintenance.

What if the program is dealing with a confined budget and older facilities and equipment? Critically document (in writing) all possible problems and legitimate concerns and give copies to the program's supervisor and/or the individual from which the program may be leasing the facility. Make this correspondence as absolute, clear, and professional as possible. Declare facts, be very lucid, and eliminate all impulsive, emotional responses. Also, furnish solutions to all conclusions brought forth in the disclosure. Copy reports to all parties concerned. As unfortunate as this process may appear, by conferring any potential dangers, one would have proactively taken steps to limit personal liability.

Does this imply that the coach or program administrator disregards potential problems and conducts activities as though there is nothing wrong? No. Sit down with the program's staff and athletes and candidly discuss potential facility and equipment risks. Make everyone mindful of the circumstances and incorporate a safety sensitive theme in the program.

PERSONNEL RISK

A service is defined as "a deed performed by one party for another . . . a service is experienced, used or consumed . . . services are not physical—they are intangible" (Perreault & McCarthy, 2007, p. 195). In transforming this description to their profession, coaches and administrators provide assistance and expertise to their subordinates and players so they, in turn, can furnish the final consumer (fan) with an intangible service (entertainment). In other words, the nature of the business involves dealing with and training people internally so they can produce externally. This type of intense training mandates personnel policies and procedures to minimize risks.

In an ideal world, all men and women would work in a utopian environment of collaboration and cohesiveness. Personal and professional antagonism and conflicts between an organization's personnel would be non-existent. Unfortunately, we do not inhabit or work in an idyllic world. As a coach and administrator, one needs to cultivate, motivate, and influence people (staff and players) to achieve the program's mission. This is the substance of personnel management.

Some of the obstacles facing business managers dealing with people include the following:

- Fair hiring and recruiting policies
- Equal pay for equal work
- Sexual harassment
- Discriminatory hiring and employment practices
- Wrongful termination disputes

- Promotion and preferential treatment
- Valid, reliable evaluation methods
- Employee job safety

Administrative Tip

A subject that has become a central issue in sports programs is fan interaction with athletes and staff. Think of fan interaction as a personnel safety issue. Have policies and procedures in place to safeguard the program's people from outside contact.

Do these uncertainties challenge coaches? Absolutely. In fact, coaches are confronted with these issues from two separate work groups—program players and staff/employees. Once again, the massive content of personnel management and the consequences involved in supervising people is beyond the scope of this text. However, there are some indispensable, common sense measures a coach can adopt to create a more risk-averse personnel system. First of all, get educated (or re-educated) in prevalent personnel topics. Browse through human resource texts, attend human resource seminars (e.g., sexual harassment, discrimination, OSHA workshops), and revisit the organization's strategic personnel plan. Secondly, develop a program manual that spells out specific expectations for the program and its members. The program manual could be composed as in Figure 1.

Systematically evaluate the program's staff and players (even if it is through scheduled verbal meetings). Give them an opportunity to voice their feeling and beliefs about any aspect of the program. Finally, maintain a file for each employee and player. Document all pertinent material for future reference. If feasible, have dates, times, and specific items recorded for reference purposes. This, in turn, can reduce any impending discrepancies and contradictions.

CONTRACT-RELATED RISK

The importance of contracts can be summed up in the following excerpt:

Mission Statement
Long-Term Objectives
(3 to 5 Years—Both Athletically and Non-Athletically)
Short-Term Objectives to Reach Long-Term Goals
Team Rules and Policies

Academics	Practices
Matches	Travel
Player Responsibilities	Player Rules

Disciplinary Policies
Staff Job Responsibilities
Head Coach/Administrator
Assistant Coaches
Trainers
Sports Information
Secretaries
Other Related Members
Staff/Player Evaluation System

Figure 1. **Program Manual Outline**

> A contract is a promise or a set of promises for the breach in which the law gives remedy, or the performance of which the law in some way recognizes as duty. Put simply, a contract is a legally binding agreement between two or more parties who agree to perform or to refrain from performing some act now or in the future. Generally, contract disputes arise when there is a promise of future performance. If the contractual promise is not fulfilled, the party who made it is subject to the sanctions of the court. That party may be required to pay damages for failing to perform the contractual promise; in limited instances, the party may be required to perform the promised act. (Jentz, Miller, & Cross, 2007, p. 189)

Contracts deal categorically with rights, responsibilities, and remuneration (compensation) between participants. The fundamental requirements for a contractual agreement (whether formal and written or informal) are listed below:

Requirements for a Contract

Agreement: An agreement includes an offer and acceptance. One party must offer to enter into a legal agreement and another party must accept the terms of the offer.

Consideration: Any promise made by parties must be supported by legal sufficient and bargained for consideration (something of value received and promised to convince a person to make a deal).

Contractual Capacity: Both parties entering into the contract must have the contractual capacity to do so; the law must recognize them as possessing characteristics that qualify them as competent parties.

Legality: The contracts purpose must accomplish some goal that is legal and not against public policy.

Genuineness of Assent: The apparent consent of both parties must be genuine.

Form: The contract must be in whatever form the law requires; for example, some contracts must be in writing to be enforceable.

(Miller & Jentz, 2002, pp. 155–156)

Agreement, Consideration, Contractual Capacity, and Legality are formally known as *elements of a contract*. The last two are possible defenses to the information or the enforcement of a contract.

It is meaningful to note that once these six criteria are met, an oral contract is just as binding as a written one. The conspicuous disadvantage is that oral transactions are much more difficult to enforce precisely because it is more difficult to prove their existence. That is why it is strongly recommended to formalize all contracts in writing.

As coaches and administrators, contracts can be applied comprehensively to minimize personal and program risks. Unless one is a contract lawyer, it is important to mention that the more critical a contractual arrangement the more apropos it is to involve an independent specialist in contract law. For example, if a coach is in a position to negotiate a long-term employment contract (which most coaches would regard as a somewhat considerable employment item), it is advisable to get a contract lawyer to counsel one as to the rights and responsibilities of the contractual obligations. On the other hand, there are contractual arrangements that in everyday program operations do not necessitate legal representation and advisement to execute. The following are a few examples.

Administrative Tip

Oral contracts and agreements are just as binding as written contracts. To enforce oral contracts and agreements, with the permission of all parties concerned, video tape the oral contract.

Program Purchasing

When interacting with vendors, it is prudent to obtain written quotes on all services and products when negotiating prices, quantities, and specifications. After both parties stipulate the services/products to be included, formal written contracts (and purchase orders if applicable) should be generated and approved by all parties. Keep copies of all documentation for future reference.

Team/Personal Travel

Maintaining comprehensive files for each trip planned and completed is essential. Files should consist of hotel contracts, rental vehicle contracts, flight receipts stubs, and competition contracts. If the organization pays a contract in advance, make a copy of the check for tangible proof of the program's fulfillment of the bilateral agreement.

Booster Clubs

If one's club or school has a booster association, generate a contractual arrangement for its enrollment. These contracts should spell out the benefits of membership as well as the financial requirements of the patrons and boosters.

Summer Camps

To minimize disorder, keep all camp business and contracts separate from normal program operations. Contracts for insurance, staff employment, state registrations, camper registration, camper insurance and medical documentation, and checking accounts are among some of the contracts that should be formalized and retained.

Scholarships

In a collegiate situation, the actual paperwork for scholarships is traditionally produced by members of the school's financial aid department. Each coach should discuss final arrangements with each player while hand-delivering (if feasible) the scholarship contract. This will avoid possible miscommunications and grievances. Keep copies of the scholarship contracts in each player's program file for future reference.

EXTERNAL RISK

External risks are environmental elements outside the control of the operation and program coach or administrator. The question then arises: If the external risks are outside coaches/program administrators' control, why do they need to acknowledge them or be preoccupied with them? This is where the concept of adaptation versus control separates the prosperous, long-term managers from the day-to-day operators. One's managerial objective to minimize risk should be to proactively adapt the program to environmental elements that affect the business but are out of one's immediate power to control or change.

In strategizing for external risk, one must be future oriented. For example, if the country is suddenly in an economic downturn that alters the business operations, the most enviable strategy would have been to anticipate this direction and retool the enterprise in advance to compensate and adapt. Unfortunately, some predicaments are simply unpredictable. The key element in successfully managing these circumstances is to try to forecast whether they are stable and likely to remain or transient and likely to change. If a coach or program administrator can foresee the situation becoming a permanent trend, then he or she needs to adapt the program's operations as quickly as possible and proactively "get out in front" of circumstances. Another solution to unforeseen events is to have an insurance arrangement that can protect the program, facilities, and so on.

The anticipatory use of insurance (for all levels of operation, not just external risk) is imperative in today's coaching and program administration environment. The following is a checklist on insurance selection and strategies:

__ never assume you are covered; always check your insurance coverage,

__ check insurance policy at least twice a year for changes and to be sure you still have adequate coverage,

__ file a report as soon as it happens and submit a proper claim to the insurance company,

__ anyone involved in an activity outside their job jurisdiction or areas of control may seek to secure more personal liability coverage,

__ be aware of potential hazards and report them to the necessary people or groups,

__ secure short-term group accident policy to cover special activities when risk is foreseeable, analyze the liability aspect of your program or area and ensure adequate coverage in these areas,

__ have release forms; they may involve small liability problems because participants acknowledge the risk they are assuming and their voluntary participation in the program, but do not rely on them to solve any negligent actions,

__ have participants in events obtain medicals. (Sawyer & Smith, 1999, p. 337)

The determination on the level of insurance protection that the program will need once again relates to the coach/program administrator's own personal perspective of risk and liability as well as the requirements of athletic administration.

Administrative Tip

As with all contractual arrangements, "shop around" for the optimum insurance policy/contract. Remember to never sacrifice the quality of coverage for a better cost. Money saved now could be money paid later.

INCIDENT TREATMENT

No matter how safety cognizant a coach/program administrator is, no matter how reliable and pristine the facility and equipment, no matter what safety measures an athletic program has in place, accidents/injuries will happen in sports programs. While accident/injury prevention is an essential athletic program component, pre-established and tested accident/injury procedures are just as crucial.

As much as possible, the steps to be taken at the time of the incident should be identified in advance. . . . Staff members in leadership positions should be given training and directions to cover such points as:

- Providing immediate care of individuals involved in the incident, both injured and uninjured
- Notifying one's supervisor or designated person as soon as possible
- Securing outside assistance, if necessary
- Writing a report on the incident, documenting as many facets as possible
- If serious, reporting to appropriate persons outside
- Diverting or organizing the persons not involved in the incident into other activities
- Referring media and determining who speaks for the organization (Ball & Ball, 2000, pp. 176–177)

The efficiency and success of accident/injury procedures falls squarely on the coach/program administrator. A coach/program administrator must do the following:

- Lead by example. If he/she takes accident/injury prevention and procedures sincerely, all internal stakeholders will.
- Have a systemized accident/injury plan in place prior to any program contacts/activities (competitions, practice, travel, etc.).
- Strongly consider having a certified athletic trainer/medical staff in attendance (or nearby) at all program activities. If this is a logistically and/or financial impracticality, the athletic program should mandate that all staff members obtain Red Cross CPR and First Aid certifications.
- Require all program staff members and coaches "carry" an accident/injury procedural card (wallet size) with them at all times. This card will have step-by-step measures to be taken in a crisis as well as emergency phone numbers. In addition, cell phones must be kept with all staff members at all program activity times. It is strongly suggested that pre-programmed emergency phone numbers be inputted into all staff cell phones.
- Keep athletic administration notified at all times of the programs schedule and activities.

- Get pre-approval from athletic administration and medical staff on all accident/injury procedures.

OTHER SAFETY AND RISK MANAGEMENT CONSIDERATIONS

The following are subsequent preventative measures (proactive) to minimize an athletic program's risk and liability.

- Cognitively examine contingencies and unforeseen possibilities . . . all scenarios necessitate some type of safety plan.
- Have all staff and coaches safety trained for sports-identifiable contingencies. Stress staff attendance in formal certifications and sanctioned training seminars.
- Not only should the athletic program conduct medical exams during the pre-season, but throughout competitive season as well. It is also recommended that staff and coaches obtain medical examinations.
- Know where medical/training staff is at all times throughout program activities . . . minutes can be decisive in minimizing long-term ramifications of accidents/injuries.
- In no way consent to non-approved individuals participating in any of the program's activities.
- Training and conditioning equipment must have the comprehensive endorsement of the medical/training staff.
- Construct an all-encompassing safety procedural manual and circulate it to all internal stakeholders.
- Be adamant on the appropriate use of all program equipment. Additionally, under no circumstances improvise with equipment or use personally devised contraptions.
- All external weather considerations must outweigh athletic program events and proceedings.
- Stay trained in the most recent sports-specialized exercise and teaching techniques.
- On no account forgo game management security . . . have security personnel inspect competitive facilities for fan/athlete contact and exchanges. Furthermore, do not assume game management security at other locations/venues. Any concerns as a visiting athletic program should be brought to the competition's administration directly.
- Never sacrifice warm-up time for the program's athletes . . . the risk and endangerment to athletes is exponentially increased in these instances.
- Always avoid "rushing" athletes back from injuries (no matter how important they are to the success of the program) . . . follow all medical/training staff counsel.

- At no time should a coach/program administrator miscalculate the significance of locker room maintenance and sanitation. Establish a timetable for cleaning and maintenance prior to all program operations.
- Analyze the athletic program's sports-exclusive health hazards. Do research on what are some emblematic sports-specific issues.
- Most accidents/injuries arise from personal inattention and carelessness . . . make staff members and athletes aware of this.
- Have health management programs (physical conditioning, dieticians, personal counseling, etc.) accessible to all athletes and staff members.

It is important to reiterate that athletic program safety and risk management is an all-inclusive concept. All program facets (from locker rooms, game management and security, facilities and equipment, personnel interactions, etc.) are all areas of program concern. A beneficial motto to live by in athletic program risk management is to "expect the unexpected."

SUMMARY

One of the central objectives of this book is to enable the reader to become a critical thinker in the area of sports administration. No topic exemplifies this underlying premise as much as risk management. Coaches and program managers' core concentration must be a philosophy of athlete and program safety. Athlete safety can be maintained through monitoring risks to facilities, equipment, and personnel. Program safety is maintained through the committed monitoring of contractual agreements and the regulation of external risks through insurance. No matter what theme of risk administration a coach accentuates, he or she must be as thorough and detail-oriented as possible. Additionally, a coach or program administrator needs to enlist others in the process of risk management. The better the collective input, the better the potential hazards can be managed.

KEY TERMS	
risk management	consideration
litigation	contractual capacity
gross negligence	legality
facility risks	genuineness of assent
equipment risks	contractual form
premise liability	external risks
personnel risks	insurance
contract-related risks	incident treatment
agreement	

Review and Discussion Questions

1. What are the four categories of risk management that affect athletic programs?

2. When examining an operational facility and its equipment (safety walk-through), what questions should a coach or program administrator ask?

3. When discussing personnel risks, what are some fundamental obstacles facing coaches and program administrators?

4. What are the requirements for a contract?

5. In strategizing for external risks, what must a coach or program administrator do to manage the external circumstances?

6. List the elements in selecting an insurance strategy.

7. In incident treatments, what are the major concerns for coaches and program administrators?

8. List some of the other safety and risk management considerations of which a coach or program administrator need to be aware.

CHAPTER

Strategic Management and Coaching

CHAPTER OUTLINE

- To introduce and define the progressive business science of strategic management
- To delineate the concepts of centralized and decentralized management as to their effects on strategic development and implementation
- To expound on managerial decision making
- To present the strategic management process
- To dissect the business concept of S.W.O.T. analysis
- To discuss the purpose of key success factor identification and analysis
- To analyze the Five Forces Model of Competitive Analysis as it relates to coaching and program administration
- To consider the internal Generic Building Blocks of Competitive Advantage as they relate to athletic programs
- To familiarize the reader with the strategic concepts of differentiation, low cost, and focus/niche strategies
- To elucidate the factors for successful strategic implementation
- To provide an overview of strategic corrections and adjustments
- To offer other generic strategic management concepts that can be utilized by coaches and program administrators

INTRODUCTION

The foundations of management discussed in Chapters 1–5 (Planning, Organizing, Human Resource Management, Leadership, and Control) are the primary building blocks of a solid business and athletic program. Strategic management, the next level beyond these indispensable functions, deals strictly with competitive positioning, critical operational analysis, and maximizing the athletic program's internal resources and capabilities. This chapter elaborates on some of the predominant strategic management business concepts as they pertain to coaching and athletic program administration.

STRATEGIC MANAGEMENT DEFINED

There are numerous interrelated interpretations of the business science of strategic management. The following definitions encompass the essential nature of strategic management:

> In being a strategic leader rather than manager, the high-value manager brings to his or her group the vision and values of the organization as a whole, shares them with the group, and directs a more focused effort to achieve his or her corporation's strategic intent. (Stone & Sachs, 1995, p. 35)

Administrative Tip

Strategic management, more than any other business function, is connected with independent and critical thought. Most decisions that one makes as a coach/program administrator involve the replication of a previous decision. Strategic management is more in line with a creative thought process. Recognize those decisions that are "no brainers" and those that take strategic reflection.

Strategic management is the way in which organizations identify and pursue the activities that make up their overall purpose. Rather than being concerned with the day-to-day operational decisions, it is designed to provide the plan which successfully unifies all of the organization's activity . . . strategic management also involves matching these activities to the resource capability of the organization, and making plans to adjust the resource capability to meet anticipated changes in activity. (Furze & Gale, 1996, p. 377)

Strategy is a deliberate search for a plan of action that will develop a business's competitive advantage and compound it . . . competitive advantage is found in differences . . . the differences between you and your competitors are the basis of your advantage. (Henderson, 1989, pp. 139–143)

From these explanations, one can understand that strategic management is the competent utilization of an athletic program's assets (whether tangible resources such as cash and facilities or intangible capabilities such as staff skills and knowledge), which leads the program to sustaining, and even increasing, its competitive strength and position. In the simplest terms, strategic management deals with how one can compete with and (hopefully) surpass the competition.

It is important to note that strategic management is a mindset as much as it is a tangible process. Coaches/program administrators must do the following:

- Actively search for all possible alternatives to athletic program situations. Coaches and program administrators must abandon rigid managerial thinking for flexible strategic assessments.
- See all possible ramifications of actions/decisions as well as understand the cascading effect of those actions/decisions throughout the athletic program.
- Concentrate their strategic thinking on long-term program goals rather than getting inundated in day-to-day minutia.
- Dynamically identify all facets of the athletic program's direct and indirect competition. Knowing the competitive environment is a crucial component in establishing a competitive advantage over it.
- Actively take every opportunity to learn about their particular sports as well as administrative methodologies.
- Steer clear of assumptions and become skilled at conducting sports-particular research. Research, in turn, will provide hard data to assist in making challenging strategic judgments.
- Enlist the entire operational staff in the strategic construction process.
- Confront all athletic program challenges as strategic opportunities rather than operational threats.

CENTRALIZED MANAGEMENT, DECENTRALIZED MANAGEMENT, AND EMPOWERMENT

Centralized, decentralized, and empowerment are three managerial concepts that have a profound affect on athletic program strategies. They can best be described by the following:

> Centralized: Little authority is delegated to lower levels of management.
>
> Decentralized: A great deal of authority is delegated to lower levels of management.
>
> Empowerment: Form of decentralization in which subordinates have the authority to make decisions.
>
> An organization is never totally centralized or totally decentralized; rather, it falls along a continuum ranging from highly centralized to highly decentralized. (Rue & Byars, 2007, p. 193)

Each managerial position has salient strategic implications for coaches and athletic program administrators.

Centralized management (that encompasses tactics, structure, and philosophy), in which a coach/program administrator retains a greater part of the athletic program's power to construct strategic decisions, has the advantage of a clear single, unambiguous vision. Decisions are definitively created by a coach/program administrator and dictated directly to the program's staff. The apparent disadvantages in centralized management lie in its inability to get subordinates vested in the program. Without a "personal stake" in the future of the athletic program, staff members can become disenfranchised and detached from strategic goal achievement. Additionally, because centralized management is a top-down attitude, coaches and program administrators could be predisposed to become autocratic micromanagers.

An athletic program with a decentralized management/structure/philosophy enlists the staff to energetically participate in the strategic process. True decentralization is not a symbolic gesture but one where the staff has legitimate authority to make program decisions that can have considerable strategic impact. Does this mean that a coach/program administrator should abandon jurisdiction over strategic decision making? No. It does underscore a cooperative strategic relationship with employees and management.

The ultimate goal of a decentralized management structure is for employees to have complete empowerment. Empowered employees are sanctioned to make decisions autonomously. In other words, the employees are given legitimate and complete control over making judgments but held accountable for those judgments. A noticeable benefit of decentralized empowerment is the utilization of the program's intellectual capital by soliciting input from a wide variety of people. Possible risks associated with decentralized empowerment relate to the difficulty of groups arriving at a strategic consensus and balancing how much empowerment the staff desires and can handle.

MANAGERIAL DECISION-MAKING PROCESS

While most managerial decisions are routine in nature, strategic decision making is a contemplative process that can have enormous future consequences to an athletic program. The strategic managerial decision-making process is made up of a seven-stage cycle. The seven stages are as follows:

1. Define the problem
2. Diagnose the problem
3. Develop alternatives
4. Consider consequences
5. Evaluate alternatives
6. Select action strategy
7. Implement the strategy (Hoy & Tarter, 1995, p. 142)

There are some distinct applications from this process that a coach/program administrator can utilize.

In the strategic decision-making process delineated above, a coach/program administrator can not overemphasize the significance of the first stage—define the problem. Since strategic management and decision making is future oriented, sometimes foreseeing a potential problem/issue/opportunity/threat can be exceptionally difficult. The true danger in this process lies with impending athletic program components that are unpredictable and uncertain. However, if a coach/program administrator can envision the future direction of his/her sport, he/she can strategize action plans to confront and make the most of that future.

Another critical stage in the strategic decision-making process is stage four—consider the consequences. Every strategic alternative developed by a coach/program administrator and his/her staff will have program implications (either single-issue ramifications or a cascading number of consequences). A beneficial technique for isolating these possible consequences is to list all of the future alternatives to the athletic program's strategic problems/issues/opportunities/threats, then bullet or sequentially number each prospective scenario from each alternative. The strength of this procedure is it provides a tangible "road map" to evaluate alternatives (stage five).

After the evaluation and selection of a strategy, it must be competently implemented (stage seven). A managerial maxim to live by is, "A strategy is only as good as its execution." In other words, a coach/program administrator and his/her staff might have correctly identified and diagnosed the future problem/issue/opportunity/threat, developed sound alternatives, considered the consequences of each alternative, and selected the correct one, but if the strategy implementation is performed incorrectly, the future strategic problem/issue/opportunity/threat will be lost.

STRATEGIC MANAGEMENT FORMULATION

In his 1994 manuscript *The Rise and Fall of Strategic Planning*, Mintzberg designs a model of the strategic management planning process. The following is a basic presentation of his work.

1. Internal Appraisal—Strengths & Weaknesses of Organization
2. External Appraisal—Threats & Opportunities in Environment
3. Key Success Factors
4. Distinctive Competencies
5. Creation of Strategy
6. Social Responsibility—Managerial Values
7. Evaluation and Choice of Strategy
8. Implementation of Strategy (Mintzberg, 1994, pp. 107–114)

This progressive representation goes from where the program is to where the program needs to be. The first step is to assess the prevailing situation from an internal and external perspective. Internally, one needs to perform a strength and weakness investigation. Very similar to the pro and con assessment, an internal strength and weakness evaluation looks critically at the athletic program's operations. The key word is "critically." Contemplate every component of the athletic program and consider whether it is a strength (operational asset) or a weakness (operational liability). It is advisable to start the strength/weakness appraisal process by prioritizing the factors of the program's operation from most crucial to least consequential. Hopefully, when the evaluation is completed, the most notable and significant operational elements will be predominantly considered strengths. A coach/program administrator's philosophy in converting the internal analysis to strategizing should be to always maximize strengths and minimize weaknesses (or even convert the weaknesses to strengths).

The second step in exploring where the program is to where it needs and desires to be is an external analysis or an opportunity/threat study. This process essentially audits all of the external environmental factors that affect the program's operation to determine if they are possibilities for growth and competitive advantage or threats to the program. Once again, prioritize the environmental elements from the most significant to the least notable. If one is fortunate, opportunities will outweigh threats. A coach's philosophy in this external analysis should be to exploit opportunities and fortify the program against threats.

To strategize from the strengths/weakness and opportunities/threats stage (also known as SWOT analysis) is straightforward logic. The best-case scenario is that the athletic program has a distinct strength that can be used to

Administrative Tip

Strategic formulation is proactive management rather than reactive crisis managing. While reactive management conditions can not be totally eradicated, constructing proactive strategies can curtail them. Inertia in strategic thinking can lead to the downfall of the program.

exploit an external opportunity. At the other end of the spectrum, the program might have a prominent weakness that coincides with an external threat. As the program administrator, one's obligation is to look at each external element as they relate to the internal operational strengths/weaknesses.

There are four primary scenarios.

Strength——————Opportunity

Take advantage of one's supremacy of the situation and strategize the exploitation of the opportunity.

Strength——————Threat

In this proposition, the program should be able to counteract this distinctive danger.

Weakness——————Opportunity

This condition needs a resolution. Does the program bolster the weakness to take advantage of the circumstance or does it pass on the opportunity? Remember, this predicament is potentially dangerous. If the program passes on the opportunity and the program's competition takes advantage of the contingency, it might then become a distinct threat.

Weakness——————Threat

This condition typically requires a prompt action to be taken. The more hazardous and powerful the threat, the more immediate and decisive is the need to respond to it.

Key success factors for athletic programs are current and future operational components that are universally critical for all athletic programs in a particular sport. For example, it is this textbook's fundamental premise that all coaches/program administrators (any level and any sport) need to have strong administrative capabilities. Administrative proficiency would be a universal key success factor for all athletic programs. A coach/program administrator and his/her staff should, through empirical observations and quantitative research, define all of the key success factors for their unique sport. Once the sport's key success factors have been clarified, a coach/program administrator and staff need to do the following:

- Evaluate how the athletic program and key success factors match up. Is the athletic program stronger, weaker, or at status quo with the sport's key success factors? The athletic program's standing in these areas will have consequential effects on current and future strategic focus.
- Compare how the athletic program's competition is doing in relation to the sport-wide key success factors.
- Analyze current key success factors for their future importance (or depreciating importance).

Administrative Tip

Another way to conceptualize SWOT analysis is to maximize the program's internal strengths, minimize the program's internal weaknesses, exploit the program's external opportunities, and defend against the program's external threats.

- Project possible future driving forces in the sport and lay the strategic groundwork on how to confront them. Driving forces can range from sport improvement (training techniques, administrative methods, game management, etc.), public perceptions of the sport and participating athletes, expansion or contraction of the sports popularity, levels of the sport's governing body regulatory authority, etc.

At this point, the program administrator needs to put together the program's strategies based on the prior analysis. When constructing them, follow these simple rules:

1. Strategy formulation should be a controlled, conscious process of thought.
2. Responsibility for the process rests with the chief executive.
3. Strategy formulation should be simple and informal.
4. Strategies should come out of the design process.
5. Strategies should be explicit and, if possible, articulated.
6. Strategies should be unique.
7. Only when strategies are fully formulated, should they be implemented. (Mintzberg, 1994, pp. 107–114)

Two more rules that need to be briefly discussed are *social responsibilities* and *manager values*. After a strategy is formulated, but preceding its implementation, a coach or program administrator needs to question it from an ethical and social context as well as from his or her own inner values and the philosophical values of the program. Both of these issues will be discussed in more detail in Chapter 13, *Ethics and Coaching*.

FIVE FORCE MODEL

As one of the country's foremost theorists in strategic management, Porter has numerous models and theories in contemporary administration and management. One of his most universally applicable models is the Five Force Model, which probes an industry's five principal external components.

Forces Governing Competition in an Industry/Five Force Model

- Threat of new entrants
- Bargaining power of suppliers
- Threat of substitute products or services
- Bargaining power of customers
- The industry: Jockeying for position among current competition (Porter, 1998, p. 22)

As previously stated, the Five Forces Model is a theoretical representation that delves into the five foremost external components in an industry. In the case of this textbook, the industry is athletics. In order to adapt this concept, coaches/program administrators must take the comprehensive categories given by Porter and focus them on their particular athletic programs.

Additionally, before elaborating on each individual factor of the model, it must be emphatically stated that the more potent and strong (or more influential power) a component has on operations, the more of a danger it is to the program. Conversely, the weaker (or more influence one has on the force), the more possibility for opportunities.

Power of Suppliers

As the model is examined, the first external segment that needs to be analyzed is the bargaining power of suppliers. Clearly stated, suppliers furnish the inputs for an organization's outputs. In fashioning this to athletic programs, the output is the team's performance. What are the inputs to produce that output? Staff, athletes, specialized equipment, etc. To illustrate, for coaches and program administrators the most significant input to produce the athletic program's output must be accomplished, quality athletes. From there, ask some of these elementary questions:

- Who provides these athletes?
- Do they control the working association or does the program's personnel?
- Do coaches need to pursue them or do they approach the coaches?

In almost every sport, athletic programs are divided into strata or tiers. If one's program is classified as a tier one program (which has a high profile and a commanding history of achievement and exposure), the coach or program administrator can characteristically dominate the relationship with the suppliers of the program's athletes. The coach will have, in most cases, the opportunity to "pick and choose" from the elite feeder programs and suppliers. However, if one's athletic program is a lower tier (not as high profile, funding, etc.), dealing with the suppliers of athletes takes on an altogether different viewpoint. Analyze all of the inputs into the program from this vantage and formulate the input strategies from there.

Back to the example above: If the program is not an upper-tiered program, what strategies can one seize to obtain the elite athlete? What strengths can be emphasized and weaknesses minimized to secure the talent? The less power, the more creatively one needs to strategize.

Bargaining Power of Buyers

As program administrators, this exterior determinant relates to funding. Funding from ticket sales or donations are two such dominant components. Along the same thoughts as the prior example, if the program is a tier one level program that has elite athletes and a solid track record, in most cases, ticket sales or fundraising activities are a distinct opportunity. Once again, if the program is a lower strata program, finding supporters and fans could be a consequential program threat. One's method of support procurement would in most cases need to be inventive and continuous.

Substitutes

The concept of substitutes relates to the convenience and accessibility of other products that the consumer can use instead of the organization's product. In our situation of athletics, fan support of the program is in direct relationship to the consumer of a business product. For example, if one's athletic program and team is located in a region where there are a limited number of other sports programs or athletic events, then direct substitutes would be less of a threat to the program's fan base. One the other hand, if one's program is located in an area with abundant substitute athletic programs and events, fan support (as well as program publicity and interest) would be a more tenuous issue. Additionally, if the athletic program is located inside an overall athletic department (one of several teams inside an academic institution), then internal substitutes are also an issue a coach would need to address for funding, staff, and fan endorsement.

Another area that was previously discussed that might preoccupy a coach is the acquisition of athletes. If recruited talent has an option of participating in other sports instead of the program's sport, this is an input substitute that will need a strategic response. To distinguish all of the possible substitutes to the program, list all of the principal components of the program, prioritize those elements, and precisely examine each for the danger of substitutes. The more meaningful and significant the ingredient of the program, the more the coach or program administrator will need specific actions to minimize the effects of any possible substitutes.

Rivalry among Existing Firms and Programs

This classification is the most discernible and tangible of the Five Forces Model. The athletic program's immediate competition is the one strategic element of which coaches tend to be mindful. The program's output and results are a direct reflection of its competitor's output and results. The stronger each of the program's direct competitors, the more of a threat those competitor are. The same comparable format for strategizing can be utilized in this category. List all of the program's legitimate competitors, prioritize them by competitive potency, and develop strategies to competitively perform against each. Additionally, do an internal strength/weakness appraisal of each competitor to form a more effective strategy.

New Entrants

The final broad segment in Porter's concept that can be adapted to athletic programs is the examination of potential new competitors entering the external environment. In other words, who has the capability to penetrate the competitive environment and what do they offer? New entrants can be start-up athletic programs with no prior history or they can be from established organizations trying to expand into different arenas. By far, this category is the most difficult to predict. Suppliers, buyers, competitive rivalry, and substitutes are already existing components that are tangible in nature and grounded in reality. New entrants require more guesswork and anticipation because of uncertainty.

In investigating this classification of the model, one needs to comprehend the concept of *barriers to entry*. The higher the barriers the more difficult it would be for a new competitor to penetrate the program's competitive environment. The opposite is also true. The lower the barriers, the more of a danger new entrants can be to the program. What are some of the barriers that sports programs might encounter? First and foremost is the financial obligation to break into the competitive environment. Another barrier could be the governing bodies' license, charter, or organizational restrictions and regulations. For example, the barriers to entry into the National Football League are uncommonly high. The NFL has exorbitant financial as well as regulatory barriers. On the other hand, an individual who might want to establish a youth sports program would encounter low barriers, such as minimal restrictions from a governing body and moderate financial commitment. To strategically dissect this section of the model, define all of the barriers to entry, then recognize who could fulfill these requirements, then finally determine if they will enter the program's competitive environment.

GENERIC BUILDING BLOCKS OF COMPETITIVE ADVANTAGE

The second consequential theory that can be related to the strategic management of athletic programs is the Generic Building Blocks of Competitive Advantage. The Generic Building Blocks of Competitive Advantage examines an organization's internal operations. The following are the components of the model:

1. Superior Quality
2. Superior Efficiency
3. Superior Customer Responsiveness
4. Superior Innovation
5. Competitive Advantage (Low Cost, Differentiation, Focus/Niche)

(Hill & Jones, 2004, p. 87)

While the Five Forces Model dealt with exploring outside environmental factors for opportunities and threats, this model investigates an organization's internal components and philosophies as they coincide with assessing its strengths and weaknesses. The position a program takes—both philosophically and in substantive actions toward the four major elements of superior quality, superior innovation, superior efficiency, and superior customer responsiveness—all lead to an overall strategic game plan for a competitive advantage (low cost, differentiation, focus/niche).

In the simplest terms, how one operates internally will furnish one with his or her strategies to compete externally. It should be emphasized that a coach/program administrator must predetermine the athletic program's philosophical base toward the four generic building blocks before he/she can structure and implement its discernible goals, strategies, and actions.

Superior Efficiency

The concept of efficiency deals strictly with the transformation of a program's inputs to produce a program's outputs. In analyzing this classification, ask, "What are our inputs/resources and how are we using our capabilities and expertise to make the best product (output)?" Acutely probe each resource and observe them from a strength/weakness standpoint to see how well they are managed. There is a universal business statement that encompasses the essence of efficiency: the less input used to produce a high quality output, the more efficient the program. Remember, maximize the program's inputs but never sacrifice high quality.

Superior Quality

Quality is a complicated concept that has quantitative, numerical elements as well as qualitative, subjective aspects. It is also an abstraction that is determined introspectively by the coaching staff in addition to externally by the program's customers. In business, quantitative quality measurements can simply coincide with the number of units being sold or the number of reworks being returned. In athletic programs, the fundamental measure of quality is wins-losses. However, in both the realms of business and athletics, quality also has people's sentiments and convictions associated with it. Both go hand-in-hand. How people subjectively feel about a product is typically linked to the quantity sold. Who determines the level of quality the program generates? It will ultimately be the people who use the product and fund the program. They will tell all stakeholders in no uncertain terms if the quality is good or not by their support. Be proactive. Ask customers, fans, and athletic administration what level of quality they desire and expect. The prevailing business statement that describes quality is, "Overwhelm the customer with quality." This, in turn, will increase the program's support and funding as well as determine who wants to be involved in the program.

Superior Customer Responsiveness

This category of the Generic Building Blocks of Competitive Advantage model can be summed up once again with the succinct, lucid statement, "The customer is everything." No matter what business or program, this declaration of customer satisfaction first and foremost should be the substructure of every aspect of the organization. Forgetting it will cause almost inescapable failure. If one does not satisfy the needs of customers and supporters, the competition most unquestionably will. One must ask the following questions:

- Who are our customers?
- Who are our supporters?
- What do they want and what do they require?
- Do our planned goals, strategies, and actions always provide customers and supporters with the greatest possible output and the highest conceivable satisfaction?
- How do they want our output and performance?
- When do they want it?
- Where do they want it?
- Why are they supporters of our program?
- Is customer satisfaction accomplished through providing the highest quality product? Is there an unconditional commitment to quality throughout our organization?
- Does the competition supply more customer and supporter satisfaction?
- What does the competition do that we have the capability of imitating to increase supporter satisfaction?

The list of questions is extensive.

Superior Innovation

In today's business world, innovation characteristically relates to technological advancements in improving the production process or the actual product itself. This can be fashioned to athletic programs by correlating innovation in the production process to new, internal training techniques and innovation in the product/output to new performance tactics. Does one's sport lend itself to supplementary and innovative training techniques? Is the program's sport one that is evolving? Is the sport conducive or receptive to new-fashioned and enhanced performance tactics? The strength/weakness evaluation of superior innovation relates to the coaching staff's ability to learn and create.

Competitive Strategic Philosophy

After the four internal components of superior quality, efficiency, innovation, and customer satisfaction are scrutinized, the model then stresses that from a strength/weakness evaluation in each category, one must choose a competitive strategy (or competitive philosophy) from the following three choices: low cost, differentiation or focus/niche.

Low Cost
A low cost strategy is when "managers try to gain a competitive advantage by focusing the energy of all the organization's departments or functions on driving the organization's cost down below the cost of its rival" (Jones &

George, 2004, p. 195). The foundation of this strategy's success relates to the concept of efficiency. As discussed previously, efficiency is the business tactic of using fewer inputs to create a quality output. The fewer inputs used equates to cost savings. With new technological advancements and understanding exactly what the customer/supporter wants, a program can utilize this strategy as its foundation. The danger lies in the obsessive competitive need to drive costs down. If quality and features are sacrificed (that the athletic program supporter wants), then the operational philosophy will damage the program.

Differentiation

A differentiation strategy is defined as "distinguishing an organization's products from the products of competitors in dimensions such as product design, quality, or after-sales service" (Jones & George, 2004, p. 196). The following figure illustrates the numerous differentiation dimensions in which a business (athletic program) can separate itself from its competition.

Quality	Functionality	Reliability	Innovation
Versatility	Marketing	Service	Size
Speed	Less Defects	Distribution	Appearance
100% Guarantee	Prestige	Selection	Durability
Brochures	Program Literature	Ambience	Personnel
Research and Development			Customer Satisfaction

Figure 1. **Factors for Differentiation**

While some of these differentiation elements might not apply to athletic programs (e.g., 100% guarantee), most can be modified from their business application to an athletic program concentration. The decisive choice on which specific differentiation factors to select is derived directly from what the customers/supporters desire. Simply put, what the athletic program supporter wants, a coach/program administrator needs to provide.

Focus/Niche Strategy

The focus/niche strategy is made up of two possible scenarios—focus low-cost and focus differentiation. They are defined by the following:

Focused low-cost strategy—Serving only one segment of the overall market and being the low-cost organization serving that segment.

Focused differentiation strategy—Serving only one segment of the overall market and trying to be the most differentiated organization serving that segment. (Jones & George, 2004, p. 196)

Due to their lack of resources and capabilities, most small athletic programs will employ a focus or niche strategy (either low-cost or differentiated). The key to utilizing this strategic philosophy is to choose a single niche based on future potential as well as current market size. The benefits are if the niche grows as projected, the athletic program will have a formidable foothold in the niche and will be unmistakably identified with it. The possible dangers associated with this strategic attitude are that the niche could "close" quickly, leaving the program with no segmentation base, or that a major competitor can come in and use its resource advantages to gain control of the niche.

Once again, modifying these three overall philosophical strategies to athletic programs is easy. Athletic programs that have strengths in relation to their uniqueness of quality, innovation, efficiency, or customer satisfaction can develop and implement a differentiation strategy. In other words, sell the program to all conceivable supporters on distinctiveness and superiority over the competition. Try to equate unrivaled strengths with the factors that electrify supporters. On the other hand, if after the analysis of the four internal elements, one concludes that the athletic program is, in general, non-distinctive and can do little (at this time) to truly segregate itself from its competition, a low-cost strategy of underselling the competition could be embraced to generate support and funding. The final strategy of focus-niche essentially takes the program's specialized strengths and focuses them on a limited target market category for support. If the program's target market group of supporters has potential for growth, this strategy is exceptional for smaller and emerging programs.

In their 2001 text *Strategic Management: An Integrated Approach,* Hill and Jones discuss the jeopardy of being "stuck in the middle" of one of these three strategies. The following is an extrapolation of their concerns.

> Each generic strategy requires a company to make a consistent choice in establishing a competitive advantage . . . [A] company must achieve a fit among one of the three possible strategies and must maintain its commitment to it. (Hill & Jones, 2001, p. 217)

In other words, as the athletic administrator, one must match the operations with one of the three possible strategic scenarios and stick primarily with that approach. Jumping from strategy to strategy negatively affects internal focus as well as conveys an outwardly confused identity. This does not mean that a coach or program administrator should retain the chosen strategy after there have been internal or external changes. By all means, choose the most effectual strategy for the circumstances (and change the operating situation). However, once one makes that determination, be resolute and diligent in its application.

Implementation

> means that the manager must act through others to execute strategy. The manager communicates the strategy to the members of the organization. The manager exercises leadership to guide the company's employees and motivates employees to cooperate with each other and to act in the interest of the company. . . . Implementation brings strategy to life, but implementation can not be effective without good strategy. (Spulber, 2004, p. 7)

Some business managers believe that strategy execution/implementation is more demanding than strategic planning. While other managers think that if the strategic plan is assembled accurately, strategy implementation should be straightforward and trouble-free. In either case, the coach/program administrator must get the strategy from "paper to application."

There are eight managerial components that are essential for strategy execution.

1. Building an organization with competencies, capabilities, and resource strengths to execute strategy successfully.
2. Marshalling sufficient money and people behind the drive for strategy execution.
3. Instituting policies and procedures that facilitate rather than impede strategy execution.
4. Adopting best practices and pushing for continuous improvement in how value chain activities are performed.
5. Installing information and operating systems that enable company personnel to carry out their strategic roles proficiently.
6. Tying rewards directly to the achievement of strategic and financial targets and to good strategy execution.
7. Shaping the work environment and corporate culture to fit the strategy.
8. Exercising strong leadership to drive execution forward, keep improving on the details of execution, and achieve operating excellence as rapidly as feasible. (Thompson, Strickland, & Gamble, 2007, p. 385)

From these eight elements, the following strategic inferences for athletic programs can be derived.

- People—An athletic program's most indispensable resource is its people. For strategy execution, they must be cultivated and treated as a significant investment.
- Capital—As a coach/program administrator, a primary function is being a resource allocator. Determining which strategies get which

internal resources (money, people, supplies, etc.) is essential in an athletic program's long term strategic success.

- Rules and regulations—For consistency in strategy execution, an athletic program will need tangible regulations and processes in place. Simply stated, established systems equate to better strategy execution.
- Avoiding complacency—To have winning strategies in which implementation improves the athletic program, a coach/program administrator and his/her staff must constantly look "outside the box" and strive for superior ways to do program activities.
- Technology—To obtain a strategic advantage, as well as to assist in strategy implementation, an athletic program needs to embrace technological advancements. A program that is deficient in technology is jeopardizing the future.
- Correct compensation—Strategic implementation can be facilitated (and accelerated) through extrinsic incentive systems. While it is necessary to have intrinsically motivated staff members, extrinsic incentive programs are always useful motivators. "The purpose of a strategic compensation plan is to establish a very careful balance between motivating ordinary operating performance and pushing strategic objectives" (Fogg, 1999, p.371).
- Athletic program environment—The atmosphere in an athletic program overtly influences strategy execution. A program environment that accentuates internal values such as fairness, commitment to excellence, and friendliness/openness has a greater likelihood for successful strategy implementation.
- Managerial leadership style—A coach/program administrator's approach to leading his/her program is a fundamental element in long- and short-term strategic implementation. A situational approach, which is the most adaptable and elastic, is typically the ideal leadership tactic to accomplish strategies.

CORRECTION AND ADJUSTMENTS TO STRATEGY

The key to making any strategic modification is investigation and analysis. A coach/program administrator with his/her staff will need to first discover what the strategy's inadequacies are, then plan the corrective actions to repair the strategy. Within most athletic programs, strategy correction and adjustment is a continuous practice rather than a one time quick fix. The attitude needs to be, "As times change, so will strategies."

The "real world" difficulty in making modifications and improvements (or even abandonment) to strategies is when a program has committed a vast amount of time and energy in developing and implementing a strategy that simply is not working. While corrections/adjustment can be simple fine-tuning, abandonment of a long established and financed strategy can be an extensive program alteration. The one danger in this scenario is when a coach/program administrator continues to finance a strategy that is long past its usefulness because of his/her emotional ties to that strategy.

OTHER STRATEGIC MANAGEMENT CONCEPTS AND TERMINOLOGY

The subsequent concepts are general strategic management representations that need an abbreviated explanation. These concepts are in no special order or priority.

Strategic Alliances

> A strategic alliance is an organizational relationship that links two or more independent business entities in some common endeavor. Although it involves a form of partnering and cooperation between businesses, technically a strategic alliance is not a legal form of organization, as it doesn't affect the independent legal status of the participating business partners. It is a way in which firms can improve their individual effectiveness by sharing certain resources. (Longenecker, Moore, & Petty, 2003, p. 255)

The keys to a good strategic alliance with an outside organization is that it adds pertinent value to the athletic program, it has the athletic program supporters in mind, it can give the program a distinct competitive edge over other sports programs, and both organizations involved in the alliance experience a reciprocal strategic gain. Major athletic programs (both professional and collegiate) have seen tremendous strategic alliances over the past 20 years with apparel manufactures, beverage companies, telecommunication conglomerates, and media outlets. The success of these alliances has trickled down into smaller athletic program as well.

Groupthink

The designation groupthink is "pressure within the group toward conformity/concurrence in thinking and action without appraising or seeing other, more realistic/appropriate alternatives" (Eitington, 1997, p. 645). As a strategic manager, a coach/program administrator must balance the need for group cohesion with the avoidance of groupthink. Developing an atmosphere of cooperation with incisive, constructive input is the fundamental strategic goal.

Contingency Planning

Contingency planning is a deliberate attempt to develop other strategies to be ready for potential circumstances. Also known as *scenario planning*, this strategic management technique looks at conceivable and impending changes, and attempts to prepare the organization for them. All conceivable future circumstances need to be planned for. For example, even if one planned course of action is estimated at 60% certainty, while another is only 40% likely, the second would warrant almost as much serious consideration as the first. However, if there is a potential likelihood of a future event/scenario with only a 10% chance of success, then having a preliminary plan would be more appropriate.

Strategic Groups

Strategic groups within an industry (in this case athletics) are competitors that are most alike in the marketing mix factors of product, price, place, and promotion. With this denotation, sports programs must define their closest competitors (e.g., within the same division, conference, etc.) and develop front-line competitive strategies to challenge them first before expanding into other competitive environments. In basic terms, the competitors in the athletic program's strategic group must be strategically prioritized over other sports programs.

Strategic Benchmarking

Benchmarking is observing other successful programs to emulate their techniques, capabilities, resources, and all other aspects that make them successful.

> Benchmarking is the detailed study of productivity, quality and value in different departments and activities in relation to performance elsewhere. The basic idea is to take or build up a database of relevant performance drawn up from looking at similar activities in other parts of the firm, and in other firms, and compare the performance of the unit being reviewed with the range of experience elsewhere. There are three different techniques that can be used in benchmarking:
>
> 1. Best Demonstrated Practice (BDP) . . . is the comparison of performance by units within one firm.
> 2. Relative Cost Position (RCP): RPC analysis looks at each element of cost structure per dollar of sales in firm x, compared to the same thing in competitor y.
> 3. Best Related Practice is like BDP but takes the comparison into related (usually not competing) firms, where direct comparisons can often be made by co-cooperation between forms to collect and compare data. (Crainer, 1995, pp. 1089–1090)

In athletics, benchmarking can be within one's sport or from sport-to-sport. Could a volleyball coach benchmark a basketball program? Absolutely. While the physical sports are incongruous, features such as practice structure, scheduling, conditioning, recruiting tactics, summer camp facilitation, sponsorships, etc. can all be scrutinized for their crossover manipulation. Benchmarking is idea generation; any source can help breed strategic knowledge as long as the coach/program administrator is willing to look for it.

The Law of Diminishing Returns

The Law of Diminishing Returns states that after a point there is less and less return for more and more effort. In athletic programs, the classic example of this is the over training conundrum. The more one trains and puts effort into producing a superior output, the worse the performance. As a coach, one must gauge how much of a strategy is enough and when is too much.

Learning Curve and Staff/Athlete Retention

The interpretation of the learning curve relates to the more repetition and time an employee (in this case, staff or athlete) does a particular task, the more competent he or she will become. Eventually, the learning curve will bottom-out due to the unmistakable fact that humans can only go as physically fast as their bodies and capabilities allow. Strategically, employee retention directly relates to the costs associated with the learning curve. The more one can maintain and retain staff members and players, the more the program can profit from premium productivity. Every time a new staff member or athlete joins the program, productivity will drop until they get up to speed and produce at the level of proficient staff and athletes.

Outsourcing

Outsourcing is "the practice of hiring an individual or another company outside the organization to perform work" (Dubrin, 2003, p. 231). In other words, outsourcing is the process of subcontracting services, operational activities, and supplies that become an ingredient of the production process and/or final product. The questions to ask when considering outsourcing: Can this outsourcing organization or individual do it more inexpensively, faster, or better than us? Can the energy and time that we conserve with outsourcing provide the athletic program with a competitive advantage? The rationale behind outsourcing is to ensure that the program will not rely on outside entities for core functional activities that have a major impact on success and survival.

Strategic Management Information Systems

Information systems are

> systems for transforming raw data into information that can be used in decision making . . . IS must first determine what information is needed . . . gather the data and provide the technology

to convert data into desired information . . . control the flow of information so that it goes only to people who need it. (Griffin & Ebert, 2002, p. 471)

As discussed previously, computer technology has been a far-reaching informational element that has assisted coaches/program administrators in athletic program decision making over the past 25 years. Video capabilities, in-game statistics, administrative records, and internal and external communication have all been affected by technology information systems. Each coach/program administrator must examine his/her sport to acquire and develop applicable systems.

Strategic Diversification

If an athletic program has the resources and desire to expand, diversification can be a great strategic means to achieve that growth. It is a strong tactical option when an athletic program's current operations are sound, there is a surplus of program capital (both financial and intellectual), the diversification would add significant overall value to the program, and there is a market opportunity in the sport that fits well with the program's overall mission. Diversification strategies

> are used to expand firms' operations by adding markets, products, services, or stages of production to the existing business. The purpose of diversification is to allow the company to enter lines of business that are different from current operations. When the new venture is strategically related to the existing line of business, it is called concentric diversification. Conglomerate diversification occurs when there is no common thread of strategic fit or relationship between the new and old lines of business; the new and old businesses are unrelated. (Helms, 2000, p. 215)

The two types of diversification, related (concentric) and unrelated (conglomerate) diversification, are strategically opposite. Unrelated diversification is when a coach/program administrator has no concern with strategically matching his/her sports program with the new venture or product. An example would be if an athletic program would diversify into agriculture. There are no cross-business activities that are the same within the two divergent products/businesses. Related diversification would be when a coach/program administrator pursues program enlargement by diversifying operation into similar (or related) products/businesses. Athletic program-related diversification is when

- the same jobs and services as well as internal structure can be used for the long-standing program as well as the new endeavor;
- there is an interchangeability of personnel (both administrative and sports specific), athletic facilities and equipment, marketing and marketing communication, suppliers, technology, etc; and

- the customer/supporter profile and target market is similar (if not identical) for the foundational program and the diversified addition.

The traditional related diversification strategy for most athletic programs (both large and small) is instructional camps.

SUMMARY

The main functional goal of the business of strategic management is to provide a coach or program administrator with the tools to achieve a superior competitive advantage. In other words, for a coach to cultivate and maintain a viable, competitive advantage, he or she must consciously become a strategic futuristic thinker. The strategic determination process is systemized through theories such as SWOT analysis, the Five Force Model, and the Generic Building Blocks of Competitive Advantage. These concepts will not only delineate macro long-term organizational strategies, but will define day-to-day micro functional actions.

KEY TERMS

strategic management	customer responsiveness
centralized management	innovation
decentralized management	low cost
managerial decision making process	differentiation
SWOT analysis	niche/focus
internal analysis	competitive advantage
external analysis	strategic alliances
key success factors	groupthink
driving forces	contingency planning
Five Force Model	strategic groups
Generic Building Blocks of Competitive Advantage	strategic benchmarking
	law of diminishing returns
new entrants	learning curve
substitutes	outsourcing
buyers	strategic management information systems
suppliers	
rivalry	related diversification
quality	unrelated diversification
efficiency	

Review and Discussion Questions

1. For athletic programs and teams, what is strategic management?

2. What are some strategic "mind-set" factors a coach/program administrator must adopt?

3. Define centralized management. Define decentralized management. Define empowerment.

4. What are the seven stages in the managerial decision making process?

5. What are the four primary scenarios of a SWOT analysis?

6. What are key success factors?

7. What are the five components of the five forces model?

8. Define the bargaining power of suppliers and describe how we can adapt this definition to sports programs.

9. What are substitutes?

10. Describe the five forces model component of new entrants.

11. What are the internal components of the generic building blocks of competitive advantage?

12. What is superior efficiency?

13. What is the most important statement when discussing customer responsiveness and why is that assertion significant?

14. From the four internal components of the generic building blocks of competitive advantage (quality, efficiency, innovation, customer responsiveness), what three competitive strategies emerge? Describe each strategy.

15. What are the eight managerial components of strategy execution? What are the strategic inferences can be drawn from these eight elements?

16. What is the "real world" difficulty in correcting and adjusting strategies?

17. What are strategic alliances?

18. What is groupthink?

19. What is benchmarking?

20. Describe the conundrum of the law of diminishing returns.

21. What are the paramount questions to ask when considering outsourcing?

22. What is related and unrelated diversification?

CHAPTER 13

Ethics and Coaching

CHAPTER OUTLINE

CHAPTER

13

OBJECTIVES

- To isolate influences on ethics
- To describe the four personality elements that impact ethics
- To define moral, immoral, and amoral mangers
- To elucidate the ethical decision-making process
- To expound on the areas of ethical decisions in business management and athletic program administration
- To describe the four social and ethical choices available to a coach or program administrator
- To exhibit universal values and ethics in most organizations
- To outline an ethical program plan
- To delineate directives for writing individual ethical codes

INTRODUCTION

From the onset, it must be emphatically stated that this chapter is not written to lecture or to righteously pronounce what behaviors are right or wrong in a particular coaching or administrative situation. Additionally, this chapter is not designed to state how everyone should conform to certain professed norms of behavior. The purpose of this chapter is to lay the groundwork for understanding business ethics (and ethical behavior) as it relates to the professions of coaching and program administration. As one will see, business and personal ethics are extremely complex and subjective components in the lives of those in the profession.

INFLUENCES ON ETHICS

Ethics is a multidimensional concept that can be examined from an individual, organizational, or cultural perspective. The philosophical literature devoted to the subjects of ethics and values is staggering. However, for the purposes of this text, start by asking what factors influence ethical behavior and conscience. Dienhart, in his text *Business, Institutions, and Ethics*, examines individual influences on ethical behavior from certain personality traits.

> Low self-esteem is not generally associated with successful executives. Executives need confidence, intelligence, and moral strength to make difficult, possibly unpopular decisions. However, when these traits are not tempered with modesty, openness, and an accurate appraisal of talents, ethical problems can arise. In other words, if executive's theories about themselves are seriously flawed, they are courting disaster . . . several ways in which people's theories of themselves tend to get flawed . . . illusion of supe-

Administrative Tip

Decisions, no matter what program type, routine, strategic, ethical, have ramifications. The more ethics are involved, the more a coach/program administrator's resolutions will be scrutinized. In making decisions of an ethical nature, one must think through all the potential ramifications of one's actions.

riority, self-serving fairness bias, and overconfidence. (Dienhart, 2000, pp. 49–50)

In the text, *Ethics, the Heart of Leadership*, Ciulla looks at ethical behavior from leadership and relational interactions.

> Morality of leadership depends on the particulars of the relationship between people. It matters who the leaders and followers are and how well they understand and feel about themselves and each other. It depends on whether leaders and followers are honest and trustworthy, and most importantly what they do and what they value. (Ciulla, 2004, p. xix)

diMauro and Grant in *Ethics: Opposing Viewpoints* look at ethical influences from a societal standpoint.

> People are impelled to act ethically simply because others in society do so. When faced with difficult decisions, this theory postulates, people tend to make choices based on what others so in similar situations. (diMauro & Grant, 2006, p. 19)

Which of the ethical perspectives is correct? Simply put, because of the dynamic nature of the subject, they all are. From an individual ethical development point of view, nearly all ethical theorists proclaim that the personality elements of (1) family upbringing and interaction, (2) moral teachings, (3) individual life experiences, and (4) personal circumstances and environmental pressure are fundamental in an individual's ethical decision making. A key observation to note is that while each of these factors is more dominant in different life stages, they are all interrelated and continual throughout the life process. In an individual's formative years, family and peers are the most potent influences in developing an ethical foundation. During this period, most ethical judgments are supported, guided, and monitored by family members and friends. As one becomes more autonomous, personal life incidences and environments dominate one's ethical development. Finally, morals, which are either influenced by a particular profession, organization, or culture/subculture group, affect the choices and beliefs in what behavior should be adopted. Through these elements, everyone develops their own perception of reality. This is why introspective values and ethics vary enormously from individual to individual.

THE FOUR-STEP ETHICAL DECISION-MAKING PROCESS

Individuals go through a four-step process for each ethical decision that is made.

Step 1
Evaluate the decision from an ethical standpoint.

Step 2
Evaluate the decision from an ethical standpoint in context of moral principles.

Step 3

Establish moral intent.

Step 4

Engage in ethical behavior. (Hill & Jones 2001, p. 67)

> Step 1: This step basically asks the question, "Who will this decision effect?"
>
> Step 2: This step is the internal evaluation of a decision and situation. Simply, what internal factors will one reference to evaluate the decision and situation?
>
> Step 3: Moral intent is the evaluation step of looking at the surroundings (whether personal or professional) and assessing if it is ethical from other stakeholders' perspective. This is the step that relates to moral intent/philosophy of the program environment.
>
> Step 4: The final step is the action (or lack of action) step. Example questions such as, "Do I engage in the activity? Do I react to an ethical situation? What decision do I make?" are all made in this final step.

It should be noted that sometimes this four-step process is instantaneous. The more consequential the decision or situation, the more deliberation and time allotted. Additionally, the consideration of whether a situation/decision is consequential varies from person to person.

From an athletic professional perspective, each individual coach/program administrator has the choice (from the above decision-making process) to be one of the following:

> Moral manager are dedicated to high standards of ethical behavior, both in their own actions and in their expectations of how the company's business should be conducted.
>
> Immoral managers have no regard for so-called ethical standards in business and pay no attention to ethical principles in making decisions and conducting the company's business.
>
> Amoral managers appear in two forms: the intentionally amoral manager and the unintentionally amoral manager. Intentionally amoral managers are of the strong opinion that business and ethics are not to be mixed. . . . Unintentionally amoral managers do not pay much attention to the concept of business ethics either but for different reasons. They are simply casual about, careless about, or inattentive to the fact that certain kinds of business decisions or company activities are unsavory or may deleterious effects on others. (Thompson, Strickland, & Gamble, 2007, pp. 323–324)

From these three ways of thinking, a coach/program administrator could perhaps consider that being a moral manager and "doing things the right way" could put his/her program at an apparent disadvantage against programs that have a disregard for moral leadership and action. This would be an erroneous assumption. Moral coaches/program administrators who strive to uphold superior principles and values throughout their athletic programs will not have to spend precious program resources (time, money, people, etc.) rectifying blatant dishonest/deceitful choices when they "come to light." Additionally, moral coaches/program administrators will maintain an indispensable program element—goodwill. Once goodwill is lost through unethical practices, it is exceptionally difficult to regain.

BUSINESS ETHICS AND COACHING

Coaches are managers in the business of athletics. No matter at what level the program operates, the coach or program administrator is bound by the indispensable concepts of sound business practice. Nearly all the rationale that applies to traditionally conceived business ventures apply to the profession. Believing this is crucial in developing a successful and ethical program.

With that in mind, it is important to recognize how today's businesses confront and tackle the growing subject (and often dilemma) of ethical behavior. Ethics and business ethics are defined as the following:

Ethics—the study of right and wrong and of the morality of the choices individuals make.

Business Ethics—the application of moral standards to business situations. (Pride, Hughes, & Kapoor, 2002, p. 37)

In other words, how do the athletic program and its people make determinations in difficult (sometimes impossible) situations? There is a remarkable similarity between the ethical circumstances that traditional business ventures and coaches or program administrators both deal with. Figure 1 outlines the similarity between these two situations.

Traditional Businesses	Coaching/Program Administration
Human Resource Planning and Staffing	Student-Athlete Recruiting
Employee Development	Athlete Training
Human Resource Educational Issues	Student-Athlete Academic Requirements
Financial Management	Financial Management
Governmental, Corporate, and	NCAA, NJCAA, NFL, MLB
Industry Reporting and Documentation	NAIA Reporting and Documentation
Customer Relations	Fan Support/Alumni
Employee Safety and Welfare	Student Athlete Safety and Welfare

Figure 1. **Business Ethics and Sports Program Ethics**

Four Social/Ethical Choices for a Coach/Program Administrator

Administrative Tip

A program that endorses social/ethical response tactics has visible side benefits. The program atmosphere will be optimistic, honest, altruistic, and healthy.

There are four social/ethical athletic program choices that managers and coaches can adopt from these ethical situations.

> Obstructionist stance: An approach to social responsibility that involves doing as little as possible and may involve attempts to deny or cover up violations.

> Defensive stance: Approach to social responsibility by which a company meets only minimum legal requirements in its commitments to groups and individuals in its social environment.

> Accommodative stance: Approach to social responsibility by which a company, if specifically asked to do so, exceeds legal minimums in its commitments to social groups and individuals in its social environment.

> Proactive stance: Approach to social responsibility by which a company actively seeks opportunities to contribute to the well-being of groups and individuals in its social environment. (Griffin & Ebert, 2004, pp. 148–149)

From the above four choices, the most socially ethical method is the proactive stance. If one is to implement this anticipatory methodology for confronting ethical situations, the most apropos tool to utilize is an ethical program plan and code of ethics.

DEVELOPMENT OF AN ETHICS PROGRAM

To begin with, an organization developing an ethical program plan and code of ethics must first explore and scrutinize its values. Values and ethics, though analogous and interrelated, are two separate concepts. The relationship between ethics and values is that "Values are stable and enduring beliefs about what an individual considers to be important. Values provide basis for meaning" (Lussier & Achua, 2007, p. 361). "Ethics are standards of right and wrong that influence behavior. Right behavior is considered ethical, and wrong behavior is considered unethical" (Lussier & Achua, 2007, p. 55). In other words, values are the introspective elements that each of us accept as true while ethics converts those beliefs into actions.

From these essential abstractions, Rue and Byars, in their 2007 text *Management: Skills and Application,* expound on areas of values and their ethical actions that are typically universal to all organizations.

- Honesty
- Adherence to the law
- Product safety and quality
- Health and safety at the workplace
- Conflicts of interest
- Employment practices

The core values of a program are the side effects of a coach/program administrator's outlook toward ethical choices. The concept of top-down flow is most evident in the concept of ethical core values. Consider oneself at the top. All ethical decisions from the top will be noted and continuously dissected as they flow down to the program's subordinates.

- Selling and marketing and marketing practices
- Financial reporting
- Pricing, billing, and contracting
- Using confidential information
- Acquiring and using information about competitors
- Security
- Payments to obtain business
- Political activities
- Protection of the environment (Rue & Byars, 2007, p. 114)

The depth and magnitude of these subjective core values and ethical actions totally depends on what the program deems intrinsically desirable. Once one has examined the program's philosophical base, then one can develop and implement an ethical program plan.

An ethical program plan is a written document that clarifies organizational values and gives miscellaneous rules that guide actions in as many foreseeable operational conditions as possible. There are eight ingredients that must be present in fostering and employing an ethical program plan:

I. A Statement of Values
II. Corporate/Program Tradition and Values
III. Tone at the Top
IV. A Code of Conduct
V. Established Procedures
VI. Ethical Training Programs
VII. Hot Line/Open-Door Policy
VIII. Ongoing Oversight Control (Hall, 1993, text concept)

Section I, Statement of Values, is the ethical equivalent to a business mission statement. This statement is a comprehensive narrative that is a broad basis for the program's ethical plan.

Section II and III, Corporate/Program Tradition and Values and Tone at the Top, are historical overviews of the past program ethical actions and values as well as the current overall atmosphere in the profession and organization.

Sections IV, V, and VI, a Code of Conduct, Established Procedures, and Ethical Training Programs, are the determined, tangible codes and procedures for ethical action in the program. The more circumscribed and tangible one can be with each definitive procedure the better.

Sections VII and VIII, Hot Line/Open-Door Policy and Oversight/Control, are the overseeing and monitoring directives in an ethical program plan.

When writing an individual and specific ethical code of conduct, there are some salient directives that should be followed.

1. Be clear about the objectives the code is intending to accomplish.
2. Get support and ideas for the code from all levels of the organization.

3. Be aware of the latest developments in the laws and regulations that affect your industry.
4. Write as simply and clearly as possible. Avoid legal jargon and empty generalities.
5. Respond to real-life questions and situations.
6. Provide resources for further information and guidance.
7. In all its forms, make it user-friendly because ultimately a code fails if it is not used. (Hartman & DesJardins, 2008, p. 126)

Because athletic programs are visible organizations in society, each coach/program administrator, when constructing singular ethical codes, must examine the ramification of each ethical codes from a public relations standpoint as well as from a right or wrong prospective. The more public an issue, the more a coach/program administrator needs to spell out in detail the ethical actions expected. All codes of conduct elements must be continuously communicated to the athletic staff. Ethical conversations should be a focal part of an athletic program's "kickoff" orientation. When it comes to ethical behavior and expectations, a good maxim is 'leave nothing to chance."

SUMMARY

A person's ethical behavior is shaped from numerous historical influences. Coaches and program administrators can regulate and manage individual ethical decisions by planning for and structuring program ethical expectations. A coach, along with his or her internal stakeholders (players and staff), should clarify the program values that, in turn, guide ethical program decisions and actions. While player and staff meetings that reiterate principles and expectations are significant in accentuating program philosophies, a written ethical program plan should be utilized to eliminate any possible misconceptions and individual ethical choice deviations.

KEY TERMS	
ethics	obstructionist stance
values	defensive stance
experiences	accommodating stance
ethical standpoint	proactive stance
moral principles	code of ethics
moral intent	ethical program plan
moral managers	statement of values
immoral managers	code of conduct
amoral managers	ethical training
ethical behavior	open-door policy

Review and Discussion Questions

1. What are some personality traits that could influence ethical behavior?

2. What are the four steps in the ethical decision-making process?

3. What are moral managers, immoral managers, and amoral managers?

4. Define ethics. Define business ethics.

5. What is the obstructionist stance to social responsibility?

6. What is the accommodating stance to social responsibility?

7. Name the values and ethical actions that are universal to all organizations.

8. What are the eight ingredients for an ethical program plan?

9. What are some salient elements when writing an individual ethical code of conduct?

CHAPTER

14

Special Topics for Coaches

CHAPTER OUTLINE

CHAPTER

OBJECTIVES

Organizational Behavior and Coaching

- To define organizational behavior
- To examine the individual and individuality in organizations
- To elucidate the concept of diversity
- To describe individual self-fulfilling prophecies and their benefits
- To discuss the concept of organizational equity
- To illuminate the intangible elements of the equity theory
- To describe the concept of group roles, which include task-related and maintenance-related roles
- To analyze group dynamics
- To present the stages of group development
- To review the elements that distinguish organizational culture

Entrepreneurship and Coaching

- To explore aspects of being an entrepreneur
- To clarify the three types of entrepreneurs
- To outline the advantages of becoming an entrepreneur
- To explore consulting and coaching
- To delve into aspects of instructional camps and coaching

Professional Career Development for Coaches

- To identify and review résumé construction
- To provide a fundamental sectional format for résumés
- To clarify aspects of reference pages
- To appraise elements of effective cover letters
- To provide a fundamental sectional format for cover letters
- To stress the importance of pre-interview research
- To consider factors of interviewing
- To discuss the importance of body language, language skills, meal interviews, phone interviews, and panel interviews
- To offer various generic interview questions

INTRODUCTION

The three core sections of this chapter encompass professional and personal subjects that can be invaluable for coaches and program administrators. The first section, which discusses the basic concepts of organizational behavior, examines the individual as part of a group and organization. Additionally, the section considers how group dynamics and corporate/organizational culture bring about the success (or failure) of an athletic program. The second section, entrepreneurship and coaching, assesses different types of entrepreneurs as well as how coaches and program administrators can utilize their distinct competencies to supplement their athletic program's financial support and personal income. The final section, professional career development, relates to coaches' and program administrators' occupational enrichment. Topics such as résumés, cover letters, and interviewing tactics are all addressed.

ORGANIZATIONAL BEHAVIOR AND COACHING

The importance of the business subject of organizational behavior to an athletic program is considerable. It is defined by the following:

> The field of organizational behavior (referred to as OB) is the systematic study of attitudes, actions, and behaviors of individuals and groups in organizations. Systematic study means identifying nonrandom patterns of individual and group behavior that contribute to, or detract from, work and organizational effectiveness. (Weiss, 2001, p. 4)

Athletic programs are comprised of the three components of organizational behavior—individuals, groups, and athletic organizations. The key to organizational behavior's usefulness/worth is understanding how each of the components (individuals, groups, and the collective whole) interrelate and shape each other.

Individual and Organizational Behavior

Once thought incongruent, over the last 50 years business leaders have come to appreciate the vital connection between individual employee growth and corporate success. Whether the theories are called humanistic, people centered, personality based, or human capital, the value of the individual has become the centerpiece of many forward thinking companies. Understanding each individual's differences (way of thinking, sentiment and feelings, introspective beliefs, personalities, etc.) is the first step in merging people into a cohesive unit that cooperatively functions and succeeds. However, having an athletic program that respects the individual goes beyond simply understanding the distinctive nature of people; valuing the individual is done through the actions of the organization and the atmosphere created by the coach/program administrator. Three major areas that can cultivate the individual and endorse a resilient people-focused atmosphere are diversity, self-fulfilling prophecies, and equity.

Diversity

Diversity "involves the overall ability to value unique individual and group characteristics, embrace such characteristics as potential sources of organizational strength, and appreciate the uniqueness of each individual" (Hellriegel & Slocum, 2007, p. 9). As the definition points out, a key to diversity in an organization (athletic program) is to welcome and respect

Because athletic programs are based on the performance of people, the individual aspect of organizational behavior has special significance. Get to know each staff member and athlete on an individual basis.

individual differences and to prize and utilize those differences for the betterment of everyone in the organization.

Sound individually focused athletic programs have coaches/program administrators who embrace human distinction, see it as a competitive advantage, and develop the individual to their utmost potential. They continually analyze all operating systems within the organization to eradicate any possible preconceptions and bias in procedures, processes, and program structure. Finally, they aggressively and proactively manage all diversity conflicts between program members.

Individual Self-fulfilling Prophecies

To develop the individual human capital in an athletic program, a coach/program administrator must create an encouraging self-fulfilling prophetic environment. Self-fulfilling prophecy can best be described by the following: "The essence of the self-fulfilling prophecy, or Pygmalion effect, is that people's expectation or beliefs determine their behavior and performance, thus serving to make their expectations come true" (Kreitner & Kinicki, 2004, p. 239). In other words, if you establish high expectation for an individual, he/she will satisfy those expectations. Unfortunately, if your expectations for an individual are low, so will be their performance. A longstanding self-fulfilling prophecy is one that states, "If you treat people like adults, they will regularly act like adults. If you treat people like children, they often will act like children." The feasible benefits of a positive self-fulfilling prophetic environment can include

- higher performance and goal achievement,
- elevated ethical actions,
- advanced self-awareness by individuals,
- improved self-esteem,
- additional job satisfaction and employee retention,
- stronger individual motivation and vested program behavior,
- willingness to be innovative, and
- enhanced ability to learn new program items.

An optimistic, affirmative self-fulfilling environment can powerfully shape every aspect of human relations in an athletic program.

In the text, *Basic Organizational Behavior*, Schermerhorn, Hunt, and Osborn outline four salient points when forming a positive self-fulfilling environment for employees. Their points are as follows:

- Create a warmer interpersonal climate between your subordinates and you.
- Give more performance feedback to subordinates—make it as positive as possible, given their actual performance.
- Spend more time helping subordinates learn job skills.
- Provide more opportunities for subordinates to ask questions. (Schermerhorn, Hunt, & Osborn, 1998, p. 58)

Administrative Tip

The best way to handle and promote diversity in an organization is through sensitivity. As the program leader, the coach/program administrator sets the "sensitivity tone" for the whole operation.

If a coach/program administrator is successful in building this type of environment, the force of it can transform and improve any athletic program.

Equity

The concept of fairness and equity in any organization is exceptionally critical for human resource interrelationships and productivity. The areas in which a coach/program administrator should be cognizant of are as follows:

> Negative inequity—comparison in which another person receives greater outcome for similar inputs.
> Positive inequity—comparison in which another person receives lesser outcomes for similar inputs.
> Equity sensitivity—an individual tolerance for negative or positive equity. (Kreitner & Kinicki, 2007, p. 244)

While there could be definitive disparities in measuring individual inputs compared to outputs, equity and fairness goes beyond the actual tangible outputs (typically salary or extrinsic rewards) and their relationship to an individual's inputs (time worked, effort expended, etc.). Organizational equity encompasses the intangible elements that are perceived by athletic program members. Some such questions relating to organizational equity are listed below:

- How are individuals being treated in contrast to each other?
- Are some program staff members treated "special"?
- Does the program have a feeling of sensitivity to all members' needs or just a select few?
- Is there a fair and impartial justice system in the organization?
- Do some staff members get more attention and guidance than others?
- Is there an unambiguous and lucid system in place that standardizes promotions?
- Is there an authoritative appeal system in place to challenge HR decisions?
- Is there a measurement system in place to determine effort and performance by all staff members?
- Are employee evaluations understandable and impartial?
- Are individual goals established by equity or arbitrarily determined?
- Are special assignments for a select few or are they obtainable by all staff members?
- Are work surroundings/conditions the same for all staff members?

These and other questions can help assist a coach/program administrator in determining if his/her program is nurturing an equitable environment or one that is beneficial for some and detrimental for others.

Groups and Organizational Behavior

Group management benefits lie in the ability to assemble complementary individuals, extrapolate their exclusive strengths, and focus those strengths

Administrative Tip

If a coach/program administrator discovers an inequitable situation, he/she should openly discuss the circumstances with all parties involved and work for an immediate resolution that is acceptable for everyone. The worst-case scenario is if a coach/program administrator tries to "sweep the inequity under the rug." Program staff and athletes will inevitably find out and the coach/program administrator will lose trust and loyalty (both essential for human resource management).

on cooperative group/organizational goals. To accomplish this, a coach/ program administrator needs to characterize and develop group roles.

> Group roles are shared expectations of how group members are to perform in their positions. Group roles are developed because activities, interactions, and sentiments of others in a group as well as self-expectations . . . roles of group members may be divided into task-related and maintenance-related roles. **Task-related roles** are those behavioral expectations that directly aid in the accomplishment of group objectives. . . . **Maintenance-related roles** are those behavioral expectations directly related to the well-being and development of the group. (Benton, 1998, p. 259)

A coach/program administrator has to definitively "spell out" all task-related roles to eliminate role confusion, wasted resources, and interpersonal conflicts. He or she also has to oversee and foster activities and behaviors that support positive group development and cohesion. These obligations are the foundation of group dynamics.

Group Dynamics

The following are focal points in promoting constructive group dynamics.

1. Individual goals must emanate from, and bond with, collective group goals. If individual objectives are out of line with group objectives, conflict and group disintegration will occur. If goals of individual members are aligned with group goals, synergetic benefits will be realized.

2. Coaches and program administrators must proactively supervise interpersonal relationships between group members. Group achievement is strengthened by internal trust and cooperation among all members.

3. Unified groups rely heavily on open-lines of communication. A coach/program administrator should scrutinize communication practices in all operational aspects of the athletic program.

4. A coach/program administrator must identify and facilitate conflict intervention and resolution. His/her talent in mediating disputes/ discord will have a direct effect on the group's productivity.

5. To ensure a quality output, a coach must balance individual rewards with group rewards. Individuals who surpass their group role expectations should receive additional compensation/incentives.

6. A coach/program administrator's decision on the group's optimal size is critical to its targeted goals. Having too many group members not only wastes the program's human resource, it can encourage members to "slack off" on group assignments. Conversely, inadequate staff can cause dissatisfaction and frustration when group responsibilities can not get completed due to a lack of human resource.

7. Coaches must have a watchful recognition of the concept of group

think. An individual's submission to the overall group consensus not only compromises the groups integrity, it weakens the group's most precious asset—original thought and problem solving.

8. A coach should not only be familiar with the group as a whole, but should recognize sub-groups and their influence on the overall group. Relationship management in this context goes beyond individual-to-individual, it encompasses sub-group-to-sub-group dynamics.

9. For group motivation, coaches/program administrators must encourage healthy inter-group competition. The fundamental premise to healthy inter-group competition is to look for as many "win-win" scenarios as possible and to have all members do well.

10. A coach should give compelling consideration to a group's hierarchical structure. Individuals must be placed in correct positions of authority and importance to make possible group harmony.

11. With technology becoming critical to all organizations, a coach must examine how technology affects (or can affect) group interactions and dynamics.

12. A coach/program administrator must gage a group's aptitude in adjusting to changes as well as their level of resistance to change. Groups that are considered rigid in their adaptability and resistance to change will need more direct assistance in altering attitudes and practices.

13. A coach must acknowledge group inertia and promote "outside the box" thinking. Creativity must be appreciated and encouraged.

14. A coach should observe external stakeholders and their influence on group dynamics. Outside influences can be just as powerful as internal influences for groups.

15. A coach should support a group in making difficult decisions. Helping a group reach a consensus decision is a major factor in group performance.

Stages of Group Development

All groups, no matter the formality or function, go through a universally recognized five-stage developmental process. The five stages are as follows:

Forming: When groups first come together, the members must get acquainted. **Forming** includes learning the traits and strengths of each potential member. . . . Preliminary identification of a leader usually occurs at this stage as well.

Storming: Once group members have had a chance to assess the human resources available in a group, several battles must be fought within the group. First, the group must decide what its goals and priorities will be. The second battle arises because the group must structure its interaction to ensure effective group functioning.

Norming: Once group functions have been (at least tentatively) decided upon and roles have been assigned, the tone of group interaction changes. Group members now identify with a common purpose, and the group has identified the human resources it needs to fulfill that purpose.

Performing: Once a group has identified its rules and roles, it has a structure within which to pursue its goals and the group has reached maturity.

Adjourning: Sometime after the group has reached maturity, it may make sense for the group to disband. **Adjourning** refers to the disbanding of a group. (Northcraft & Neale, 1994, pp. 241–242)

From an athletic program perspective, the group development process can have the following elements:

Forming—Groups within athletic programs can come into being by official channels (coaches design) or through casual alliances (happenstance). Either way, group formation must be supervised and monitored.

Storming—Coaches must acknowledge that groups need to go through a period of storming. There is an intrinsic necessity about having the group members "jockeying" for status and authority. The hazard in this stage is when groups can not get past the power struggles and get stuck in the stage. Another threat associated with storming is when there is an apparent (but not valid) positioning and norming of the group and conflicts are not in actuality solved. Because there was no true resolution to group issues, the group will falsely progress through the development process and convert back to storming at any time.

Norming—This occurs when there is is a "coming together" and everyone in the group knows his/her position/role. Once a group differentiates its norms, a coach/program administrator must be knowledgeable about the norms upon which the group has decided. Hopefully, the norms are in the best interest of the athletic program. If not, the coach may possibly have to re-assemble a new group of individuals and start the developmental process again.

Performing—This stage depends heavily on the previous three stages. If a group has had effectual development in forming, storming, and norming, then performing should be sound. The group will be stable and should be able to handle any possible obstacles. Unfortunately, the reverse is also true. If forming, storming, and norming are inadequate, then any difficulties will divide the group and performance will suffer (if not utterly fail).

Adjourning—Every group disbands. It is the natural progression of organizational behavior. The key to adjourning is to know that the process is circular. Once one group adjourns, another will take its place and start the group developmental process again.

Administrative Tip

The group development process is not time specific . . . different groups will go through the process at different speeds. If there are time restrictions for a group's performance, a coach/program administrator should assist the group (through discussion, incentives, leadership, etc.) in getting to the performance stage.

Organizational Culture

After a coach/program administrator has examined the individual and group aspects of organizational behavior, he/she must look at how the organization and its culture can affect productivity and success.

Organizational culture refers to a system of shared meaning held by members that distinguishes the organization from other organizations . . . the most recent research suggests that there are seven primary characteristics that, in aggregate, capture the essence of an organization's culture.

1. Innovation and risk taking
2. Attention to detail
3. Outcome orientation
4. People orientation
5. Team orientation
6. Aggressiveness
7. Stability (Robbins, 1998, p. 596)

There are no universal formulas for determining what the organizational culture is like in an athletic program. Each coach must reflect on the seven points introspectively and decide if the values, background, and traditions are conducive to goals achievement. Other requisites that determine an athletic program's culture are:

Distinctiveness—What separates the athletic program's philosophy from other programs?

Dedication—What level of dedication do current program members have?

Permanence—How solid is the philosophical foundations of the athletic program?

Adaptability—Is there a feeling of "whatever it takes" in the athletic program?

Honesty—Is the program up-front with all of its operations?

Esteem—Does the program have internal and external goodwill?

Vision—Is the organizational culture geared toward the future, not the past?

Accountability—Is there a feeling of mutual accountability in the program?

Regulations—Is there a balance between policies and procedures and individual freedoms?

Accomplishment—Is success the cultural standard?

Community—Is there a sense of kinship in the athletic program?

Counseling—Is constructive guidance the paradigm in the program?

Affiliation—Do all athletic program members feel a commitment and connection with each other (no matter who and what their position is)?

Autonomy—Is there empowerment and independence in the athletic program?

Quality—Is quality prioritized in all aspects of the athletic program?

Stimulus—Does the program's culture inspire program members?

Dignity—Does the program's culture arouse pride and self-esteem?

These are just some of the cultural conditions that can be examined by a coach and his/her program members. It must be unconditionally stated that a program's culture begins with the coach/program administrator. He/she sets the tone for all of the aspects of the program customs, ethos, and philosophy. As a leader, a coach must lead the culture, not be subject to it.

ENTERPRENEURSHIP AND COACHING

Entrepreneurship is a concept that goes beyond simply saying that one is a business owner. It is a mindset that emphasizes freedom and independence, creativity and innovation, strategic risk taking, goal setting (both personal and professional), and self-gratification. A major component that relates to each of these dimensions/attitudes is the desire for continuous improvement and growth. While it is possible to be successful with a single business or product strategy, most coaches/program administrators will strive to eliminate operational inertia with growth and entrepreneurial diversification.

Successful entrepreneurs are individuals who are opportunistic and exploitive. While the connotation for the words *opportunistic* and *exploitive* is not always encouraging, in this instance they are a positive trait. Entrepreneurs envision the future and take advantage of the potential conditions sometimes only they can anticipate and foresee. They derive personal satisfaction from not only making a profit but from realizing their intrinsic goals. For some entrepreneurs, profit is a secondary consideration. Their inner drive to accomplish objectives gives them a self-confidence that permits them to take risks that others would consider and avoid.

There are actually three types of entrepreneurs:

1. Artisan Entrepreneur—A person who starts a business with primary technical skill and little business knowledge.
2. Opportunistic Entrepreneur—A person who starts a business with both sophisticated managerial skill and technical knowledge.
3. Entrepreneurial Team—This is two or more individuals who work together as entrepreneurs to complement each other. (Longenecker, Moore, & Petty, 2003, pp. 14–16)

These three classifications are crucial to understand as a prospective entrepreneur. Simply stated, a coach or program administrator needs to know what type and level of entrepreneur he or she is in order to distinguish his or her future potential and limitations. Not consciously accepting one's

Administrative Tip

A coach/program administrator should enlist key program members in reinforcing positive cultural objectives. The more members are involved in the cultural directives, the greater the internal commitment to the desired culture.

current limitations could be the ultimate factor in the demise of one's impending entrepreneurial operation.

Some of the advantages to coaches/program administrators emerging as entrepreneurs are as follows:

- Coaches/program administrators who take advantage of entrepreneurial opportunities have less long-term career risks. These supplementary entrepreneurial options can often become the primary career (and financial) focus for coaches/program administrators.
- Entrepreneurial growth is important for the survival of the athletic program. Entrepreneurial ventures "tied into" the athletic program's name can have huge public relations benefits that, in-turn, will provide the program with a distinct competitive advantage.
- Entrepreneurial activities can help eliminate inertia in an athletic program. Once a program is established and operating at a desired level, a coach/program administrator should consider, in order to motivate his/her staff, external ventures to provide opportunities for staff development, organizational enthusiasm, and financial gain. This relates to the strategic management philosophy of continuous improvement.
- If there is a strong strategic fit between the athletic program and a new entrepreneurial endeavor, an athletic program can see benefits such as the following:
  - Capacity utilization benefits
  - Additional resources (tangible: equipment, facilities, human, land, and intangible: goodwill, brand name recognition, etc.) for the athletic program
  - The development of new capabilities/skills
  - Augmenting the current customer base as well as tapping new customers/athletic program supporters

There is a new resurgence in small business ownership and the coaching profession is no different than any other. The two primary types of entrepreneurial ventures for coaches are consulting and instructional camps.

Consulting

Consulting, in its most original form, is selling one's proficiency and intelligence in a discipline to another individual or organization that needs it. From a more technical standpoint, consultants are "a person who consults someone or something . . . a person who gives professional or expert advice" (Random House College Dictionary, p. 289). The depth and intensity of one's consulting business depends greatly on ambition and expectations. For coaches, consulting enterprise can be as casual as helping colleagues with general, informal advice and insight to as official as setting up a separate business entity, establishing a proposal sales system, wide-ranging marketing activities, structuring consulting procedures, etc.

Before taking into consideration the challenges of being a consultant, a coach or program administrator must consider the exceptional value that he or she can offer as a coach. Ask the following questions:

- Do I truly have the level of knowledge and comprehension of my particular coaching specialty to provide a benefit to other coaches?
- Do I have good written and oral skills?
- Am I completion oriented?
- Can I be objective and unbiased in my consultation?
- Am I a good instructor?
- Am I willing to accept the hard work that goes along with being a consultant?
- Can I maintain a high level of confidentiality?
- Am I a skillful time manager?
- Can I market and sell myself and my services?
- Do I have the aptitude to observe, analyze, and then solve problems?
- Do I have the financial resources to initiate a consulting venture?
- Where will my clients come from? What is my market niche and targeted segment?
- Will my target market of clients be potentially profitable?
- How much worth can I place on my services?
- What is the competitive atmosphere for coaching consultants?

These are just a few of the daunting questions one will have to ask before jumping into consulting. The upside of launching and operating a consulting venture is substantial. In general, most of the start-up overhead is limited to basic office equipment and promotion of the venture. The work is very dynamic and literally differs from situation to situation. Finally, facilitating someone else's achievement has very ample intrinsic rewards.

If one feels that functioning as an entrepreneurial coaching consultant would be desirable, one should utilize the business concepts in this text to set up, plan, and manage the operation.

Instructional Camps

From a coaching outlook, the most popular venue to delve into one's entrepreneurial spirit is through instructional camps and clinics. If one wants to thrive in these small business ventures, there are some recognized keys that are universal to all sports camps and clinics. The ensuing directives are in no particular arrangement and will need to be focused explicitly on one's particular sport and its precise operating methodology.

1. It is strongly recommended to regard all camp operations (and all entrepreneurial undertakings) as absolutely separate and autonomous from one's core coaching job. To integrate camp operations with

the program's normal processes could be at best confusing and at worst destructive.

2. Follow the indispensable managerial principals (discussed in Chapters 1–5) in conducting all camp business. All of the business theories and practices that pertain to one's athletic program also apply to one's camp venture.

3. It is soundly recommended that the camp business be incorporated. Incorporation creates a distinct, separate business entity with a life of its own. The primary advantage to incorporating is the coach or program administrator's personal liability, as a rule, is limited to the corporation and excludes his or her personal assets. The foremost disadvantage is double taxation. Not only is the camp business taxed but any income that one derives from the camp operation will then also be taxed. Confer with a tax accountant about the implications and setup of the camp corporation.

4. Never forget: *The customer is everything.* All of one's camp aspirations and actions should always have this in mind.

5. For fruition and future camp expansion, offer superior customer satisfaction to all attending one's camps. To do this, provide the highest quality product one's resources can provide. This, in turn, will generate positive word of mouth and enhance future operations.

6. Under the same foundations as quality, hire the most competent staff and instructors. Their compensation should fit and (if the resources allow) surpass their expectations. Supply camp staff with additional perks to retain them for future camp seasons.

7. Be hands-on and visible at camp sessions. Even if one is not acting as a clinician, walk the facility and communicate with the participants. Show an allegiance and commitment to the product.

8. Have a structured, controlled camp atmosphere. It will convey professionalism as well as lessen campers' anxieties. Post schedules and instructional sites whenever possible. Additionally, have pre-camp staff conferences to scrutinize schedules, locations, activities, and job responsibilities. The more systematic the camp business, the better flow and atmosphere the camp will have.

9. At the end of each camp, survey the campers (either informally through walk-around discussions or through formal survey techniques). Ask them about their experiences at camp and what other services and training they may perhaps want in the future. If the parents are involved, solicit their assessments. Additionally, enlist the camp staff through a recap session and get its input. Feedback is the salient key to improving quality in the future.

10. Keep the camper-to-staff ratio as low as financially practical. The lower the ratio, the more superior the customized quality of the instructional camp.

11. Develop an appealing, enlightening camp brochure. Triple check all final prints before circulating it to the public. Once again, the up-front financial resources and camp projections will shape a great part of the promotional and admission brochure.

12. Follow a stringent risk management philosophy (imparted in Chapter 11). Be, if anything, over insured.

13. Maintain the most advantageous, straightforward record keeping system. Utilize any number of computer software programs for precise accounting. Plan on the camp being audited. This attitude will intensify the camp's system integrity. If one is not detail oriented, outsource this administration function to someone who is. Medical records, insurance forms, emergency contact information, employment contracts, and specialized sports-specific information are all detail-oriented materials that need compulsory maintenance. Special note: By no means consent to a child or clinic member participating in any event or activity without his or her entire records being on file. This could be construed as gross negligence and may be a cause for loss of protection under the camp's insurance carrier.

14. Have top skilled training and medical personnel on staff. Have them assist in all medical and insurance considerations.

Other alternatives one would need to contemplate are more sports specific and personal. Items such as

- operating of day camps or overnight camps,
- providing food plans or having campers independently obtain food,
- running specialty camps or administering comprehensive, overall skill camps,
- running an all-inclusive total camper session or breaking down the camp into age and skill groups,
- allowing camp sessions to be open to the general public or closing training sessions, and
- providing auxiliary activities or keeping the camps sports specific only.

All of these issues (and more) are the individualized concern of one's camp and necessitate planned strategies.

PROFESSIONAL CAREER DEVELOPMENT FOR COACHES

Résumés

General Information
The following are general tips in the construction of a professional coaching/athletic program administrator's résumé:

- Do a SWOT analysis on yourself before beginning the résumé process. It will help illuminate one's personal strengths to highlight, weaknesses to minimize and explain, opportunities to pursue, and threats to one's professional developmental goals.

- Establish a timeline for your job hunting activities. To keep oneself on task, create definitive points in time to accomplish job searching responsibilities.
- Recognize the importance of the internet in job searching. Become familiar with coaching/program administration-specific sites such as the NCAA, NAIA, NJCAA, and high school association web pages.
- Realize that the résumé does not get one a job . . . it gets one an interview. It is just a single step in the entire career search process.
- For a general job search, understand that résumés are typically examined between 30–45 seconds. Make the résumé something that will catch a prospective employer's eyes. Learn the many ways one can highlight/accentuate information on a résumé.
- Obtain a separate e-mail account for job hunting. Keeping it disconnected from one's personal e-mails will eliminate the possibility of missed opportunities (spam blocker, unrecognizable addresses, etc.).
- Tailor your résumé for each specific employer. Do extensive research before sending résumés and underscore any qualifications that the prospective employer may be looking for. In other words, illustrate the bond between your competencies, depth, and accomplishments and the needs of the prospective employer.
- Show the whole person, not just the working side. Demonstrate abilities and activities outside professional functions.
- Sell yourself without "selling yourself." This is the fine line of résumé construction . . . knowing how far to push qualifications and responsibilities.
- For continuity, eliminate substantial time gaps in the résumé. Time gaps could be described as non-productive interruptions in one's professional or personal development.

Administrative Tip

Exude refinement and class in résumé presentation. One's résumé is a profound statement of who he/she is.

Formats

- No right or wrong . . . just some are better than others
- Unlimited layouts/designs—check textbooks for ideas
- Profession dictates which ones would be appropriate
- Typical are Chronological or Functional

Fundamental Guidelines

- Entry level coaching/program administration career jobs—try to limit to one page
- Use action-oriented words rather than passive language
- Appropriate font (business)
- Free of spelling and grammatical errors
- Flow and spacing should help in the aesthetic appeal of the document

- Reverse chronological in all categories
- Use 20–24 lb. bond paper with matching envelopes
- Never lie! Enhance but do not tell untruths

Heading
- Name
- Title
- Addresses
- Phone
- E-mail (Business)

Administrative Qualifications/Managerial Qualifications
- Chance to get attention
- Chance to show direct correlation between you and job

Job Objective
- The résumé's mission statement

Education/Certifications
- No high school
- Relevant coursework if work experience is weak
- Academic awards
- Watch GPAs—if you list one, you should list all

Professional Experience
- Date (years)
- Local (city/state)
- Description of position should list at least four major job responsibilities (with action words, not passive) that relate toward job you are applying for
- Narrative or bullet—your choice
- Show career progression (if possible) as well as stability
- Internships

Military Service (if applicable)

Entrepreneurial Ventures (if applicable)

Publications (if applicable)

Honors/Activities/Awards
- Associations/campus activities/community activities/professional memberships
- Red Cross, United Way, Habitat for Humanity, school clubs, student government, etc.
- Show leadership if possible

Figure 1. Résumé Sectional Format

Reference Page

A separate reference page is different from employment references. Reference pages are made up of the references one chooses voluntarily give to prospective employers. There are some prominent areas in their composition:

- Choose correctly your professional and personal references. The more the professional/personal reference is tied into career choice, the better.
- Contact each reference to make sure that it is OK. While this might seem to be common sense, it is often forgotten.
- Do check-in calls with references to see if there are any inquiries and to remind them that they are still a professional/personal reference.
- Triple check to make sure that the information for each reference is updated and correct. Having a wrong phone number or e-mail could show the prospective employer that one is not detailed oriented.
- By and large, the reference page should be a separate page.

Cover Letters

Some general elements of a cover letter encompass the following:

- Formal business format (date, inside address, salutations, body, closing, signatures, etc.) . . . 1-inch margins, block format, etc.
- Two to four paragraphs (three is standard—intro, body, conclusion).
- Short, crisp action paragraphs.
- Complete name and title of recipient (don't misspell).
- Reason one is interested in company . . . schmooze.

First Paragraph
- Introduce yourself
- Position (and position number if applicable)
- Where you found out about the position
- If unsolicited position, re-work opening to include interest in specific company and how your talents match what the company does
- Brief statement of interest and consideration . . . gain attention

Body/Second Paragraph
- Get the reader interested in meeting you . . . highlight your strengths
- Skill, duties, and accomplishments (related to the job)
- No salary requirements
- Current information to supplement résumé
- Refer to résumé (if applicable)

Conclusion/Third Paragraph
- Indicate action/request for interview (without being pushy)
- Indicate a follow-up contact
- Make it easy for reader to respond
- Complimentary closing (e.g., Sincerely, Yours Truly, Respectfully)
- Legible signature
- Four spaces between complimentary closing and typed name
- Typed name with titles
- Two spaces below . . . enclosures

Figure 2. **General Cover Letter Template**

- Demonstrate research on company in narrative portion of cover letter.
- Reiterate tangible benefits one can offer the prospective employer.
- Match skills acquired with skills required for the position.
- Enthusiasm and positive writing.
- Brevity and little or no "fluff."
- Once again, error free.

Interviews

Pre-Interview Research

The first question associated with interviewing is when does the interview process start? The interview starts the second one gets notified that an interview will take place. Simply stated, researching a company prior to the interview is critical to the success of the interview. The more one knows about an athletic organization prior to an interview, the more the interviewer will be impressed by that person. The sources one could you use to research the athletic organization include

- on-line websites,
- media guides,
- program catalogs,
- athletic newsletters,
- promotional materials, and
- sports-specific periodicals.

Once the organizational data has been collected, an athletic organizational profile should be constructed. An athletic organizational profile is a one-page synopsis of an organization's operations. The parts of an athletic organizational profile include the following:

- Athletic organization's name
- Athletic organization's parent company (if applicable)
- Job position(s) available
- Job descriptions
- Salary range
- Size and locations of athletic organization
- Number of staff members and breakdown of athletic department's workforce
- Athletic organization's product line
- Sales volume/booster support
- Athletic organization's market position
- Future plans for the athletic organization
- Direct competitor information
- Athletic organization's concerns in future

Actual Interview Preparation

Some basic guidelines for interview preparation are listed below.

Time of interview: It is standard interviewing protocol to arrive early for an interview. However, arriving too early can be a detriment to the interview. A generally accepted policy is to arrive 15 minutes prior to the scheduled time.

Place of interview: Know precisely where the interview is. If possible, do a "dry run" to find the exact location (especially if the interview is in a new city). Good directions are essential.

Parking: Plan on a parking charge. Keep an interview emergency $20.00 for parking fees and tolls.

Names: Be familiar with the people involved in the interview. Know their organizational position, titles, and the pronunciation of their names.

Projected length of interview: One should allot at least fours hours for each interview. If the interview is going well, one could be shown around, introduced to other staff members, taken to lunch/dinner, etc.

Prepare questions in advance: An interviewee should have prepared relevant questions in advance to be answered and asked.

Prepare your briefcase in advance: Items should include the following:
- Work samples
- Copies of résumé (5 minimum)
- Leather portfolio with pad, pens, etc.
- Breath mints, comb, lint remover, deodorant, etc.
- Copies of transcripts
- Copies of references and reference letters

Professional image: Focus on the following:
- Over dress rather than under dress
- Be pressed and fuzz free (pet fur)
- Know that one only has a few seconds to make a good first impression.
- Items
  - Suit: black, blue, brown
  - Shirt/Blouse: white
  - Conservative ties
  - Socks/stockings: matching outfit
  - Shoes: conventional
  - Watches: no sport watches
  - Jewelry: moderate

– Hair: business professional

– Grooming/make-up: traditional in nature

It is recommended that a classy and conservative style will work best for most interviewing situations.

The Interview

Interviewers look for the following:

- Competence related to the position
- Career goals
- Communication skills
- Enthusiasm
- Leadership and charisma
- Interpersonal skills
- Problem solving and independence
- Appearance and poise
- First impression
- Body language (to be discussed)
- Positive, positive, positive attitude
- Preparation
- Rapport
- Spontaneous, not "canned"
- Confidence

Body Language

An interviewee needs to be cognizant of the following body language factors:

- Eye contact
- Facial expressions
- Natural gesture
- Walk confidently
- Sitting: straight but relaxed
- Voice control: volume and inflection
- Smiling

Language Skills

Since communication is essential for almost every profession, language skills are critical in career development. At an interview, one must

- display a good vocabulary,
- limit jargon/buzz words,
- eliminate slang, slurs, fillers (e.g., you know, like, umm),
- eliminate loaded words (e.g., honey, dear),
- use direct and assertive language,
- avoid/be conscious of rambling,
- utilize humor (if appropriate), and
- never talk about politics, family, and religion.

Administrative Tip

It is important to remember that the interview process is a "two-way street." The coach/program administrator is interviewing the athletic organization just as the athletic organization is interviewing the coach/program administrator. One should ask relevant questions that will determine if he/she is interested in the organization.

Meal Interviews

Some salient factors in preparing and participating in a meal interview:

- Remember, it is an interview not a meal
- Mental preparation is critical
- Concentrate on interview, not food
- Eat before going
- Order light, neat food
- Table manners
  - Let interviewers pick chairs; let them lead group to the table
  - Pull out chairs (if you feel appropriate)
  - Napkin immediately on lap
  - Wait to eat unless told to start
  - Proper silverware
  - Take your time
  - Small bites
  - Use your napkin, it is there for a purpose
  - Elbows off the table, forearms
  - Don't gulp
- Never
  - Order alcohol
  - Smoke
  - Reach for the check

Phone Interviews

Because of the mobility in the job market and limited resources of most athletic organizations, more and more interviews are conducted over conference call or video phone. Elements that will help in phone interviews encompass the following:

- Environmental preparation is key
- Noise free
- Table preparation
  - Copy of résumé
  - Your questions
  - Blank note pad and pens
  - Company profile
- Phone selection: hand held or hands free
- Comfortable chair

Panel Interviews

Panel interviews are customary in interviewing for athletic positions in colleges and universities. Panels could consist of administrators, athletes, administrative support staff, and fellow coaches. A major consideration in participating in one is to remember that it is an interview and that all previous interviewing rules apply. It is also helpful to have a proper mindset; one should act as if he/she is being interviewed by one person. Use the circular eye contact technique to keep the entire group in the process. If possible, know names of all panel members.

---

1. Tell me about yourself.
2. Tell me about _____ college/university.
3. How would you rate your education?
4. What courses did you take that are relevant to the position you are interviewing for?
5. Do you currently work? No, why not? If yes:
   a. What do you like about your job?
   b. What do you dislike about your job?
   c. What is your typical day like?
   d. Why do you want to leave your current job?
6. Do you like team projects? Why or why not?
7. What people do you like to work with?
8. Describe a difficult person.
9. What are your biggest strengths? Weaknesses?
10. What would you classify as a stressful situation?
11. Describe the worst superior you have ever had.
12. Where do you want to be in five years?
13. Why should I hire you? Are you willing to travel? Relocate? Extra training/education?
14. What questions do you have for me?

Figure 3. Generic Interview Questions

SUMMARY

The concepts of organizational behavior, entrepreneurship, and professional career development are indispensable components to the success of an athletic program and a coach/program administrator's future. The essential comprehension of each will provide a coach/program administrator with insights into individuality and productivity inside a group and organizational structure, opportunities to increase both program and personal revenue, and definitive tactics to advance one's career. If these concepts are incorporated into one's operational and personal philosophies, they can transform an individual's future in coaching and program administration.

organizational behavior

diversity

self-fulfilling prophecy

equity

negative inequity

positive inequity

equity sensitivity

group roles

task-related roles

maintenance-related roles

group dynamics

group development

forming

storming

norming

performing

adjourning

organizational culture

entrepreneurship

artisan entrepreneur

opportunistic entrepreneur

entrepreneurial team

consulting

instructional camps

résumés

reference page

cover letters

pre-interview research

interview preparation

body language

language skills

meal interview

phone interview

panel interview

Review and Discussion Questions

1. Define organizational behavior.

2. What is organizational diversity?

3. What are the feasible benefits of a positive self-fulfilling prophetic environment?

4. Define negative inequity. Define positive inequity. Define equity sensitivity.

5. What are group roles? What are task-related roles? What are maintenance-related roles?

6. What are the five stages in group development?

7. What are some of athletic program requisites for cultural determination?

8. What are the three types of entrepreneurs?

9. What are some of the benefits an athletic program can receive from external entrepreneurial activities?

10. What are the considerations a coach/program administrator must reflect on before becoming a consultant?

11. What are some fundamental guidelines in constructive a professional résumé?

12. What are some general cover letter elements?

13. What are some of the sources a coach/program administrator can use to research athletic organizations?

14. What are the parts of an athletic program profile?

15. When interviewing, what are some items that should be included in one's briefcase?

16. What do interviewers look for in an interviewee?

17. What are some language skills that an interviewee must display or avoid in an interview?

18. What are some salient factors in a meal interview?

References

Abrahams, J. (1995). *The mission statement book: 301 corporate mission statements from America's top companies.* Berkely, CA: Ten Speed Press.

Adams, J. D. (1986). *Transformational leadership: From vision to results.* Alexandria, VA: Miles River Press.

Agor, W. H. (1989). *Intuition in organizations: Leading and managing productively.* Newberry Park, CA: Sage.

Alesandrini, K. (1992). *Survive information overload: The 7 best ways to manage your workload by seeing the big picture.* Homewood, IL: Business One.

AMA board approves new marketing definition. (1985, March). *Marketing News, 1,* 1.

American Marketing Association: Committee on Definitions. (1960). *Marketing definitions: A glossary of marketing terms.* Chicago, IL: AMA.

Anderson, L. (1997). Good will: Are your employees loyal ambassadors of your company. *Entrepreneur, 25,* 96.

Anthony, R. N., & Govindarajan, V. (2007). *Management control systems* (12th ed.). New York, NY: McGraw-Hill/Irwin.

Anthony, W. P., Perrewe, P. L., & Kacmar, K. M. (1993). *Strategic human resource management.* Fort Worth, TX: Dryden Press.

Babcock, P. (2004). Is your company two faced. *Human Resource Magazine, 49*(1), 44–45.

Baird, J. E. (1977). *The dynamics of organizational communication.* New York, NY: Harpers Row.

Baird, J. E., & Stull, J. B. (1988). *Business communication: Strategies and solutions.* New York, NY: McGraw Hill.

Ball, A., & Ball, B. (2000). *Basic camp management.* Martinsville, IN: American Camping Association.

Bateman, T. S., & Snell, S. A. (2004). *Management: The new competitive landscape.* New York, NY: McGraw-Hill/Irwin.

Batten, J. D. (1989). *Tough-minded leadership.* New York, NY: AMACOM.

Becker, F., & Steele, F. (1995). *Workplace by design: Mapping the high-performance workscape.* San Francisco, CA: Jossey Bass.

Beckwith, S. (2003). *Complete publicity plans: How to create publicity that will spark media exposure and excitement.* Avon, MA: Adams Media Corporation/Streetwise Publishing.

Bedeian, A. G. (1993). *Management.* Fort Worth, TX: Dryden Press.

Belch, G. E., & Belch, M. A. (1998). *Advertising and promotion: An integrated marketing communication perspective.* Boston, MA: McGraw Hill/Irwin.

Bellman, G. M. (1990). *The consultant's calling: Bringing who you are to what you do.* San Francisco, CA: Jossey Bass.

Bennett, P. D. (1988). *Dictionary of marketing terms.* Chicago, IL: American Marketing Association.

Benton, D. A. (1998). *Applied human relations: An organizational and skill development approach.* Upper Saddle River, NJ: Prentice Hall.

Berkowitz, E. N., Kerin, R. A., Hartley, S. W., & Rudelius, W. (1992). *Marketing.* Homewood, IL: Irwin.

Bermont, H. (1989). *How to become a successful consultant in your own field.* Rocklin, CA: Prima.

Black, J. S., & Porter, L. W. (2000). *Management: Meeting new challenges.* Upper Saddle River, NJ: Prentice Hall.

Blackwell, R. D., Miniard, P. W., & Engel, J. F. (2001). *Consumer behavior* (9th ed.). Orlando, FL: Harcourt College Publishers.

Blake, R. R., & Mouton, J. S. (1978). *The managerial grid.* Houston, TX: Gulf Publishing.

Bohlander, G., Snell, S., & Sherman, A. (2001). *Managing human resources.* Cincinnati, OH: South-Western Publishing.

Bond, W. J. (1997). *Going solo: Developing a home based consulting business from the ground up.* New York, NY: McGraw-Hill.

Booher, D. (1985). *Cutting paperwork in the corporate culture.* New York, NY: Facts on File.

Boone, L. E., & Kurtz, D. L. (1995). *Contemporary marketing plus.* Fort Worth, TX: Dryden Press.

Boone, L. E., & Kurtz, D. L. (2006). *Contemporary business 2006.* Mason, OH: Thompson South-Western.

Bragg, T. (2002). Improve employee commitment. *Industrial Management, 44*(4), 18–20.

Brandt, J. R. (2004). Staying together. *Industry Week, 253*(9), 27.

Branham, L. (2001). *Keeping the people who keep you in business: 24 ways to hang on to your most valuable talent.* New York, NY: AMACOM.

Broce, T. E. (1986). *Fundraising: The guide to raising money from private sources.* Norman, OK: University of Oklahoma Press.

Brodsky, N. (2002). Street smarts. *Inc., 24*(10), 52–54.

Browning, G. (2002) Cheers, ears – How to listen well. *People Management, 8*(24), 106.

Butler, J. E., Ferris, G. R., & Napeir, N. K. (1991). *Strategy and human resource management.* Cincinnati, OH: South-Western Publishing.

Byars, L. L., & Rue L. W. (2006). *Human resource management.* New York, NY: McGraw-Hill/Irwin.

Carlisle, H. M. (1987). *Management essentials: Concepts and applications*. Chicago, IL: Science and Research Associates.

Carson, M. (2006). Saying it like it isn't: The pros and cons of 360-degree feedback. *Business Horizons, 49*(5), 395–402.

Caywood, C. L. (1997). *The handbook of strategic public relations and integrated communications*. New York, NY: McGraw-Hill.

Certo, S. C. (1994). *Modern management: Diversity, quality, ethics and the global environment* (6th ed.). Boston, MA: Allyn and Bacon.

Certo, S. C., & Peter, J. P. (1990). *Strategic management: A focus on process*. New York, NY: McGraw-Hill.

Charski, M. (2005). It's safe to return home. *Adweek, 46*(21), 38.

Cheek, L. M. (1977). *Zero based budgeting comes of age*. New York, NY: AMA.

Child, J. (2005). *Organization: Contemporary principles and practices*. Malden, MA: Blackwell.

Chisholm, D. (1989). *Coordination without hierarchy: Informal structures in multi-organizational systems*. Berkeley, CA: University of California Press.

Churchill, G. A., & Peter, J. P. (1998). *Marketing: Creating value for customers*. Boston, MA: Irwin-McGraw Hill.

Ciulla, J. B. (2004). *Ethics, the heart of leadership* (2nd ed.). Westport, CT: Praeger.

Clow, K. E., & Baack, D. (2002). *Integrated advertising, promotion, and marketing communication*. Upper Saddle River, NJ: Prentice Hall.

Cohen, W. A. (1990). *The art of the leader*. Upper Saddle River, NJ: Prentice Hall.

Collier, A. T. (1992, March/April). Business leadership in a creative society. *Harvard Business Review, 70*, 159.

Conger, J. A. (1989). *The charismatic leader: Behind the mystique of exceptional leadership*. San Francisco, CA: Jossey Bass.

Cooper, R. K. (1991). *The performance edge: New strategies to maximize your work effectiveness & competitive advantage*. Boston, MA: Houghton Mifflin.

Craig, R. L. (1996). *The ASTD training and development handbook*. New York, NY: McGraw-Hill.

Crain, D. P. (1986). *Personnel: The management of human resources*. Boston, MA: Kent.

Crainer, S. (1995). *The financial times handbook of management*. London, GB: Pittman.

Cross, R., & Colella, S. (2004). Building vibrant employee networks. *Human Resource Magazine, 49*(12), 101.

Cummings, T. C. (1980). *Systems theory for organizational development*. New York, NY: John Wiley and Sons.

Curzon, S. C. (1995). *Managing the interview: A how-to-do-it manual for hiring staff*. New York, NY: Neal-Schuman.

Cutlip, S. M., Center, A. H., & Broom, G. M. (2000). *Effective public relations* (8th ed.). Upper Saddle River, NJ: Prentice Hall.

David, F. R. (1997). *Cases in strategic management*. Upper Saddle, NJ: Prentice Hall.

DeNisi, A. S., & Griffin, R. W. (2001). *Human resource management*. Boston, MA: Houghton Mifflin.

Dessler, G. (1977). *Human resource management*. Upper Saddle River, NJ: Prentice Hall.

Di Mauro, L., & Grant, T. (2006). *Ethics: Opposing viewpoints*. Farmington Hills, MI: Greenhaven Press.

Dibble, S. (1999). *Keeping your valuable employees: Retention strategies for your organization's most important resource*. New York, NY: John Wiley and Sons.

Dienhart, J. W. (2000). *Business, institutions, and ethics: A text with cases and readings*. New York, NY: Oxford University Press.

DiGaetani, J. L. (1986). *The handbook of executive communication*. Homewood, IL: Dow-Jones-Irvin.

Dilenschneider, R. L., & Forrestal, D. J. (1987). *The Dartnell public relations handbook*. Chicago, IL: Dartnell.

Donnelly, J. H., Gibon, J. L., & Ivancevich, J. M. (1987). *Fundamentals of management*. Plano, TX: Business Publication.

Dougherty, N. J., & Bonanno, D. (1985). *Management principles in sport and leisure services*. Minneapolis, MN: Burgess Publishing.

Draft, R. L., & Marcic, D. (2006). *Understanding management*. Mason, OH: Thompson South-Western.

Dressier, G. (1982). *Organization and management*. Reston, VA: Reston Publishing.

DuBrin, A. J. (2006). *Essentials of management* (7th ed.). Mason, OH: Thompson South-Western.

Edmonds, T. P., Tsay, B., & Olds, P. R. (2008). *Fundamental managerial accounting concepts* (4th ed.). New York, NY: McGraw-Hill/Irwin.

Eitington, J. E. (1997). *Winning management: Leadership skills for general innovation, quality, and employment commitment*. Houston, TX: Gulf Publishing.

Evans, J. R., & Berryman, B. (1984). *Essentials of marketing*. New York, NY: McMillian.

Evans, J. R., & Berryman, B. (1997). *Marketing*. Upper Saddle River, NJ: Prentice Hall.

Ferrett, S. K. (2003). *Strategies: Getting and keeping the job you want*. New York, NY: McGraw Hill/Glencoe.

Filing . . . like the beat . . . goes on . . . and on. (2001). *Journal of Accountancy, 192*(5), 24.

Finney, R. G. (1993). *Powerful budgeting for better planning and management*. New York, NY: AMA.

Finney, R. G. (1994). *Basics of budgeting*. New York, NY: AMA.

Fisher, C. D., Schoenfeldt, L. F., & Shaw, J. B. (1999). *Human resource management*. Boston, MA: Houghton Mifflin.

Flanagan, J. (1982). *The grass roots fund raising book: How to raise money in your community*. Chicago, IL: Contemporary Books.

Flanagan, J. (1993). *Successful fundraising: A complete hand-*

book for volunteers and professionals. Lincolnwood, IL: Contemporary Publishing.

Fogg, C. D. (1999). *Implementing your strategic plan: How to turn "intent" into effective action for sustainable change.* New York, NY: AMACOM.

French, W. L. (1994). *Human resource management.* Boston, MA: Houghton-Mifflin.

Friedman, J. P. (1987). *Barron's dictionary of business terms.* Hauppage, NY: Barron's Educational Series.

Fuqua, D. R., & Newman, J. L. (2002). Creating caring organizations. *Consulting Psychology Journal: Practice and Research, 54,* 131–140.

Fuqua, D. R., & Newman, J. L. (2004). Moving beyond the "Great Leader" model. *Consulting Psychology Journal: Practice and Research, 56,* 146–153.

Fuqua, D. R., & Newman, J. L. (2005). Integrating structural and behavioral leadership strategies. *Consulting Psychology Journal: Practice and Research, 57,* 126–132.

Furze, D., & Gale, C. (1996). *Interpreting management: Exploring change and complexity.* London, GB: International Thomson Business Press.

Galbraith, J. R. (1978). *Organizational design.* Reading, MA: Addison-Wesley.

Garcia, J. E., & Haggith, C. (1990, September). Organizational development: Interventions that work. *Personnel Administrator, 69,* 90–92.

Garrison, R. H., & Noreen, E. W. (2003). *Managerial accounting* (10th ed.). New York, NY: McGraw-Hill/Irwin.

Grasty, W. K., & Sheinkept, K. G. (1982). *Successful fundraising.* New York, NY: Charles Scribbners and Sons.

Gray, D. A. (1986). *Start and run a profitable consulting business.* British Columbia, Canada: International Self-Counsel Press.

Gray, J. L., & Starke, F. A. (1988). *Organizational behavior: Concepts and applications.* Columbus, OH: Merril.

Griffin, R. W. (1990). *Management* (3rd ed.). Boston, MA: Houghton Mifflin.

Griffin, R. W. (1996). *Management* (5th ed.). Boston, MA: Houghton Mifflin.

Griffin, R. W., & Ebert, R. J. (1993). *Business* (3rd ed.). Upper Saddle River, NJ: Prentice Hall.

Griffin, R. W., & Ebert, R. J. (2002). *Business* (6th ed.). Upper Saddle River, NJ: Prentice Hall.

Griffin, R. W., & Ebert, R. J. (2004). *Business* (7th ed.). Upper Saddle River, NJ: Prentice Hall.

Griffin, R. W., & Moorehead, G. (1986). *Organizational behavior.* Boston, MA: Houghton Mifflin.

Gumpert, D. (1990). *How to really create a successful business plan.* Boston, MA: NC Publishing.

Guy, M. E. (1990). *Ethical decision making in everyday work situations.* New York, NY: Quorum Books.

Hacker, C. A. (1996). *The cost of bad hiring decisions and how to avoid them.* Delray Beach, FL: St. Lucie Press.

Hackman, M. A., & Johnson, C. E. (1991). *Leadership: A communication perspective.* Prospect Heights, IL: Waveland.

Hackman, M. A., & Johnson, C. E. (2004). *Leadership: A communication perspective* (4th ed.). Long Grove, IL: Waveland.

Hahn, F. E. (1988). *Do it yourself advertising: How to produce great ads, brochures, catalogs, direct mail, web sites, and more.* New York, NY: John Wiley and Sons.

Hall, W. D. (1993). *Making the right decision: Ethics for managers.* New York, NY: John Wiley and Sons.

Hallowell, E. M. (2007, January Suppl.). Finding connection and creativity in craziness. *Associations Now,* 11–14.

Hamilton, C., & Parker, C. (1987). *Communication for results: A guide for business and the professions* (2nd ed.). Belmont, CA: Wadsworth.

Harrel, G. D., & Frazier, G. L. (1999). *Marketing: Connecting with customers.* Upper Saddle River, NJ: Prentice Hall.

Harris, D. A., Engen, B. W., & Fitch, W. E. (1991). *Planning and designing the office environment.* New York, NY: Van Nostrand.

Harris, O. J., & Hartman, S. J. (2002). *Organizational Behavior.* New York, NY: Best Business Books.

Hart, N. A. (1988). *Practical advertising and publicity: Effective promotion of products and services to industry and commerce.* London, Great Britain: McGraw Hill.

Hartman, L. P., & DesJardins, J. (2008). *Business ethics: Decision-making for personal integrity and social responsibility.* New York, NY: McGraw-Hill/Irwin.

Hellriegel, D., & Slocum, J. W. (2007). *Organizational behavior* (11th ed.). Mason, OH: Thompson South-Western.

Hellriegel, D., Slocum, J. W., & Woodman, R. W. (1986). *Organizational behavior.* St. Paul, MN: West Publishing.

Helms, M. M. (2000). *Encyclopedia of management* (4th ed.). Farmington Hills, MI: Gale Group.

Henderson, B. (1989, November/December) The origin of strategy. *Harvard Business Review,* 139–143.

Hersey, P., & Blanchard, K. H. (1982). *Management of organizational behavior: Utilizing human resources.* Upper Saddle River, NJ: Prentice Hall.

Hiam, A. (1997). *Marketing for dummies.* Foster City, CA: IDG Books.

Hiebing, R. G., & Cooper, S. W. (1997). *How to write a successful marketing plan* (2nd ed.). Chicago, IL: NTC Business Books.

Hill, C. W. L., & Jones, G. R. (2001). *Strategic management: An integrated approach* (5th ed.). Boston, MA: Houghton-Mifflin.

Hill, C. W. L., & Jones, G. R. (2004). *Strategic management: An integrated approach* (6th ed.). Boston, MA: Houghton Mifflin.

Hindle, T. (1994). *Field guide to strategy: A glossary of essential tools and concepts for today's manager.* Boston, MA: Harvard Business School Press.

Hingston, P. (2001). *Effective marketing*. New York, NY: Dorling Kindersley.

Hisrich, R. D. (1990). *Marketing*. New York, NY: Barrons.

Hodgetts, R. M. (1999). *Modern human relations at work* (7th ed.). Fort Worth, TX: Dryden Press.

Holt, D. H. (1990). *Management: Principles and practices*. Upper Saddle River, NJ: Prentice Hall.

Holtz, H. (1999). *The concise guide to becoming an independent consultant*. New York, NY: John Wiley and Sons.

House, R. J., & Mitchell, T.R. (1974, Autumn). Path goal theory of leadership. *Journal of Contemporary Business*, 81–94.

Hoy, W. K., & Tarter, J. C. (1995). *Administrators solving the problems of practice: Decision-making concepts, cases, and consequences*. Needham Heights, MA: Allyn and Bacon.

Janal, D. S. (2000). *Dan Janal's guide to marketing on the internet: Getting people to visit, buy, and become customers for life*. New York, NY: John Wiley and Sons.

Janus, L. R., & Jones, S. K. (1982). *Time management for executives: A handbook from the editors of Execu-Time*. New York, NY: Charles Scribner and Sons.

Jefkins, F. (1993). *Planned press and public relations*. London, Great Britain: Blackie Academic and Professional.

Jenner, M. (2005). How to . . . lead leadership development. *People Management, 11*(25), 44–45.

Jennings, M. M., & Shipper, F. (1989). *Avoiding and surviving lawsuits: The executive guide to strategic legal planning for business*. San Francisco, CA: Jossey Bass.

Jentz, G., Miller, R. L., & Cross, F. B. (2007). *West's business law: Alternative edition*. Mason, OH: Thompson South-Western.

Jones, G. R. (2007). *Organizational theory, design, and change* (5th ed.). Upper Saddle River, NJ: Pearson Prentice Hall.

Jones, G. R., & George, J. M. (2004). *Essentials of contemporary management*. New York, NY: McGraw-Hill/Irwin.

Jones, G. R., & George, J. M. (2006). *Contemporary management* (4th ed.). New York, NY: McGraw-Hill/Irwin.

Jucius, M., Dietzer, B., & Schlender, W. (1973). *Elements of managerial action*. Homewood, IL: Irwin.

Karlson, D. (1988). *Marketing your consulting or professional services: A step-by-step program of proven marketing techniques*. Menlo Park, CA: Crisp Publications.

Kast, F. E., & Rosenzweig, J. E. (1979). *Organization and management: A system and contingency approach*. New York, NY: McGraw-Hill.

Kaumeyer, R. A. (1982). *Planning and using a total personnel system*. New York, NY: Van Nostrand-Reinhold.

Keding, A., & Bivins, T. (1990). *How to produce creative advertising: Proven techniques & applications*. Lincolnwood, IL: NTC.

Kendall, R. (1996). *Public relations campaign strategies: Planning for implementation* (2nd ed.). New York, NY: Harper Collins.

Keown, A. J., Martin, J. D., Petty, J. W., & Scott, D. F. (2001). *Foundations of finance: The logic and practice of financial management* (3rd ed.). Upper Saddle River, NJ: Prentice Hall.

Kinicki, A., & Williams, B. K. (2003). *Management: A practical introduction*. New York, NY: McGraw-Hill/Irwin.

Kinnear, T. C., Bernhardt, K. L., & Krentler, K. A. (1995). *Principles of marketing* (4th ed.). New York, NY: Harper Collins.

Kotler, P. (1986). *Principles of marketing* (3rd ed.). Upper Saddle River, NJ: Prentice Hall.

Kotler, P. (1994). *Marketing management: Analysis, planning, implementation, and control* (8th ed.). Upper Saddle River , NJ: Prentice Hall.

Kotler, P. (2003). *Marketing management* (11th ed.). Upper Saddle River, NJ: Prentice Hall.

Kotler, P., & Armstrong, G. (1993). *Marketing: An introduction* (3rd ed.). Upper Saddle River, NJ: Prentice Hall.

Kotler, P., & Armstrong, G. (1997). *Marketing: An introduction* (4th ed.). Upper Saddle River, NJ: Prentice Hall.

Kotter, J. P. (1988). *The leadership factor*. New York, NY: Free Press.

Kouze, J. M., & Posner, B. Z. (1993). *Credibility: How leaders gain and lose it, why people demand it*. San Francisco, CA: Jossey Bass.

Kouzes, J. M., & Posner, B. Z. (1997). *The leadership challenge* (2nd ed.). San Francisco, CA: Jossey Bass.

Kratz, E. F. (2004). The grey flannel office. *Fortune, 150*(12), 152–160.

Kreitner, R. (1995). *Management* (6th ed.). Boston, MA: Houghton Mifflin.

Kreitner, R., & Kinicki, A. (2004). *Organizational behavior* (6th ed.). New York, NY: McGraw-Hill/Irwin.

Kreitner, R., & Kinicki, A. (2007). *Organizational behavior* (8th ed.). New York, NY: McGraw-Hill/Irwin.

Lal, R., Quelch, J. A., & Kasturi Rangan, V. (2005). *Marketing management*. New York, NY: McGraw-Hill/Irwin.

Lamb, C. W., Hair, J. F., & McDaniel, C. (1992). *Principles of marketing*. Cincinnati, OH: South-Western Publishing.

Lamb, C. W., Hair, J. F., & McDaniel, C. (2003). *Essentials of marketing* (3rd ed.). Mason, OH: Thompson South-Western.

Lane, M. J. (1989). *Legal handbook for small businesses*. New York, NY: AMACOM.

Lasher, W. (1994). *The perfect business plan made simple*. New York, NY: Doubleday.

Laurie, J. (1990, March). The ABC's of change management. *Training and Development Journal, 44*, 87–88.

Lazer, W., & Layton, R. A. (1999). *Marketing of hospitality services*. Lansing, MI: Educational Institute of the American Hotel and Motel Association.

Leonard, B. (1999). Cyberventing. *HR Magazine, 44*(12), 34–39.

Leonard, H. S. (2003). Leadership development for the postindustrial, postmodern information age. *Consulting Psychology Journal: Practice and Research, 55*, 3–14.

Lindenberger, J. (2007). Feedback without fear. *Associations Now, 3*(3), 34–38.

Lindsey, L. L., & Beach, S. (2000). *Sociology: Social life and social issues.* Upper Saddle River, NJ: Prentice Hall.

Locker, K. O. (2006). *Business and administrative communication* (7th ed.). New York, NY: McGraw-Hill/Irwin.

Longenecker, J. G., Moore, C. W., & Petty, J. W. (2002). *Small business management: An entrepreneurial emphasis* (12th ed.). Cincinnati, OH: South-Western Publishing.

Luck, D. J., & Ferrel, O.C. (1985). *Marketing strategies and plans* (2nd ed.). Upper Saddle River, NJ: Prentice Hall.

Lussier, R. N. (2006). *Management fundamentals: Concepts, applications, skill development* (3rd ed.). Mason, OH: Thompson South-Western.

Lussier, R. N., & Achua, C. F. (2007). *Leadership: Theory, application, and skill development* (3rd ed.). Mason, OH: Thompson South-Western.

Lyden, D. P., Reitzel, J. D., & Roberts, N. J. (1985). *Business and the law.* New York, NY: McGraw-Hill.

Madura, J. (2007). *Introduction to business* (4th ed.). Mason, OH: Thompson South-Western.

Malcolm, H. B. M., & Keegan, W. J. (1997). *Marketing plans that work.* Newton, MA: Butterworth-Heinemann.

Mallory, C. (1989). *Publicity power: A practical guide to effective promotions.* Menlo Park, CA: Crisp Publications.

Manz, C. C., & Simms, H. P. (1989). *Super leadership: Leading others to lead themselves.* New York, NY: Berkeley Books.

Marconi, J. (1999). *The complete guide to publicity: Maximize visibility for your product, service, or organization.* Lincolnwood, IL: NTC Business Books.

Marks, R. B. (1997). *Personal selling: A relationship approach* (6th ed.). Upper Saddle River, NJ: Prentice Hall.

Maslow, A. (1954). *Motivation and personality.* New York, NY: Harper and Row.

Mathis, R. L., & Jackson, J. H. (1982). *Personnel: Contemporary perspectives and applications* (2nd ed.). St. Paul, MN: West Publishing.

Mayer, J. (1995). *Time management for dummies.* Foster City, CA: IDG Books.

McCarthy, E. J., & Perreault, W. D. (1994). *Essentials of marketing: A global managerial approach.* Burr Ridge, IL: Irwin.

McGhee, W. (1977). Training and Development Theory: Policies and Practices. *A.S.P.A. Handbook of Personnel and Industry Relations, Volume 5.* Washington, DC: Bureau of National Affairs.

McGregor, D. (1960). *The human side of the enterprise.* New York, NY: McGraw Hill.

McLaughlin, P. (2007) Giving good feedback. *Supervision, 68*(2), 7–8.

Megginson, L. C., Byrd, M. J., & Megginson, W. L. (2006). *Small business management: An entrepreneur's guidebook.* New York, NY: McGraw-Hill/Irwin

Megginson, L. C., Mosley, D. C., & Pietri, P. H. (1983). *Management: Concepts and applications.* Cambridge, MA: Harper and Row.

Mescon, M. H., Albert, M., & Khedouri, F. (1985). *Management: Individual and organizational effectiveness* (2nd ed.). Cambridge, MA: Harper and Row.

Milkovich, G. T., & Boudreau, J. W. (1991). *Human resource management.* Homewood, IL: Irwin.

Miller, L. K. (1997). *Sports business management.* Gaithersburg, MD: Aspen Publishing.

Miller, R. L., & Jentz, G. A. (2002). *Fundamentals of business law* (5th ed.). Austin, TX: West Publishing.

Mintzberg, H. (1983). *Power in and around organizations.* Upper Saddle River, NJ: Prentice Hall.

Mintzberg, H. (1994). The rise and fall of strategic planning. *Harvard Business Review, 72,* 107–114.

Mondy, R. W., Holmes, R. E., & Flippo, E. B. (1983). *Management concepts and practices.* Boston, MA: Allyn and Bacon.

Moore, H. F., & Kalupa, F. B. (1985). *Public relations: Principles, cases, and problems* (9th ed.). Homewood, IL: Irwin.

Murphy, H. A., & Hildebrant, H. W. (1988). *Effective business communication* (5th ed.). New York, NY: McGraw Hill.

Murphy, P. E. (1998). *80 exemplary ethical statements.* Notre Dame, IN: University of Notre Dame Press.

Mutz, J., & Murray, K. (2000). *Fundraising for dummies.* Foster City, CA: IDG Book.

Nanus, B. (1989). *The leader's edge: The seven keys to leadership in turbulent times.* Chicago, IL: Contemporary Books.

Newstrom, J. W., & Davis, K. (1997). *Organizational behavior: Human behavior at work* (10th ed.). New York, NY: McGraw-Hill.

Nilson, C. (1990). *Training for non-trainers: A do-it-yourself guide for managers.* New York, NY: AMACOM.

Northcraft, G. B., & Neale, M. A. (1994). *Organizational behavior: A management challenge* (2nd ed.). Fort Worth, TX: Dryden Press.

Northouse, P. G. (2004). *Leadership: Theory and practice* (3rd ed.). Thousand Oaks, CA: Sage.

Nystrom, P. C., & Starbuck, W. H. (1981). *Handbook of organizational design, volume 2: Remodeling organizations and their environments.* London, GB: Oxford Press.

O'Keefe, S. (1997). *Publicity on the internet.* New York, NY: John Wiley and Sons.

O'Brien, J. A. (1994). *Introduction to information systems* (7th ed.). Burr Ridge, IL: Irwin.

Page, S. B. (1984). *Business policies and procedures handbook.* Upper Saddle River , NJ: Prentice Hall.

Paley, N. (2000). *How to develop a strategic marketing plan: A step-by-step guide.* Boca Raton, FL: St. Lucie Press.

Parkhouse, B. L. (1996). *The management of sport: Its foundations and applications* (2nd ed.). St. Louis, MO: Mosby.

Pearce, J. A., & Robinson, R. B. (1989). *Management.* New York, NY: Random House.

Perreault, W. D., & McCarthy, E. J. (2006). *Essentials of mar-*

keting: A global-managerial approach (10th ed.). New York, NY: McGraw-Hill/Irwin.

Perreault, W. D., & McCarthy, E. J. (2007). *Essentials of marketing: A global-managerial approach* (11th ed.). New York, NY: McGraw-Hill/Irwin.

Peterson, R. B., & Lane, T. (1979). *Systematic management of human resources.* Readington, MA: Addison-Wesley.

Pollar, O. (1992). *Organizing your workspace: A guide to personal productivity.* Menlo, CA: Crisp Publications.

Porter, M. E. (1980). *Competitive strategy: Techniques for analyzing industries and competitors.* New York, NY: Free Press.

Porter, M. E. (1985). *Competitive advantage: Creating and sustaining superior performance.* New York, NY: Free Press.

Porter, M. E. (1998). *On competition.* Boston, MA: Harvard Business Review Books.

Pride, W. M., & Ferrell, O.C. (1993). *Marketing: Concepts and strategies* (8th ed.). Boston, MA: Houghton Mifflin.

Pride, W. M., Hughes, R. J., & Kapoor, J. R. (1993). *Business* (4th ed.). Boston, MA: Houghton Mifflin.

Pride, W. M., Hughes, R. J., & Kapoor, J. R. (2002). *Business* (7th ed.). Boston, MA: Houghton Mifflin.

Rachlin, R., & Sweeny, H. W. A. (1994). *Handbook of budgeting.* New York, NY: John Wiley and Sons.

Ramacitti, D. F. (1990). *Do it yourself publicity.* New York, NY: American Marketing Association.

Ramsey, J. E., & Ramsey, I. L. (1985). *Budgeting basics: How to survive the budgeting process.* New York, NY: Franklin Watts.

Random House College Dictionary (1982). New York, NY: Random House.

Renzetti, C. M., & Curran, D. J. (1998). *Living sociology.* Needham Heights, MA: Allyn and Bacon.

Rich, S. R., & Gumpert, D. (1987). *Business plans that win $$: Lessons from the MIT Enterprise Forum.* New York, NY: Harpers Row.

Robbins, S. P. (1998). *Organizational behavior: Concepts, controversies, applications* (8th ed.). Upper Saddle River, NJ: Prentice Hall.

Robertson, I. (1987). *Sociology* (3rd ed.). New York, NY: Worth.

Ross, S. D. (2007). Segmenting sports fans using brand association: A cluster analysis. *Sports Marketing Quarterly, 16*(1), 15–24.

Rothwell, W. J., & Kazanas, H. C. (1988). *Strategic human resource planning and management.* Upper Saddle River, NJ: Prentice Hall.

Rue, L. W., & Byars, L. L. (2004). *Management: Skills and applications* (11th ed.). New York, NY: McGraw-Hill/Irwin.

Rue, L. W., & Byars, L. L. (2007). *Management: Skills and application* (12th ed.). New York, NY: McGraw-Hill/Irwin.

Russell, J. T., & Lane, W. R. (1999). *Advertising procedures* (14th ed.). Upper Saddle River, NJ: Prentice Hall.

Russell, N. (2006). It's not about time. *Business Credit, 108*(9), 58.

Ruvolo, C. M., Petersen, S.A., & LeBoeuf, J.N.G. (2004). Leaders are made, not born: The critical role of a developmental framework to facilitate an organizational culture of development. *Consulting Psychology Journal: Practice and Research, 56,* 10–19.

Sawyer, T. H., & Smith, O. (1999). *The management of clubs, recreation and sport: Concepts and applications.* Champaign, IL: Sagamore Publishing.

Schermerhorn, J. R., & Hunt, J. G. (1988). *Managing organizational behavior* (3rd ed.). New York, NY: John Wiley and Sons.

Schermerhorn, J. R., Hunt, J. G., & Osborn, R. N. (2001). *Basic organizational behavior* (2nd ed.). New York, NY: John Wiley and Sons.

Schewe, C. D., & Hiam, A. (1998). *The portable M.B.A. in marketing* (2nd ed.). New York, NY: John Wiley and Sons.

Schmidt, W. H., & Finnigan, J. P. (1993). *TQ manager: A practical guide for managing in a total quality organization.* San Francisco, CA: Jossey Bass.

Schoell, W. F., & Guiltman, J. P. (1988). *Marketing: Contemporary concepts and practices* (3rd ed.). Boston, MA: Allyn and Bacon.

Schoell, W. F., & Guiltman, J. P. (1990). *Marketing: Contemporary concepts and practices* (4th ed.). Boston, MA: Allyn and Bacon.

Schoell, W. F., & Guiltman, J. P. (1995). *Marketing: Contemporary concepts and practices* (6th ed.). Boston, MA: Allyn and Bacon.

Segal, J. A. (2005). Shatter the glass ceiling: Dodge the shards. *HR Magazine, 50*(4), 121–126.

Shank, M. D. (2005). *Sports marketing: A strategic perspective* (3rd ed.). Upper Saddle River, NJ: Prentice Hall.

Sharon, B. (2006). Risk management: Worry about other things that need to go right. *Business Credit, 108*(8), 62–63.

Shelly, G. B., Cashman, T. J., & Vermaat, M. E. (2001). *Microsoft Office 2000: Introductory concepts and techniques* (2nd ed.). Boston, MA: Course Technology Thompson Learning.

Shenson, H. L., & Wilson, J. R. (1993). *138 quick ideas to get more clients.* New York, NY: John Wiley and Sons.

Shim, J. K. (2006). *Dictionary of business terms.* Mason, OH: Thompson.

Smith, J. (1991). *The publicity kit: A complete guide for entrepreneurs, small businesses and non-profit organizations.* New York, NY: John Wiley and Son.

Smith, L. Y., & Roberson, G. G. (1985). *Business law: 6th edition.* St. Paul, MN: West Publishing.

Soderberg, N. R. (1986). *Public relations for the entrepreneur and the growing business.* Chicago, IL: Probus.

Spulber, D. F. (2004). *Management strategy.* New York, NY: McGraw-Hill/Irwin.

Stanton, W. J., Etzel, M. J., & Walker, B. J. (1994). *Fundamentals of marketing* (10th ed.). New York, NY: McGraw Hill.

Stearns, T. M., & Aldag, R. J. (1987). *Management.* Cincinnati, OH: South-Western.

Stedry, A. C. (1960). *Budget control and cost behavior.* Upper Saddle River, NJ: Prentice Hall.

Steinmetz, L., & Todd, R. H. (1986). *First line management: Approaching supervision effectively* (4th ed.). Homewood, IL: Irwin.

Stone, F. M., & Sachs, R. T. (1995). *The high-value manager: Developing the core competencies your organization demands.* New York, NY: AMACOM.

Stoner, J. A. F. (1978). *Management.* Upper Saddle River, NJ: Prentice Hall.

Sudhalter, D. L. (1980). *The management option: Nine strategies for leadership.* New York, NY: Human Services Press.

Synder, N. H., Dowd, J. J., & Houghton, D. M. (1994). *Vision, values, and courage: Leadership for quality management.* New York, NY: Free Press.

Szilagy, A. (1981). *Management and performance.* Santa Monica, CA: Goodyear.

Tannenbaum, R., Margulies, N., & Massarik, F. (1985). *Human systems development.* San Francisco, CA: Jossey-Bass.

The Secrets of Employee Turnover. (2005). *Buildings, 99*(8), 30–32

Thompson, A. A., Strickland, A.J., & Gamble, J. E. (2005). *Crafting and executing strategy: The quest for competitive advantage: Concepts and cases* (14th ed.). New York, NY: McGraw-Hill/Irwin.

Thompson, A. A., Strickland, A.J., & Gamble, J. E. (2007). *Crafting and executing strategy: The quest for competitive advantage: Concepts and cases* (15th ed.). New York, NY: McGraw-Hill/Irwin.

Tiffany, P., & Peterson, S. D. (1997). *Business plans for dummies.* Foster City, CA: IDG Books.

Time management: Your secret weapon in the year ahead. (2007). *H.R. Focus, 84*(1), 3.

Tracy, J. A. (1997). *Accounting for dummies.* Foster City, CA: IDG Books.

Trewatha, R. L., & Newport, M. G. (1979). *Management: Function and behavior* (3rd ed.). Dallas, TX: Business Publication.

Tuller, L. W. (1992). *The independent consultants Q&A book.* Holbrook, MA: Bob Adams.

Wallace, C. W. (1990). *Great ad! Low-cost do-it-yourself advertising for your small business.* Blue Ridge Summit, PA: Liberty Hall Press.

Warren, C. S., Reeve, J. M., & Fess, P. E. (2002). *Accounting* (20th ed.). Mason, OH: Thompson South-Western.

Merriam-Webster's Online Dictionary. (n.d.a). Retrieved March 27, 2008, from http://www.merriam-webster.com/dictionary/fundraiser

Merriam-Webster's Online Dictionary. (n.d.b). Retrieved March 27, 2008, from http://www.merriam-webster.com/dictionary/fundraising

Weinstein, A. (1994). *Market segmentation: Using demographics, psychographics and other niche marketing techniques to predict and model consumer behavior.* Chicago, IL: Probus.

Weiss, J. W. (2001). *Organizational behavior and change: Managing diversity, cross-cultural dynamics, and ethics* (2nd ed.). Cincinnati, OH: Thompson South-Western.

Wells, W., Burnett, J., & Moriarty, S. (1992). *Advertising principles and practices* (2nd ed.). Upper Saddle River, NJ: Prentice Hall.

Wendroff, A. L. (1999). *Special events: Proven strategies for nonprofit fund raising.* New York, NY: John Wiley and Sons.

Werther, W. B., & Davis, K. D. (1989). *Human resource and personnel management* (3rd ed.). New York, NY: McGraw-Hill.

Westwood, J. (1998). *The marketing plan: A practitioner's guide.* Dover, NH: Kogan Page.

Wilcox, D. L., Ault, P. H., & Agee, W. K. (1998). *Public relations: Strategies and tactics* (5th ed.). New York, NY: Longman.

Wilcox, D. L., Ault, P. H., Agee, W. K., & Cameron, G T. (2000). *Public relations: Strategies and tactics* (6th ed.). New York, NY: Longman/Addison Wesley.

Williams, C. (2000). *Management.* Cincinnati, OH: South-Western Publishing.

Williams, M. (2006). *Mastering leadership* (2nd ed.). London, Great Britain: Thorogood.

Winston, S. (1985). *The organized executive.* New York, NY: Warner Books.

Wortman, C. B., & Loftus, E. F. (1988). *Psychology* (3rd ed.). New York, NY: Borzoi Books.

Wright, P., Knoll, M. J., & Parnell, J. A. (1996). *Strategic management: Concepts and cases* (3rd ed.). Upper Saddle River, NJ: Prentice Hall.

Wright, P., Pringle, C. D., & Kroll, M. J. (1994). *Strategic management: Text and cases* (2nd ed.). Boston, MA: Allyn and Bacon.

Young, A. (1986). *The management handbook: The practical guide to successful management.* New York, NY: Crown Publishing.

Zikmund, W. G. (2000). *Business research methods* (6th ed.). Fort Worth, TX: Dryden/Hardcourt College.

Zikmund, W. G. (2003). *Essentials of marketing research* (2nd ed.). Mason, OH: Thompson South-Western.

Suggested Readings

Advertising

Felton, G. (2006). *Advertising: Concept and copy.* New York, NY: W.W. Norton.

Granat, J. P. (1994). *Persuasive advertising for entrepreneurs and small business owners.* New York, NY: Hawthorne Press.

Hahn, F. E., & Mangun, K. G. (1997). *Do it yourself advertising and promotion.* New York, NY: John Wiley and Sons.

Irwin, R. L., & Sutton, W. A. (2002). *Sports promotion and sales management.* Champaign, IL: Human Kinetics.

Jackall, R., & Hirota, J. M. (2000). *Image makers.* Chicago, IL: University of Chicago Press.

Zimmerman, J. (2002). *Marketing on the internet: Seven steps to building the internet into your business.* Gulf Breeze, FL: Maximums Press.

Budgeting

Dickey, T. (1994). *Budgeting for small businesses.* Menlo Park, CA: Crisp.

Finney, R. G. (1993). *Powerful budgeting for better planning and management.* New York, NY: AMACOM.

Kemp, S., & Dunbar, E. (2003). *Budgeting for managers.* New York, NY: Mc-Graw-Hill.

Shim, J. K., Siegel, J. G., & Simon, A. J. (1996). *Handbook of budgeting for non-profit organizations.* Englewood Cliffs, NJ: Prentice Hall.

Tracy, J. A. (1996). *The fast forward M.B.A. in finance.* New York, NY: John Wiley and Sons.

Vinter, R. D., & Kish, R. K. (1984). *Budgeting for not-for-profit organizations.* New York, NY: Free Press.

Consulting

Bond, W. J. (1997). *Going solo: Develop a home-based consulting business from the ground up.* New York, NY: McGraw-Hill.

Chung, E., & Slepicka, J. (2002). *Vault career guide to consulting.* New York, NY: Vault Inc.

Gray, D. A. (1996). *Start and run a profitable consulting business.* North Vancouver, Canada: Self-Counsel.

Holtz, H. (1999). *The concise guide to becoming an independent consultant.* New York, NY: John Wiley and Sons.

Riddle, J. (2001). *Entrepreneur magazine's consulting business.* Irvine, CA: Entrepreneur Press.

Shenson, H. L., & Wilson, J. R. (1993). *138 quick ideas to get more clients.* New York, NY: John Wiley and Sons.

Thomas, M. A. (2003). *High-performance consulting skills and internal consultant's guide to value added performance.* London, Great Britain: Thorogood.

Control

Brokaw, L. (1995). *301 great management ideas.* Boston, MA: INC Publishing.

Evans, J. R. (1999). *The management and control of quality.* Cincinnati, OH: South-Western Publishing.

Townsend, P., & Gebhardt, J. (2006). *Quality makes money.* Milwaukee, WI: American Society for Quality, Quality Press.

Vinten, G. (2004). *Achieving managerial control.* Bradford, Great Britain: Emerald Group Publishing.

Ethics

Boatright, J. R. (1997). *Ethics and the conduct of business.* Upper Saddle River, NJ: Prentice Hall.

Mackall, D. D. (2004). *Professional ethics and etiquette.* New York, NY: Ferguson.

Pratley, P. (1995). *The essence of business ethics.* London, Great Britain: Prentice Hall.

Preiffer, R. S., & Forsberg, R. P. (2000). *Ethics on the job.* Belmont, CA: Wadsworth.

Velasquez, M. G. (2002). *Business ethics: Concepts and cases.* Upper Saddle River, NJ: Prentice Hall.

Wines, W. A. (2006). *Ethics, law, and business.* Mahwah, NJ: Lawrence Erlbaum Associates.

Fundraising

Allen, J. (2000). *Event planning: The ultimate guide to successful meetings, corporate events, fundraising galas.* New York, NY: John Wiley and Sons.

Bray, I. M. (2005). *Effective fundraising for nonprofits: Real world strategies that work.* Berkeley, CA: NOLO.

Copeland, B. W. (1995). *Funding sources in physical education exercise and sports science.* Morgantown, WV: Fitness Information Technology/West Virginia University.

Edles, L. P. (1992). *Fundraising.* New York, NY: McGraw-Hill.

Flanagan, J. (1999). *Successful fundraising: A complete handbook for volunteers and professionals.* New York, NY: McGraw-Hill.

Stier, W. F. (1994). *Fundraising for sport and recreation.* Champaign, IL: Human Kinetics.

Warwick, M. (2001). *How to write successful fundraising letters.* San Francisco, CA: Jossey Bass.

General Management

Ballard, C. (2005). *Business performance management meets business intelligence.* San Jose, CA: IBM.

Boyett, J., & Boyett, J. (1998). *The guru guide: The best ideas of the top management thinkers.* New York, NY: John Wiley and Sons.

Crainer, S. (1999). *The 75 greatest management decisions ever made . . . and the 21 worst.* New York: AMACOM.

DeSensi, J. T., & Rosenberg, D. (2003). *Ethics and morality in sports management.* Morgantown, WV: Fitness Information Technology/West Virginia University.

Drucker, P. F. (1999). *Management challenges for the 21st century.* New York, NY: Harpers.

Gillentine, A., & Crow, R. B. (2005). *Foundations of Sports Management.* Morgantown, WV: Fitness Information Technology/West Virginia University.

Klopp, H. (1998). *The complete idiot's guide to business management.* New York, NY: Alpha Books.

Human Resource Management

Barbeito, C. L. (2004). *Human resource policies and procedures for nonprofit organizations.* Hoboken, NJ: John Wiley and Sons.

DeVine, G. (1997). *Managing your employees.* Englewood Cliffs, NJ: Prentice Hall.

Murphy, K. R., & Cleveland, J. N. (1995). *Understanding performance appraisals: Social, organizational, and goal-based perspectives.* Thousand Oaks, CA: Sage.

O'Connor, B. N., Bronner, M., & Delaney, C. (1996). *Training for organizations.* Cincinnati, OH: South-Western Publishing.

Wilson, R. F. (1997). *Conducting better job interviews.* New York, NY: Barrons.

Leadership

Blanchard, K., Carlos, J. P., & Randolph, A. (1996). *Empowerment takes more than a minute.* San Francisco, CA: Berrett-Koehler.

Peters, T. (1994). *The pursuit of wow!* New York, NY: Vintage Books.

Pitino, R. (2000). *Lead to succeed: The ten traits of great leadership in business and life.* New York, NY: Broadway Books.

Putzier, J. (2001). *Get weird!:101 innovative ways to make your company a great place to work.* New York, NY: AMACOM.

Quigley, J. V. (1993). *Vision: How leaders develop it, share it, and sustain it.* New York, NY: McGraw-Hill.

Marketing

Cook, K. J. (1993). *Small business marketing.* Lincolnwood, IL: NTC Business Books.

Hingston, P. (2001). *Effective marketing*. New York, NY: Dorling Kindersley.

Luther, W. M. (2001). *The marketing plan*. New York, NY: AMACOM.

Muckian, M. (2001). *Prentice Hall's one-day M.B.A. in marketing*. Paramus, NJ: Prentice Hall.

Mullin, B. J., Hardy, S., & Sutton, W. A. (2007). *Sports marketing*. Champaign, IL: Human Kinetics.

Pitts, B. G., & Stotlar, D. K. (2007). *Fundamentals of sports marketing*, 3rd Edition. Morgantown, WV: Fitness Information Technology/West Virginia University.

Stevens, R. E. (2006). *Marketing planning guide*. New York, NY: Best Business Books.

Stotlar, D. K. (2005). *Developing successful sports marketing plans*, 2nd Edition. Morgantown, WV: Fitness Information Technology/West Virginia University.

Organization

Bacon, T. R. (2003). *Winning behavior: What the smartest, most successful companies do differently*. New York, NY: AMACOM.

Bruce, R., & Wyman, S. (1998). *Changing organizations: Practice, action, training and research*. Thousand Oaks, CA: Sage.

Carron, B., Hausenblas, H., & Eys, M. (2005). *Group dynamics in sport*, 3rd Edition. Morgantown, WV: Fitness Information Technology/West Virginia University.

Cell, E. (1998). *Organizational life: Learning to be self directed*. Lanham, MD: University Press of America.

Hellrieger, D., Slocum, J., & Woodman, R. W. (2001). *Organizational behavior*. Cincinnati, OH: South-Western Publishing.

Sims, R. R. (2002). *Managing organizational behavior*. Westport, CT: Quorum Books.

Planning

Barrow, P. (2001). *The best laid business plans: How to write them, how to pitch them*. London, Great Britain: Virgin.

Forsyth, P. (2002). *Business planning*. Oxford, Great Britain: Capstone Publishing.

Henricks, M. (1999). *Business plans made easy*. Irvine, CA: Entrepreneur Media.

Pinson, L. (2001). *The anatomy of a business plan*. Chicago, IL: Dearborn.

Public Relations

Beckwith, S. L. (2006). *Publicity for nonprofits: Generating media exposure that leads to awareness, growth, and contributions*. Chicago, IL: Kaplan Publishing.

Chajet, C., & Shachtman, T. (1991). *Image by design*. Reading, MA: Addison-Wesley.

Green, A. (2006). *Effective communication skills for public relations.* London, Great Britain: Kogan Page.

Haig, M. (2000). *The essential guide to public relations on the internet.* London, Great Britain: Kogan Page.

Hall, A., Nichols, W., Moynahan, P., & Taylor, J. (2007). *Media relations in sport,* 2nd Edition. Morgantown, WV: Fitness Information Technology/ West Virginia University.

Marconi, J. (1996). *Image marketing: Using public perceptions to attain business objectives.* Lincolnwood, IL: NTC.

Marconi, J. (2002). *Reputation marketing: Building and sustaining your organization's greatest asset.* New York, NY: McGraw-Hill.

Risk Management

Doherty, N. A. (2000). *Integrated risk management: Techniques and strategies for managing corporate risk.* New York, NY: McGraw-Hill.

Goodden, R. L. (1996). *Preventing and handling product liability.* New York, NY: Marcel Dekker.

Haimes, Y. Y. (2004). *Risk modeling assessment, and management.* Hoboken, NJ: John Wiley and Sons.

Hopkins, B. R. (1994). *Nonprofit law dictionary.* New York, NY: John Wiley and Sons.

Maloy, B. P., & Higgins, C. R. (2000). *No excuse risk management.* Carmel, IN: Cooper Publishing Group.

Nader, R., & Smith, W. J. (1990). *Winning the insurance game.* New York, NY: Knightsbridge.

Stettner, M. (1994). *Buyers beware: How to win at the insurance game.* Chicago, IL: Probus.

Strategic Management

Heller, R. (2000). *Peter Drucker: The great pioneer of management theory and practice.* New York, NY: Dorling Kindersley.

Heller, R. (2000). *Tom Peters: The best selling prophet of the management revolution.* New York, NY: Dorling Kindersley.

Hickman, C. R. (1994). *The strategy game.* New York, NY: McGraw-Hill.

Hindle, T. (1994). *Field guide to strategy.* Boston, MA: Harvard Business.

Jocobs, R. W. (1994). *Real time strategic change.* San Francisco, CA: Berrett-Koehler.

Lawrie, G. (2004). *Strategic performance management.* Bradford, Great Britain: Emerald Group Publishing.

Sadler, P. (2003). *Strategic management.* Sterling, VA: Kogan Press.

Index

About the Author

Richard Leonard

Coaching

For six seasons, Dr. Richard Leonard was the Head Women's Volleyball Coach at Georgia State University in Atlanta, Georgia. Under Leonard, whose career record as a head coach stands at 144-69, the Lady Panthers hold the best winning percentage in school history at .676. For his efforts, Leonard was named Trans American Coach of the Year in 2000 and the Atlantic Sun Conference Coach of the Year in 2001 and 2003.

Prior to Georgia State, Leonard spent four seasons as Associate Head Coach at Saint Louis University. During his tenure at Saint Louis University, the Billikens developed into one of the best volleyball programs in the Midwest. They compiled a 91-59 mark, including a 29-10 record and a trip to the Volleyball National Invitational Tournament.

Leonard's first coaching position was at the University of North Florida. The Ospreys went to the NAIA National Championship in both of their first two years of intercollegiate competition. In the team's first season as an NCAA Division II member, North Florida gained a top 15 national ranking and a number 1 ranking in the Southeastern United States Region.

Leonard was a member and player in the United States Volleyball Association from 1980 to 1997 and was AA rated. He has been on four USVB regional championship teams and seven USVB semifinalist and finalists. During his playing career, his teams have won more than 125 tournaments and league championships.

Academic/Administrative

A native of Pittsburgh, Pennsylvania, Leonard has earned a bachelor's degree in accounting from Robert Morris University, an MBA in management from Florida Metropolitan University—Tampa College, and a PhD in administration and management from Walden University. He has certifications in Strategic Management and Leadership from the American Management Association as well as certification in Professional Learning, Collaborative Learning, and Classroom Management. He has served as a regional tournament director and been the owner-operator of numerous summer camps, and has authored various national articles on sport administration. He is US Volleyball CAP Level II certified and US Volleyball Critical Thinking Seminar certified. He has also achieved his ACEP certification.

Over the past 14 years, in addition to his coaching duties, Leonard has served as an adjunct and assistant professor of business for numerous colleges and universities. He has taught classes in entrepreneurship, all levels of management, and a range of marketing classes. He is currently the Chair of the Department of Business Administration and Accounting at Flagler College in Tallahassee, Florida.